BEHIND THE RED DOOR

BEHIND THE RED DOOR

*How Elizabeth Arden's Legacy Inspired
My Coming-of-Age Story in the Beauty Industry*

Louise Claire Johnson

gatekeeper press

Published by Gatekeeper Press
2167 Stringtown Rd, Suite 109
Columbus, OH 43123-2989
www.GatekeeperPress.com

Library of Congress Cataloging-in-Publication Data
Title: Behind the Red Door : How Elizabeth Arden's Legacy Inspired My Coming-of-Age Story in the Beauty Industry / Louise Claire Johnson.
Names: Johnson, Louise Claire, author.
ISBN (hardcover): 978-1-66290-908-5
ISBN (paperback): 978-1-66290-909-2
ISBN (ebook): 978-1-66290-910-8
LCNN: 2021935290
Subjects: Biography & Memoir, Women, Historical

The views and opinions expressed in this book are solely those of the author and do not reflect the views or opinions of Gatekeeper Press. Gatekeeper Press is not to be held responsible for and expressly disclaims responsibility of the content herein.

In order to protect the privacy of those involved, certain names and locations have been changed. In some instances timelines have been condensed for narrative clarity.

Jacket Design: milagraphicartist.com
Map Illustration: Lexi McKenna, Paper & Poste

First Edition

For Mom, Dad, Grace, Meredith, and Geoff—you are my whole heart. This book wouldn't exist without your unwavering support. Thank you for believing in me before I believed in myself. I love you beyond measure.

For Florence Nightingale Graham—the woman whose legacy inspired all of this.

For you, Dear Reader—I turn this tale over to you. Take what resonates (leave what doesn't), and let it marinate as you move through life to become your best self.

**Florence Nightingale Graham reading on her
porch outside of Toronto, Canada.**
(circa 1905, age 27)

Portrait of Elizabeth Arden in New York City.
(1947, age 69, but by this time, she refused to disclose her actual age)

"I'm not interested in age. You're as old as you feel."
- Elizabeth Arden

Louise in New York and Switzerland.
From Manhattan to the Matterhorn.

Contents

Liz & Low's NYC

1. 689-691 FIFTH AVENUE
2. 834 FIFTH AVENUE
3. 509 FIFTH AVENUE
4. 200 PARK AVENUE S.
5. 529 BROOME ST.
6. 67 EAST 2ND ST.

Upper West Side

CENTRAL PARK

2.
LIZ'S PENTHO...

1. LIZ'S FIRST RED DOOR.

3.
ELIZABETH HUBBARD'S SALON (1910)

NYPL

4.
ELIZABETH ARDEN NY OFFICE (2008-2015)

5. "THE DOLLHOUSE"

WASHINGTON SQUARE PARK

DELI

SoHo

STRAND BOOK STORE

6.
EAST VILLAGE APARTMENT

East Village

Geneva

London

THIS WAY TO EUROPE

Financial District

THE SINGER BUILDING

THE BROOKLYN BRIDGE

N
W — E
S

"You're in another world when you come through the red door of Elizabeth Arden. And the world is based on one exclusive object—you."
—*Elizabeth Arden*

Preface

We all have a fictitious self; a façade we wear like a mask. This version of ourselves is constructed over time as we intuitively process how to perceive the world and how the world perceives us. Our self-image is punctuated by the perceptions of others but ultimately shaped by the stories we tell ourselves.

All of this, I only now recognize in retrospect.

In 2008, at the age of eighteen, I moved from the suburbs of Toronto, Canada to Manhattan to begin my dream internship at the cosmetic giant, Elizabeth Arden. I knew nothing about the beauty industry but was enamored by the woman who built it. Full-time marketing roles at the company headquarters in New York and Geneva followed, but behind the glamorous lifestyle I *appeared* to be leading, I was struggling to reconcile who I really was with who I purported to be.

In 1908, exactly one hundred years earlier, Florence Nightingale Graham moved from the suburbs of Toronto, Canada to Manhattan with dreams of becoming a self-made woman. Within two years she opened her first beauty salon on Fifth Avenue and adopted the same name as her new company: Elizabeth Arden. At a time when women didn't have the right to vote she went on to pioneer the global beauty industry (valued at over half a trillion dollars today). She empowered women in the workplace during an era when their opinions were silenced, and opportunities were few. Elizabeth would become one of the wealthiest women in the world, the first businesswoman to grace the cover of *TIME* magazine and the first woman inducted into the U.S. Business Hall of Fame. By the end of the 1930s, it was said, "There are only three American names known in every single corner of the globe: Singer Sewing, Coca Cola, and Elizabeth Arden." And yet—so few know her story.

1

Before my internship at Elizabeth Arden, I admittedly knew nothing about the woman behind the brand. While my grandmother's generation was readily familiar with Arden's heyday, and the name "rang a bell" amongst my mother's demographic, the majority of millennials had never heard of the company *or* its female founder.

When my mom gave me a copy of the book *War Paint* by Lindy Woodhead, I was surprised to discover that Elizabeth was Canadian, raised near my hometown, and one of the most powerful businesswomen in the world for nearly three decades, from the 1930s through the 1960s. With such an impressive legacy, I was perplexed as to why the story of this trailblazing feminist wasn't more prominent on official records. The richest men of her era, like John D. Rockefeller, Cornelius Vanderbilt, J.P. Morgan Jr., and Henry Ford had buildings, monuments, universities, and museums named after them. Why was Elizabeth Arden's story hidden in history? Was it because of her gender that she faded from public consciousness? Was it her working-class Canadian roots?

War Paint was published in 2004, long after Elizabeth's lifetime, and turned out to be a *dual* biography with more than half the pages dedicated to Helena Rubinstein. While I devoured the details of Elizabeth's life, I didn't like that the book pitted the two titans against each other. The narrative that successful women in power must criticize and condemn one another to get to the top felt antiquated. Despite the tired typecast, *War Paint* was the foremost resource on my newfound heroine and the catalyst that sent me down a research rabbit hole.

When I wanted to learn something, I started with books. After I dog-eared and tattered the cover of *War Paint* from rereading it so many times, I accessed library archives and scoured every last corner of cyberspace for old newspaper clippings, article mentions, vocal recordings, personal letters, and vintage photographs. On eBay, I tracked down an out-of-print 1972 edition of *Miss Elizabeth Arden* by Alfred Allan Lewis and Constance Woodworth and a rare copy of the 1946 *TIME* magazine featuring Elizabeth on the cover. I framed the magazine and hung it above my desk as a tangible reminder of my goals, perpetually asking myself: *WWED? What would Elizabeth do?*

Plan Ahead + Work Hard = Achieve Goals. This was my motto. It was the only formula I knew for accomplishing anything in life. I was fascinated by Elizabeth's rise to riches, but it was the unwritten, in-between moments of the former Florence Nightingale's life trajectory that would have the greatest impact on me.

Most of humanity is drawn to how things *appear.* Wearing makeup, for example, is sometimes about trying to *look* different, but most often, it is about *feeling* your best self. The key is figuring out what the best version of you ("your best self") actually looks *and* feels like. One of the ways we do that is by observing other people. Maybe you love a certain color of lipstick or hairstyle on someone else; you might find when you try it on that it doesn't do anything for you, or you might find it's exactly what you've been looking for.

At eighteen, I wanted to try Elizabeth's successful lifestyle, of a big career in a big city, on for size. Although we lived a century apart, Elizabeth became my invisible guide and her life story my road map. I assumed the career accolades of status, wealth, and power were what I needed to feel fulfilled. I thought I had to *do* something big to *be* somebody of importance; doing was the prerequisite of being. Moving to Manhattan to become a marketing maven in the beauty industry sounded "impressive" and was an aspiration approved by my parents and society. Suddenly, Elizabeth Arden 2.0 was who I was supposed to be. In hindsight, she was a multifaceted mirage, an illusion of her own and other people's making.

In today's climate of change, Elizabeth Arden's legacy is as poignant as ever. Even if you don't aspire, as I did, to follow directly in her footsteps, we can all glean inspiration from her on how to pursue professional and personal goals as we move through life.

This book brings you behind the red doors of Arden, while my story serves to highlight how much (or how little) has changed a century later. The following account is told with as much histori-cal accuracy as research, records, and archival resources provided. In some instances, thoughts, feelings, and events have been surmised and timelines condensed for narrative clarity. Memories are also fallible. Personal anecdotes from my past are reconstructions of reality filtered through my mind; a subjective snapshot of events as told through my lens. Some names have been changed for privacy.

What began as a desire to preserve Elizabeth's place in history evolved into an examination of my own coming of age in the beauty industry and a cultural excavation on a much larger thread that connects us all.

Ultimately, this book is about identity and how we learn to navi-gate the world to find our best self, even if it's on a different path than we originally anticipated.

Part I
NEOPHYTE
New York, New York

"Hold fast to life and youth."

—Elizabeth Arden

Chapter 1

The Most Striking Woman in the Room

Toronto and New York

1908–1909

Smoke billowed along the station platform overlooking Lake Ontario as Florence waited to board the train. She pulled a loose thread from her worn wool dress, adjusted the straw cartwheel hat atop her head that once belonged to her mother, and gripped tightly to the trunk in her hand containing a few possessions and a one-way ticket to Grand Central Station in Manhattan. She looked on in earnest as the Pullman porters escorted first-class patrons to their luxurious sleeper cars, while she could barely afford the $30 third-class fare for the days-long trek from Toronto to St. Lambert, Quebec. From there she would change lines and travel south through Vermont to the "Capital of the World," as E.B. White called New York City at the time.

In 1908, Florence Nightingale Graham was on the cusp of her thirtieth birthday when she left her family farm behind to make a new life in Manhattan. "It was the beginning of my real life, my coming-of-age, as it were," she said.

Unmarried and childless in her late twenties, Florence was considered a spinster by societal standards. It was unheard of for a single woman of limited means to travel anywhere unaccompanied, but she sought to stake her destiny outside of domesticity.

Florence's upbringing was full of hardship, but it fostered an unwavering work ethic and iron-willed determination to succeed. Her parents, William and Susan Graham, had immigrated from Liverpool, England in the 1860s, as the Canadian government eagerly sponsored people from Great Britain to cultivate undeveloped farmland. After docking in Canada, the Grahams moved to a small settlement outside of Toronto in a newly-established agricultural community called Woodbridge. Mr. Graham rode his worn-down horse and buggy to Toronto's St. Lawrence Market to sell seeds and crop vegetables, but despite his hopes for a prosperous future, the family struggled to get by.

Florence Nightingale was born in 1878, the fourth of five children, and named after the prolific writer and war heroine who pioneered modern nursing. Mrs. Graham had high aspirations for her daughter, who had a clever mind from birth, and hoped she would follow in the footsteps of her namesake to become a nurse. Unfortunately, Florence's father adhered to an opposing thought principle: a woman's sole purpose was to bear children and cater to the homestead.

When Florence was six, her mother died of tuberculosis. A single father of five after his wife's death, Mr. Graham succumbed to alcoholism and angry outbursts. The four girls had to leave school and take over the housework and farm chores. Florence's innate love of learning and appreciation for academics would never leave her, and being forced to quit school would become her single greatest regret. Willie Jr., the only son, was allowed to continue his education, with the hope that he would someday be rich enough to provide for his aging father and sisters.

Florence was the most organized and responsible of her siblings and became a mother figure to her younger sister of six years, Gladys. The silver lining of life on the farm were the horses. Florence's adoration of the majestic creatures started young and would remain a constant source of companionship and great comfort throughout her life.

Along with her domestic duties, Florence worked various jobs in town, including as a stenographer and cashier, to help financially support the family. Despite the exhausting workload, she was a lifelong insomniac and is said to have spent her sleepless nights reading and journaling about her dreams for the future. Any extra pennies earned were spent on books and nickelodeons starring female protagonists. She loved romantic escapism and being immersed in the glamour of another life, far different from the one she led. Florence was twenty-seven when *The House of Mirth* by Edith Wharton was published in 1905 to instant success, about an impoverished woman at the end of her marriageable years (mid-twenties) attempting to navigate New York's high society. This novel would have inspired Florence and potentially planted the notion of Manhattan in her mind. However, (spoiler alert), Lily, in *The House of Mirth*, ends up tragically lonely on the margins of society. Perhaps this should have served as a foreboding that "success" has a variable viewpoint.

Florence was a forward-thinker who exuded confidence, although years later she admitted to suffering from self-doubt as a nonconformist. A petite five-two, her big dreams, larger-than-life personality, and ambitious attitude compensated for her small stature. She had enviable hourglass curves, yet hid her assets for fear of not being taken seriously. Her gregarious extroversion masked an inner introvert. Outwardly, she wanted everyone to believe she was bold, brash, and bubbly—yet underneath, she was shy, naïve, and reserved.

Described as possessing a "peaches-and-cream complexion," Florence was gifted with a naturally youthful appearance, something she sought to preserve her entire life. While some historians remark that she was rather plain to look at, her aura was so enchanting she was often said to be the most striking woman in the room.

The difference between being striking and beautiful is that the former is unusual, something you don't see every day; unforgettable in a way that stops you in your tracks, whereas the latter insinuates a conventional attractiveness. A striking woman embraces her beauty imperfections and flaws while commanding attention with her presence. Florence radiated an allure that dared you not to look away. Years later, she harnessed this idea to inspire other women to celebrate their individual beauty—one not dictated by the male gaze. She would go on to reclaim the word "beautiful" and created the famous mantra "to be beautiful is the birthright of *every* woman."

Back at Toronto's Union Station, the whistle blew, and Florence stepped into the train car. She sat forward, facing her future, never to look back. Her father disowned her upon departure, supposedly for abandoning the family and the farm. Soon, she would renounce her former identity altogether.

When Florence set off for Manhattan at the turn of the twentieth century, the history of cosmetics in North America was in its burgeoning stages. Ancient civilizations in the Eastern, African, and European worlds had used cosmetics for thousands of years as part of religious ceremonies, sun protection, class indication, and artistic expression. The concept of "painting one's face" was the earliest form of a ritual, dating back to 10,000 BC when both men and women decorated themselves with homemade hues and potted paints. They were resourceful in using rice powder for the face, crushed mulberries for red lips and cheeks, paste from henna plants for hair dye, and kohl to enhance the eyes.

In the middle ages, during the Crusades, essential oils were imported from the Middle East to Europe. By 1400–1500, Italy and France were the epicenters of cosmetic manufacturing worldwide, but only the aristocracy had access. Queen Elizabeth I of England used white lead paint for a paler complexion, but by 1800, Queen Victoria declared makeup was improper and immoral.

In the early 1900s, cosmetics were still considered the sinful markings of prostitutes. In Stevenson's 1934 *Book of Quotations,* he wrote, "Face: painted. See also under Whore." Men claimed ownership over women's appearances and saw makeup as a devilish attempt to seduce other males, while vanity was viewed as a sign of selfishness. *True* ladies catered only to the whims of others; they never indulged their own. Secretly, women of all social classes were creating homemade recipes for a more youthful appearance that still looked "natural." They used egg whites and honey on the face, beads of candle wax and burnt matchsticks to tinge eyelashes, and ash from the fire to darken eyebrows.

Florence arrived just as the birth of North American beauty culture was about to burst out from behind closed doors.

At the time, women wore long, full skirts that kissed the ground, with tailored blouses hugging the neck. Corsets were tightly tapered for structure and postural support, but offered a softer figure than the previous contorting S-shaped bodices. Fashionable evening dresses fell in a slender silhouette with short puff sleeves and a hint of the bust. Draped in lace, beading, chiffon, or silk, the romantic ballgowns had high empire waists and came in light pastels like lilac and rose for summer, and deep tones like emerald and burgundy for winter.

Broad-brimmed hats decorated with feathers, ribbons, flowers, and the occasional stuffed bird (hummingbirds were a sign of the ultra-wealthy) sat atop "Gibson Girl" hairstyles. If women didn't have long, wavy hair to sweep into the up-do *du jour,* they used horsehair pads called "rats" and added volume with a "switch" (the original weave).

As the world transitioned from the Victorian age into the Edwardian era, a trend called the 'New Woman' emerged around the First World War. Encouraged by the growing women's suffrage movement, the New Woman was driven, smart, and steadfast about questioning the gender roles assigned to her. She wanted to pursue higher education and corporate employment. She wore less restrictive, more streamlined clothing so that she could participate in active outdoor sports like her male counterparts. But the rise of the New Woman faced harsh criticism and swift backlash. In a *New York Times* editorial, she was described as a woman who "dresses like a man, thereby making herself hideous…the next step will be to wear her hair short, and she will want to work by a man's side, on his level, and still be treated with chivalry…it will produce a storm of indignation and wrath beyond the sex she is endeavoring to emulate."

It would be another two decades before white women received the right to vote in 1920 and not until The Voting Rights Act of 1965 for discriminatory voting practices to be outlawed against black men and women in America. The quest for parity was only just beginning, but Florence was empowered by the shifting ideologies the New Woman presented.

Florence was one of many determined to make it big in "the Big Apple," a term coined by Edward S. Martin in his book *The Wayfarer in New York* in 1909. When she first arrived in 1908, Manhattan was bursting with optimism and possibility. The city had rapidly transformed from a small seaport town, with its natural harbor, into a prosperous commercial metropolis and destination for dreamers. New York's growth was accelerating at an astonishing speed. City blocks were built in a chronological grid, with numbered avenues running north to south and cross streets from west to east. It was a visionary move that heralded the future of urban development.

New York City's first official subway line was in its infancy. Fare cost five cents. Riders in the early 1900s were skeptical about this newfangled technology that traveled below the bedrock like a coal miner's wagon. Automobiles were also newly popular. The Ford Model T, colloquially called the "Tin Lizzie," was released in October 1908. It was the first affordable, mass-produced car for the middle class and would change the way people traveled. Despite the influx of modern motorcars and a subway system, horse and carriage were still the preferred means of transportation. New York's iconic taxi cabs wouldn't be invented until 1915 when John D. Hertz, an Austrian-Hungarian born businessman raised in Chicago, founded the Yellow Cab Company, first in Chicago and then franchised to New York City. Mr. Hertz painted his fleet of taxis yellow after reading a study that said it was the color most visible from a distance. Years later, when Florence flagged down her first taxi, she would have no idea that someday she would race thoroughbreds against the Yellow Cab creator.

Grand Central Station was operational but under heavy construction when Florence disembarked from her long journey. Outside the terminal, the unpaved streets were teeming with horse-drawn carriages driven by handsome drivers in black ties and top hats. She would have merely fluttered her lashes to be offered a ride.

New York icons included the Brooklyn Bridge, an industrial marvel and the longest suspension bridge in the world when it was completed in 1883. The Williamsburg Bridge was only five years old (completed in 1903), and the Manhattan Bridge was a year shy of its grand opening in 1909. The Statue of Liberty had been living a life of leisure on Bedloe Island in the harbor since 1885 and looked spry for a twenty-three-year-old, still shiny brown, like a freshly minted copper penny.

At the corner of Liberty Street and Broadway in lower Manhattan's Financial District, Florence's driver would have surely pointed out the brand new forty-seven-story office building: the dazzling headquarters of the Singer Sewing Manufacturing Company. Standing at six hundred and twelve feet, it was the tallest building in the world from 1908 to 1909. (The world's tallest building today, Dubai's Burj Khalifa is four times the size). Looking at the stunning Singer Building would have spurred the ambitious Florence to dream about someday opening a business of her own in an architectural beauty with a glamorous New York City address.

I get chills thinking about Florence soaking in the sights, smells, and sounds of her first day in Manhattan, with no idea she would someday be synonymous with the greats—or that a century later, another young girl from Canada would be looking up in amazement at a dazzling headquarters with Florence's name on it.

***

Florence desperately needed two things: a job and a place to live. Verifiable records are scarce, but it is presumed she moved into a female boarding house. Only men could rent an apartment or get a hotel room, so nearly every working-class, single woman lived in a boarding home in the nineteenth and twentieth centuries.

For Florence, the cost of living in the early 1900s would have been approximately $2.50 a week for a shared room, light housekeeping, and three hot meals a day. On the luxury end of female residences was the Barbizon Hotel, which opened in 1926, and required three letters of recommendation, known pedigree, and fancy attire to be granted accommodation. The Barbizon later housed Joan Crawford, Grace Kelly, Sylvia Plath, and Joan Didion. Florence would have likely lodged at the more modest Martha Washington Hotel for Women (simply referred to as "the Women's Hotel") at the corner of Fifth Avenue and 30th Street in Midtown, which housed nearly five hundred women.

Despite the opportunity to make friends, Florence had little use for female companionship. She was determined to be somebody of importance, and socializing was a frivolous indulgence. To her, relationships were nothing but a distraction.

With housing solidified, employment was next. Having ruled out the medical field—despite her namesake, Florence found she couldn't stand the sight of blood—and shifted her career focus elsewhere.

Scanning the classifieds, "CHAMBERMAIDS, NANNIES, and SECRETARIES WANTED," Florence would have come across the term "millionaire," which had recently begun circulating to describe New York's wealthy elite—male elite, that is. One million dollars seemed like such an astronomical sum that some people thought millionaire was a made-up word, like "zillionaire" today. Even when it was printed in the gospel ink of the *New York Times*, it was unfathomable to think anyone could earn that money without inheriting it. The accumulation of wealth, largely due to real estate, oil, and financial investments, grew so rapidly over the course of the next century that today, one out of every twenty-five New Yorkers is a multimillionaire. But in 1908, an unmarried woman who aspired to that elite status was better off trying to become president (a laughable impossibility at the time).

For the moment, Florence understood she had to play by the rules of society, which meant starting at the bottom in one of the few pink-collar positions available. At every opportunity, she keenly observed and attempted to adopt the mannerisms of Manhattan social-ites, from how they spoke to how they dressed. She was astute enough to recognize it was the wealthy wives who managed their husband's fortunes. They had the spending power and controlled the social skel-eton of the city.

The last thing Florence wanted was to be mistaken for who she was: a rough-and-tumble farm girl from Canada. Her quest to fit in extended to the manipulation of her voice to sound more "breathy and childlike." In an effort to shed her Canadian accent and small-town slang, she eventually enrolled in enunciation lessons (which she contin-ued for the rest of her life). Her new voice helped her to maintain an air of feminine sophistication, which she associated with Manhattan's elite. The issue with her vocal transformation was that sometimes she would slip back into her old self, particularly when angered. "Swearing like a trooper, her voice would rise to what long-suffering associates described as a squealing shriek," wrote Woodhead in *War Paint*. "I didn't want them to love me; I wanted them to fear me," Florence later said of her staff.

That was the trouble with adopting a new persona: when her defenses were lowered, people caught a glimpse of her old self hiding behind the curtain. (I used to think it was over-the-top for Florence to change her voice, but I would soon alter my Canadian vocabulary and drop my rounded "o's," too, in the hope of fitting in).

Careers as "culturists" were gaining popularity amongst women in New York. Culturists took a mind, body, and soul approach to improving a woman's exterior appearance and interior well-being. They were the first to understand the benefits of self-care, decades before the concept became trendy. Makeup, as we know it today, was still only worn conspicuously by "ladies of the night," so beauty culturists focused on facials, skincare products, and massage treatments.

Florence answered an ad for a bookkeeping position with Mrs. Eleanor Adair, a beauty culturist, at her salon on West 39th Street. Mrs. Adair specialized in "Ganesh Strapping," where a leather strap was hooked under the chin, tied over the head, and electric currents were used to lift and firm facial muscles. At first glance, the contraption looked like a torture device, but the modern technology fascinated young Florence. Skincare would go on to become her favorite focus. Skin was the natural canvas; cosmetics were the enhancement tools.

Mrs. Adair hired Florence on the spot. Her wages averaged $6 a week. On off-hours, Florence begged Mrs. Adair to teach her how to mix ointments and administer the "Ganesh" technique. Within a few months, clients began requesting Florence so often she was promoted from bookkeeper to treatment girl.

The idea that beauty began on the *inside* was an awakening moment for Florence. She went on to champion the concept of "holistic beauty." Exercise, meditation, healthy food, skin nourishment, cosmetics, and fragrance were all essential to a well-rounded beauty regime. One of her many mantras: "to achieve beauty, one must first achieve health," was derived from this notion.

Florence absorbed everything about pampering, the preservation of youth, and the art of business. She was skilled at sales and convinced women to purchase products by demonstrating how they could use them at home (the concept of "morning and night routines" was new at the time). Florence had an eye for branding and a knack for reading people. She always remembered personal details that made every customer feel special when they walked in and out of the door. Her innate understanding of how the 4Ps—price, product, placement, and promotion—affected profitability made her a natural marketer.

After a year working for Mrs. Adair, often seven days a week, Florence was her top treatment girl, but the achievement left her feeling unfulfilled. She'd reached the ceiling of opportunity and wanted to *do* more, to *be* more.

With new beauty culturists cropping up daily, Mrs. Adair tasked Florence with checking out the local competition. It was common practice for culturists to keep tabs on each other, but thus far, Mrs. Adair was the benchmark to beat. On her routine visits to other salons, Florence feigned interest as a prospective customer, sampling products and taking notes on unique services the competition offered.

Mrs. Elizabeth Hubbard was a new Manhattan culturist with a small product line. Mrs. Hubbard mentioned she was looking for someone to help with packaging and promotion of her preparations. With Florence's aptitude for the business side of beauty, she saw the potential for the perfect partnership. Unbeknownst to Mrs. Adair, Florence began courting Mrs. Hubbard, flattering her with compliments and inviting her on lunch dates. Although Florence's motives were opportunistic, Mrs. Hubbard became the closest semblance of a friend Florence had in the city.

A year after she moved to Manhattan, Florence handed in her resignation to Mrs. Adair. Over a boozy lunch, she toasted with Mrs. Hubbard to the beginning of their professional partnership.

Florence's pocketbook was still a far cry from millionaire status, but her dreams continued to consume her. Her former life on the farm was a distant memory. Florence recognized the correlation between cosmetics and the rise of female emancipation—and it didn't take long before she realized the beauty business was the door she had been waiting for.

Chapter 2

Little Lou, Big City

New York
2006–2008

From above, Manhattan looked like an island of misfit toys—remnants of a child's playroom with board game pieces strewn haphazardly and forgotten figurines tucked in nooks, the buildings stacked like Lego blocks. Central Park's rectangular green space reminded me of a Monopoly board, with hotels and houses fringing its edges.

I had read that most of New York City's population came from somewhere else. A diverse island built on a shared dream. I pictured people invading like pawns in chess, motivated to succeed. I wasn't sure what the prize was, but the possibilities seemed endless: *status, wealth, power*? I guessed it was up to each player to find out, and I was eager to make my first move. I had come to New York, as everyone does, in search of something bigger than myself.

I saw Lady Liberty for the first time from the air. The pilot had to queue before landing at LaGuardia, so we circled close enough to see the darkened streaks running down her cyan cheeks. She reminded me of the woman behind the company I was about to work for—an emblem of independence and freedom. I was captivated, awestruck by the embodiment of a strong female figure at the height of her potential. I thought the Statue of Liberty looked contemplative, even a little scared, as though underneath her powerful pose, she, too, was terrified of the unknown.

When the plane finally landed, wheels digging deep, skidding across the tarmac, the enormous expanse of what I was undertaking began to set in. I felt a *whoosh* of excitement tinged with trepidation.

Arriving felt like a literal check off "Lou's Life List" pinned on my bulletin board back home, yet I was plagued by the sense I didn't deserve to be there. I knew little about the ways of the world beyond the bubble I had just come from, only that I aspired to be a part of the corporate climb, to reach the apex of a professional career.

After picking up my luggage at the airport, I waited outside for a taxi. The line moved quickly as people hopped into the endless parade of yellow cabs. Soon the Manhattan skyline tumbled into tangible view.

"Excuse me, sir, may I roll down the window?" I asked the cab driver.

"You can do whatever you want," he said.

I can do whatever I want, his words echoed. The liberation from that sentence was overwhelming for someone who had always followed a singular, planned path set out before her, but maybe that's what it meant to be an adult: multiple routes with variable outcomes.

New York has a way of making you feel like it's exclusively yours, yet it belongs to no one. "Absorb everything the city has to offer!" my dad said before I left. I had set off like a sponge, ready to soak up every last secret. However, I would soon discover it was the city that absorbed you.

The traffic was thick the rest of the ride from LaGuardia into Manhattan. I didn't mind. It gave me a chance to catch up on the present facts. It was the summer of 2008; I was eighteen and had secured an internship at one of the biggest beauty companies in one of the greatest cities in the world. *Who the hell did I think I was? Lauren Conrad on The Hills?* Coming from a small pocket of Canada, my life was far from an MTV reality show, so getting this kind of dream internship opportunity was monumental to me. I'd spent the last eighteen years seeking approval from my parents, teachers, coaches, and peers. Progressing from gold stars in kindergarten to good grades in high school, my self-worth was wrapped up in academic achievements.

I felt the weight of the high expectations placed upon me. Earning praise for doing well on an exam or essay encouraged me to keep reaching for more, to keep raising the bar, to keep achieving. I was cognizant of my privilege, that not every kid had the foundational support of others who believed in them, so I felt guilty if I wasn't always striving to do more, to be more. There was no reason for me *not* to succeed, other than my own shortcomings, which I mitigated with the belief that if I planned ahead and worked hard enough, harder than anyone, my efforts would be rewarded. *Plan Ahead + Work Hard = Achieve Goals.* That was my formula for success.

The problem with this theory, I would later discover, was that in the real world, there are some things you can't plan for, and some things, no matter how hard you work, won't result in external praise or achievement of goals.

Ever since I was little, I had the inclination that *something big* was on the verge of happening. I never knew quite what it would be, but I thought if I worked hard enough, *something big* would manifest itself. In the fourth grade I developed insomnia, a curse that would return sporadically in my adult life. My parents were deeply concerned about my inability to fall asleep and the dark circles under my nine-year-old eyes, so after consulting with my teachers and principal, we eventually went to see a psychologist. My memories are patchy from this period, but I remember we determined the main cause of my insomnia was because I worried too much about the future: upcoming recitals, races, and tests—any event that I perceived would set me up for success in adulthood. From a young age, I was always on a quest to accomplish the impossible, to do everything perfectly and make my parents proud. Even before my tenth birthday, I worried I wasn't doing enough in the present to prepare for *something big* in my future.

Books were my greatest comfort. Reading gave me a refuge from the torrent of thoughts; a place to escape when the pressure I placed on myself to achieve became overwhelming. I cared deeply about what other people thought of me. Through their eyes I constructed an identity of who I thought I was supposed to be. My confidence relied on the validation of others, and I was gripped by self-doubt without it. As a perfectionist, I feared failure most of all. *Who am I if I don't get good grades in school? Who will I be if I don't rise to the top of the corporate ladder as an adult? Who am I if I don't accomplish what I set out to do, what others expect me to do? Who am I if I don't succeed?*

My parents taught me early on that what others often perceived as "luck" was actually preparation meeting opportunity. Preparation was what happened behind closed doors, while opportunity was being courageous enough to open those doors and walk through. Getting an internship in New York City was my "lucky break" to some, but I believed my preparation had met opportunity. Even though deep down, I didn't truly believe in myself, I was buoyed by the influences that had shaped me to that point. Now, it wasn't only my parents and teachers who thought I had the potential to be somebody; strangers in another country thought I was worthy enough to be offered a coveted stepping stone to the corporate door.

To me, my Manhattan internship wasn't a one-off adventure that would end in four months. It was a rung on a much larger ladder. And all I wanted, or thought I wanted, was to get to the top. I wanted to be CEO of the company, to transition from academic to corporate achievement, to reap the rewards the city dangled: *status, wealth, power.* It was what others expected of me, so I expected it of myself.

***

A year and a half before I moved to Manhattan, a chance encounter would set my life's path in motion.

As much as I loved school, I wasn't top-of-my-class level smart. This was a valuable realization. To compensate, I worked really, really, ridiculously hard. *Plan Ahead + Work Hard = Achieve Goals.* I stayed up past midnight to memorize material like I was the lead understudy in a Broadway play. I read, rehearsed, and reviewed until my eyelids rebelled. I learned the patterns of what teachers looked for on tests and which regurgitated textbook answers elicited full marks. This repeated practice allowed me to read people, decipher what they want, and find a resourceful way to present it to them. In essence, I faked it 'til I made it. Now, I realize I was strengthening a muscle that would help me once I entered the real world. At first, I resented the extra effort it took to excel, but soon, the process for success became as habitual as blinking.

In high school, English was my favorite subject; however, at the time, I never thought of reading and writing as a plausible career. They were activities I liked to do for fun, and I didn't equate *job* with *joy*. I loved books with strong female characters, like Jo in *Little Women*, who weren't afraid to follow a different path than society set out for them, largely because at that age it was a trait I did not possess.

When I was young, I had many ideas of what I was going to be. On one of my elementary school assignments, I wrote that I was going to be a Spice Girl (zigga-zig-ah), Briefcase Woman (I think I meant businesswoman), and a Wizard Writer (*Harry Potter* had just come out). I didn't overanalyze or question the steps it would take to be that bizarre combination of a triple threat, and neither did anyone else. *I could be anyone! I could do anything!* No one laughed, judged, or criticized my choices. The options were limitless.

As I aged, I became subject to "logic" and "realism," accompanied by new emotions of fear and self-doubt. Now that I was faced with adult decisions about what I wanted to be when I grew up, I wished I could go back to being a kid, where if you wanted to be something, you were whimsically blind to the obstacles and breezily transparent about your innermost desires.

The dream of writing a book someday never went away, but faced with the pressure to make a decision about my future, I chose to pursue a more practical, direct path to financial and societal success. For university, I studied "business." The vague umbrella term felt safe and broad enough to give me an array of job prospects after graduation.

It also felt weighted with importance. When kids asked, "What does your dad do?" The answer: "He's a businessman" always elicited the most impressive responses. I wanted to feel that kind of significance in the world, to be a self-made businesswoman. Oddly, the same question was rarely asked about what my mom did. The subtle innuendos of a patriarchal society, lost on me then, grew clearer as I got older.

***

Late October 2006, there was a torrential downpour on the day I tagged along to my dad's twenty-fifth class reunion. A large white tent was assembled like a classy circus on the lawn in front of the Richard Ivey School of Business. Corralled like cattle, we sought refuge from the rain under the cozy canopy beneath patio heaters.

It was early morning, but the bar area was packed. Circular tables and folding chairs were scattered aimlessly. On my tiptoes, I could see a small wooden stage with a podium and an older gentleman in a navy suit with a paisley pocket square muffling into the microphone about donations for a new building.

"Nice mullet," my dad said as he surveyed the scene.

"Who's got a mullet?" I said, rubbernecking.

"The school! Business in the front, party in the back," my dad joked. He made every situation seem less intimidating.

Time dripped on like molasses as I followed my dad around the tent while he reunited with former classmates. Between sips of beer and stories from their glory days, they all seemed to repeat the same opening line: "Wow, you sure have changed, but your wife hasn't aged one bit." My dad played along before introducing me as his eldest daughter. This seemed to make them all feel old.

I was still in that naïve state where I found age to be a deterrent. I wanted to be old enough to drink alcohol and recount amusing anecdotes along with them. They held their whiskey and wore their wealth with the ceremony of a coronation. I was desperate for maturity, to make something of myself like these people had.

"Three daughters? Poor guy. Must have done something wrong in a past life to get dealt that hand," one man snorted, ignoring the fact that I, one of his three daughters, was standing there.

"You mean he must have done something *right*," I shot back playfully, careful to convey my correction while still being "in on the joke." Playing along with male bravado was sometimes exhausting. The pity party for a dad with three daughters felt anachronistic. After a while, even sexism gets boring.

My dad got lost in another conversation. I tuned out and scanned the scene. One man across the tent, around my dad's age, caught my attention. He had the aura of an Old Hollywood golden boy, like a young James Dean or Clint Eastwood. His bronzed tan, immaculately coiffed blond hair, and piercing blue eyes stood out among the muted hues of the gray day. It wasn't just his appearance that caught my attention so much as his confidence and charisma. My impression of him was infused with automatic authority. I continued to watch in eager observance, as though by sheer surveillance, his magnetism would waft through the air and latch onto me.

"Who's the blond silver fox?" I poked my dad softly in the ribs and motioned in the movie star's direction.

"Oh, that's Scott Beattie. You should go talk to him," my dad suggested, more as a way to shed me as his shadow, before diving back into his conversation.

With Diet Coke pumping through my veins, and nothing better to do, I glided across the room and hovered on the outer edge of the circle surrounding him.

"Well, my glass won't refresh itself," said a woman wearing a Pepto-Bismol shade of lipstick. The rest of the troops retreated to the bar along with her, opening up a space in front of Scott Beattie. I sidled into the open spot.

"Hi, Mr. Beattie, I'm Eric Johnson's daughter. He was class of '81. I'm interested in Ivey's business program, so I'm tagging along to check it out. I just wanted to introduce myself." I stuck my hand out to shake his like I was running for public office. Even in the moment, I was mortified at how uncool I was playing it, but the words tumbled out of my mouth like Olympic gymnasts.

"Well hello, Eric Johnson's daughter," he said, unruffled by my precociousness. "Is your mom Denise, by any chance? She must be. You look just like her," he said, answering his own question.

"Yep, that's my mom," I acquiesced. *Talking about my parents was not helping me to appear more mature.* "I'm Louise, their eldest daughter," I offered, hoping that my primary rank would add an air of authority.

"Nice to meet you," he said. "Oh, and please call me Scott. Mr. Beattie makes me feel old," he said as he finally shook my outstretched hand, which had nearly turned limp from hanging in anticipated suspension. What was with everyone complaining about being old?

Looking back, I can't pinpoint what possessed me to approach Mr. Beattie (I could never level us by calling him Scott), or what I expected from my keen introduction, just that I was so strongly compelled to meet him that day. It was as if I were pushed by a giant gust of wind, or an invisible guiding hand, powerless against fate.

The band started playing in the background as Mr. Beattie handed me a business card and said, "My company offers internships every summer. You should consider applying if you're interested."

"Oh, thank you," I said, stuffing it quickly into my leather jacket so that I could duplicate the gesture. "Glad I finally have an excuse to use these," I replied, as I dug into my purse and handed over one of my homemade "business cards," a scrap of paper I'd hand-cut into uneven rectangles with my name and email: write_to_lou@hotmail. com, to keep in touch with other prospective Ivey students I had hoped to encounter that day. So far, I'd only met old dudes, so Mr. Beattie was my first recipient.

"Thanks," he said, with a bemused chuckle, for some reason.

Later that night, I emptied the contents of my leather jacket, and his business card fell out. I turned it over, thumbing the embossed red door logo and read: *Scott Beattie, Chairman, President and CEO of Elizabeth Arden*. My mouth dropped open.

***

For over a year after my fateful encounter with Mr. Beattie, his Elizabeth Arden business card stayed tacked beside "Lou's Life List," the handwritten list of goals I hoped to accomplish someday. That was when my mom gave me *War Paint,* and my Elizabeth Arden obsession skyrocketed. During bouts of homework procrastination, I sat at my desk and stared at the red door logo stamped on the business card, envisioning a day where I might walk through it in real life.

My grandmothers were the most impressed when I mentioned my chance meeting with Mr. Beattie and urged me to apply for an internship. Having grown up in the zenith of Arden's makeup monopoly, Elizabeth Arden was as beloved by them as Queen Elizabeth II (they were royal fanatics). Both of my grandmothers weren't encouraged to work outside of the home once they became pregnant in their late teens and early twenties, so in a way, it felt like sending in my résumé to Elizabeth Arden was fulfilling a generational dream.

The company's loyal consumers, like my grandmothers, were aging out of the category, and with increased competition and changing shopping habits (Sephora > department stores), the name Elizabeth Arden was starting to fade from the mainstream.

I bought a red Moleskine notebook as a catchall to document my thoughts during this chapter of life—which quickly became a place to house my notes and research on Elizabeth Arden. I had recently gone through a heavy Joan Didion phase, and inside the hardcover I wrote, "I write entirely to find out what I'm thinking, what I'm looking at, what I see and what it means." Joan Didion's use of writing as a tool for observation and self-reflection rekindled the romanticism of journaling for me. Writing offered an exploration of the mind. I'd kept diaries on and off growing up, but addressing my inner thoughts to "Dear Diary" always made me feel as though I was spiraling into madness talking to an inanimate object. Anne Frank dedicated her diary entries to "Dear Kitty," a fictional friend she confided in and sought advice from, and to me, addressing someone outside of yourself was a genius act of catharsis. I adopted this format for my own journals and found putting my feelings onto paper provided a profound emotional release.

As I became obsessed with following in Elizabeth's footsteps, I dedicated my diary entries to "Dear Liz." Although it was a one-way correspondence, it made me feel less alone. In psychological effect, I was writing to myself, an audience of one, but because journaling wasn't intended for public consumption, it became a private place to confess my thoughts to "a real person" who had forged the path before me.

***

Two years after I met Mr. Beattie, I had graduated from high school and was nearing the end of my first year of university (taking prerequisite courses for the Ivey business program). While most students were making the most of their newfound adolescent freedom, attending keg parties and sipping from red Solo cups, all I could think about was securing an internship at Arden.

At the time, I thought "business emails" meant limiting my use of multiple exclamation marks (!!!), so after a few drafts, I sent the following along with my résumé:

Dear Mr. Beattie,

I don't know if you will remember me, but we spoke briefly at Ivey's homecoming a couple years ago. You mentioned your company offered internships, and I would love to be considered. Please let me know with whom I should contact for next steps in the application process.

Thank you,

Louise

I never heard from him (and I thought "with whom" made me sound so sophisticated), so I mailed a hard copy of my cover letter and résumé to the New York City address on Mr. Beattie's business card. Snail mail also resulted in silence.

Undeterred, I went so far as to call the Elizabeth Arden head office and requested to speak with the human resources department. The receptionist couldn't connect me since I didn't have an extension number or know anyone in the department's name. A few weeks later I tried calling again, but it went to an automated voice message. I stopped calling, paranoid they would dial *69 and blacklist me for being a stalker.

As the last patches of snow vanished on campus, my cell phone buzzed loudly in my backpack in the middle of my economics lecture. There was no caller ID, but I bolted outside (luckily, I was sitting in the top row near the exit).

"Hello?" I answered.

"Hi, is this Louise Johnson?" chimed a female voice on the other line.

"Yes, it is," I responded, trying to match her mature tone.

"My name is Anne. I work in HR at Elizabeth Arden," the woman said. "We received your email *and* your letter and would like to set up a phone interview next week. Ideally, we like our intern applicants to come into the office; however, you're our first international candidate, so we'll have to interview you by phone," she said.

OH MY GOD. NEW YORK WAS (QUITE LITERALLY) CALLING. The freak out happening in my head was deafening.

"Anytime next week works for me!" I squealed, shattering my faux composure.

The next week, my phone interview was a blur, but I must have said something right because three long weeks later, Anna called to let me know I had secured one of six places in Elizabeth Arden's summer internship program.

"You'll receive an official offer package in the mail shortly," said Anna. "You will be responsible for your own accommodations; however, many interns stay at New York University (NYU) Summer Housing. It gets quite competitive, so I suggest you apply for a spot soon. Also, as our only Canadian intern, we will sponsor your J-1 visa if you procure the paperwork for us to sign," she relayed.

Getting a visa to work in the United States was one thing Elizabeth was lucky she didn't have to worry about. In the early 1900s, she didn't even need a passport to travel to Canada's southern neighbor.

"Congratulations and welcome to Arden!" she concluded.

***

Looking back, my relentless approach to getting an Arden internship seemed out of character. As a girl who lived for indoor recess so she could read, I was always more passive than aggressive. It was as though another person living inside of me was the one who wouldn't take no for an answer.

Once the high wore off, the reality of leaving my safety net of support—family, friends, and boyfriend—set in. For longer than I care to admit, I toyed with the idea of turning down the internship to hostess at the restaurant where I'd worked throughout high school in my hometown. As a teenager, the space-time continuum outside of my familial comforts felt like an infinite abyss. I still had three years of university ahead of me. Why didn't I just slow down, enjoy being eighteen, and relax a little? Slowing down and relaxing were skills I desperately needed to work on. But deep down, I knew I couldn't turn it down; my *something big* had finally come to fruition.

***

Back in the cab, zooming toward my future, pinching myself seemed pointless, but I did it anyway for effect. My NYU housing placement was at 200 Water Street in the Financial District across from the South Street Seaport. It was a swanky spot with panoramic views of all three "BMW" bridges (a trick my aunt had taught me to remember their names: Brooklyn, Manhattan, and Williamsburg). At first, I assumed everyone in Manhattan must live in a scene out of *Gossip Girl* if that was what an intern salary afforded, but the next year NYU sold the building, and my "dorm" turned into a multimillion-dollar celebrity condo. I realized I had inadvertently paid peanuts to live in a penthouse my first summer in Manhattan, which was most definitely *not* the norm.

My roommate, Laura, was interning at the Bank of New York Mellon. Our parents had grown up together and encouraged us to apply for summer residence as a pair to help our chances of getting accepted. Laura was twenty-one, and I was still three years shy of the legal drinking age in America, which back then, felt like a large gap in terms of life experience. I was nervous she would think I was too square, and as a people pleaser, I wanted her to like me—but I reminded myself of Elizabeth's first rule of success: relationships were a distraction from your goals. I wasn't in New York to make friends; I was there to work. Or so, I intended.

In preparation for my internship, my mom helped me raid the sales rack at Winners (a Canadian version of Marshalls or TJ Maxx). Finding clothes that hid my natural cleavage and met "professional standards" was a challenge. Hillary Clinton and Elizabeth Arden were my style icons for what successful women wore in the workplace, so I chose multicolored pantsuits, tasteful skirt suits (below the knee), and high-necked tops (anything that covered my chest). For my first day, I picked a red skirt suit, white blouse, and my go-to beige sports bra that was like Spanx for breasts, squishing them into a flattened uni-boob. Elizabeth and I were both Canadian, so I secretly applauded my subliminal patriotic nod to our home country with the red-and-white combo. Red also felt "on brand," even though Elizabeth's favorite color, I had read, was actually pink.

I wore minimal makeup at the time and worried a swipe of Maybelline mascara might be considered contraband, so I didn't prep much in that department. My hair was mousy and flat, so I planned to shower and blow dry it for that "working girl" volume on my first day.

Everything up until that point had been a breadcrumb along the trail to adulthood, but the internship was my lightning in a bottle, stars aligning, World-Series-kind-of-stuff moment. My preparation had met opportunity. The portal to the professional realm of my dreams was in front of me. I was finally about to walk through the red door in real life.

Chapter 3

Florence Becomes Elizabeth

New York
1909–1912

Florence and her new business partner, Mrs. Elizabeth Hubbard, knew *location, location, location* mattered if their salon was going to have a shot at success. Fifth Avenue was one of New York's most sought-after streets for upscale boutiques. Luxury jeweler, Tiffany & Co., had just moved onto the block (Audrey Hepburn wouldn't star in a movie about it for another fifty years) and the Plaza Hotel had newly opened at the base of Central Park. Florence and Mrs. Hubbard secured the third floor of a brownstone building at 509 Fifth Avenue and 42nd Street, with the help of Mr. Hubbard, as only men could sign leases.

Mr. Hubbard fronted $500 for the pair to start the salon. He also owned the University Hotel on West 47th Street and allowed Florence to live there under the stipulation that she would forego her salary as payment for room-and-board. The agreement was that once the business was profitable enough and Florence's share of the advance was paid off ($250), Mrs. Hubbard and Florence would split the profits equally. Florence agreed to keep the salon name, ELIZABETH HUBBARD, for fear women would mistake FLORENCE NIGHTINGALE as a hospital ward. Also, given Mr. Hubbard's financial backing of his wife's "hobby shop," he wanted his surname above the door.

Florence's loyal clientele followed her from Mrs. Adair's to the Hubbard salon and she quickly added value to the company by building up their patronage, but Mrs. Hubbard was more set in her ways than Florence had anticipated. It soon became evident that Mrs. Hubbard wasn't fussed about growth or expansion. She was content to keep the product line niche and collect her monthly "pocket money," as she called it. Mrs. Hubbard took control of the books, but left the heavy lifting of running a business to Florence—who handled all client treatments during the day and mixed tinctures at night, not to mention packaging the product and cleaning the salon. Florence worked herself to the bone, but was willing to do whatever it took to make their business a success.

Six months into their new beauty venture, sales were sweet, but the partnership had soured. The corporate divorce revealed an ugly side to the beauty business that Florence hadn't foreseen. Mr. and Mrs. Hubbard refused to disclose the books and pay Florence a fixed salary, despite having paid off her portion of the advance within the first two weeks of opening. An article in the *New York Tribune* on August 20, 1910 made the mess public. The dissolution of their partnership hardened Florence and taught her that trust and trepidation went hand in hand. It would be the first, but not the last time she was deceived by appearances that seemed too good to be true.

NEW YORK TRIBUNE

August 20, 1910

LAWYER RUNS BEAUTY SHOP: Partners Quarrel, Court Appoints a Receiver

Beauty culture is not exactly aligned with the practice of law, but Justice Goff appointed [lawyer] Charles K. Allen as temporary receiver of a "beauty parlor" at No. 509 Fifth Avenue.

The receivership for the beauty parlor was made necessary by a misunderstanding between Mrs. Elizabeth A. Hubbard and Miss Florence N. Graham, the former supplying the money, the latter the experience in beautifying.

Miss Graham said Mrs. Hubbard agreed if Miss Graham gave her best professional attention and talent, she could have half the profits and assets. Miss Graham complained that after she spent much time and some money in building up a patronage, Mrs. Hubbard took charge of the business and refused to permit her to see the books of concern.

Mrs. Hubbard said in reply: the arrangement was that the assets were to remain in her property at all times. She said Miss Graham was not an expert "beautifier," but a former bookkeeper at a "beauty parlor." Mrs. Hubbard said she had boarded her partner at the University Hotel until the time should arrive when the complexion business became profitable. Then, according to the defendant, Miss Graham left the hotel and sent word she would not work anymore unless she received a fixed salary. Miss Graham also threatened to open a rival establishment, said Mrs. Hubbard.

Florence was desperate to keep the beauty salon; it was all she had in the world. She offered to settle the court disputes by buying Mr. and Mrs. Hubbard out, which they agreed to for $1000 (the equivalent of nearly $30,000 today). The only problem: banks did not allow women to open accounts or apply for loans. Female financial independence was prohibited until the Equal Credit Opportunity Act in 1974, when it was legal for a woman to get a credit card without her husband's permission. As a single woman in 1910, Florence found herself in a dire financial state. She hated to admit it, but she needed a man's help.

Florence knew through correspondence with her younger sister, Gladys, that their older brother, Willie Jr., had moved to Manhattan to pursue a career on Wall Street. Florence and Willie Jr. had never been close, but desperate times call for desperate measures. Florence asked Gladys for their brother's contact information. Lo and behold, Willie Jr. (who now went by William), agreed to meet with his sister. It was a humbling experience for the fiercely independent Florence who prided herself on never relying on anyone for anything.

William co-signed the lease at 509 Fifth Avenue and lent Florence $1500 to buy out Mrs. Hubbard and enough to begin her own business. Grateful for William's help, their strained relationship turned cordial, and Florence vowed to repay her debts. Mrs. Hubbard exited the beauty business and helped her husband manage the University Hotel.

Florence was ready to start fresh in the third-floor salon at 509 Fifth Avenue, but the sign still read ELIZABETH HUBBARD above the door. It was time to create a new name and shed her former identity altogether.

Florence decided to keep "Elizabeth" due to the brand recognition she had already built, but Hubbard needed to go. It also saved money to change half, not all, of the sign. Why Florence chose the surname, "Arden," was, and still is, a mystery. Most reported histories believe the name Arden came from Florence's favorite Tennyson poem, *Enoch Arden*, a copy of which she kept on her bedside table. Another assumption is that she saw the name in the obituary of E.H. Harriman, a multimillionaire railroad executive from New York, who left behind a lush estate called "Arden," with ponds, stables, and magnificent gardens—aligned with Elizabeth's aspirations of becoming a self-made millionaire and a nod to her country roots. Shakespeare's *As You Like It* is another theory, as the heroine flees her family's court to find safety and love in the Forest of Arden. Perhaps, the surname Arden was derived from all three theories.

Before committing to the permanent name change, Florence mailed herself a letter with the moniker "Miss Elizabeth Arden" handwritten on the envelope. She wanted to see how the full name suited her in ink. Evidentially, she was pleased with the postman's delivery. Elizabeth Arden was a strong name for a strong woman looking to reinvent herself—and so Florence was reborn.

The newly self-appointed Elizabeth—*(for clarity, I will now refer to Elizabeth Arden, the person, as **Elizabeth**, and Elizabeth Arden, the company, as **Arden**)*—was in survival mode following the dissolution of her former partnership. The extra funds from her brother helped cover rent for a little while, but it wouldn't last long and she also needed to pay him back. Since Elizabeth moved out of the University Hotel, she slept on a cot in the back office as she couldn't afford rent for both an apartment and the salon. Financially, Elizabeth was in the red, but "you've got to spend a little money, to make a little money," she wrote in an update to her sister Gladys.

After replacing HUBBARD with ARDEN, Elizabeth gave the interior décor a minor facelift by painting the walls a blush pastel and adding gold accents. Elizabeth relished in solo entrepreneurship and had a newfound pep in her step. She accelerated her efforts to repay her brother and was determined to make Arden a household name.

Elizabeth began taking out newspaper advertisements, a renegade move for beauty culturists who had previously relied on word-of-mouth referrals. In a *New York Times* ad, she called the shop, "Salon d'Oro" in an effort to appeal to Manhattan's elite:

Elizabeth Arden Triumphs with the New Salon d'Oro!

Women everywhere recognize the necessity of expert guidance in caring for their looks. The Salon d'Oro is home to the exclusive Arden treatments appreciated by New York Society Women.

To help offset the hefty rent and utility costs, Elizabeth leased one of the rooms on the third-floor of the Fifth Avenue brownstone to two hairdressers, the Ogilvie sisters, Jessica and Clara. Elizabeth prided herself on helping enterprising women who would have been unable to secure such a lease on their own and allowed them to pay in cash. The arrangement was a win-win. In addition to helping with rent, the Ogilvie sisters sent their hairdressing clients to Elizabeth for beautifying services and vice versa. Jessica and Clara begged Elizabeth to go drinking and dancing with them—experience the razzle-dazzle of New York nightlife, flirt with unsuitable men, smoke cigarettes, show their ankles, and twirl under the bright lights of Times Square in the wee hours of the morning. But Elizabeth politely declined their offers so many times they eventually stopped asking. The financial strain and sting of the Hubbard's betrayal had made her all work, no play—even in a playground as enticing as Manhattan.

After doing facials and massages on clients all day, Elizabeth scrubbed the floors, updated the books, and retreated to her "laboratory" (her bedroom) to prepare inventory. Elizabeth created a small range of skin tonics (astringents) and skin foods (creams). She believed holistic beauty required a rejuvenation of the entire ecosystem: mind, body, and soul. Her new ad copy emphasized that what we put *on* our bodies should be as nourishing as the foods we put into them: "Your skin should have a balanced diet," and "Extracted from rare imported herbs, my special skin food has high nutritive value to rebuild worn tissues and active the glands." Elizabeth also began recommending at-home exercises and meal plans for customers looking to feel as good on the inside as they looked on the outside. She touted fruit in the morning and to avoid full-fat dairy products. "Cream is meant to go *on* the face, not in it," Elizabeth said.

Most beauty culturists named their tinctures simply: "tonic" or "cream," but Elizabeth was among the first to brand her products as a complete skincare line, called *Venetian Ardena*:

- *Venetian Ardena Pore Cream*: "reduces the pores 'til the skin has an exquisite satiny quality"

- *Venetian Ardena Skin Tonic*: "a mild astringent; a real tonic for the skin, imparting smoothness and brilliance to the complexion"

- *Venetian Ardena Crystalline Eye Tonic*: "comforts and strengthens the eyes when they are tired and aching; in many cases helps overcome the necessity for glasses"

To extend beyond brick-and-mortar sales, Elizabeth began promoting the purchase of her products by mail order in her newspaper ads:

GET VENETIAN ARDENA PORE CREAM $1 JAR BY MAIL

Write to "Elizabeth Arden" and request a $1 jar of Venetian Pore Cream. I will personally reply and send you my free booklet "The Quest of the Beautiful" on how to obtain good looks and keep them!

The "Quest of the Beautiful" booklet was included with every sale and detailed how to live a more holistic life with instructions on Elizabeth's revolutionary three-part skincare system—cleanse, nourish, and tone (a regimen still touted by the industry today):

There are three fundamental things to keep your skin smooth and the curves of your face firm and young. The wonderful treatments given in my famous salons are based on **cleansing, toning, and nourishing**. If you will do these three things at home, according to my scientific method, faithfully and thoughtfully, morning and night, you can have the loveliest skin that ever blossomed. Pay a visit to my Arden Salon d'Oro on Fifth Avenue for a muscle-strapping treatment to further tighten the skin.

Elizabeth sought to make the *Venetian Ardena* packaging as luxurious as her salon décor and the services she provided. Elizabeth understood the importance of cohesive branding to sell not just products, but a *lifestyle*.

Ingredients were sourced in bulk from a local drug house called Parke, Davis & Co. Elizabeth mixed, filled, labeled, and corked every glass bottle herself. Her skin tonic elixir was a combination of water, ethyl alcohol, boric acid, and essential oils. She attached pastel pink bows, and her detailed, deluxe packaging soon became a coveted item with customers who eagerly displayed the craftsmanship on their vanity tables. Elizabeth adhered to the adage that people *do judge* a book by its cover, so how her products *looked* mattered just as much as the formula inside.

Word began to spread through Manhattan's high society luncheons and galas about *Venetian Ardena* and the luxury "Salon d'Oro" on Fifth Avenue. Soon enough, high-end department stores caught wind of the buzzed about skincare products. Stern Brothers, on 42nd Street, and Bonwit Teller, at Fifth and 38th, were two of the most prominent women's retailers in the city and asked Elizabeth if she would do a test-run of *Venetian Ardena* in their stores. Elizabeth was over-the-moon, but stifled her inner excitement and coolly obliged the offer. She cleverly included her "Quest of the Beautiful" pamphlet to teach women about her three-part skincare regimen and incline customers to buy all *three* products, instead of one, and proudly display the matching trio on their dressing tables. Stern Brothers and Bonwit Teller sold out overnight and foot traffic soon doubled at the Arden Salon d'Oro.

After what happened with Mrs. Hubbard, Elizabeth remained skittish of partnerships, but as business grew, she made her first hire with Irene "Lanie" Delaney as a bookkeeper. It was a shrewd move, as Lanie would remain dedicated to the company for the rest of her life. She never married and would become one of Elizabeth's closest companions and most loyal employees—but Elizabeth didn't play favorites with Lanie at work. She was strict about keeping her personal and professional lives separate.

Elizabeth was finally able to hire treatment girls to take over the day-to-day client pampering, so she could focus on the big picture expansion strategy. It was no coincidence her staff uniforms were gilded pink smocks with matching silk hair ribbons that mimicked both the salon's décor and product packaging. Subliminal branding became Elizabeth's specialty. As *Fortune* later affirmed, "Arden built her business on swank, ultra-exclusiveness and a line beautifully packaged and styled."

Makeup was still taboo, so Elizabeth kept her salon focused on skincare and holistic beauty treatments. Publicly, Elizabeth played by societal rules, but privately, she dabbled in creating her own makeup products and began offering them as finishing touches for select clients: *Venetian Flower Powder* ("an exquisitely fine face powder") and *Venetian Rose Color* ("a smart rouge in liquid form for the lips").

By 1912, less than three years after the horrible ordeal with Mrs. Hubbard, Elizabeth had paid back her brother's loan and was a household name in New York. The former farmgirl turned marketing maven was on the move, and there was no stopping her.

- LOU -

The night before my first day of work, my new roomie Laura asked if I wanted to grab dinner and drinks. My initial plan was an indulgent evening of self-care: face mask, hot shower, moisturize my skin, call my boyfriend Logan, journal in my red notebook, and read in bed before an early lights out. I knew I wouldn't sleep from nerves and excitement, but I wanted to at least go through the motions of feeling prepared for my first day as a real-life Manhattan intern.

The humidity in New York City in the summer sometimes felt like living inside a giant rubber glove; I soon looked forward to the *whoosh* of wind from an approaching subway to cool down. Our apartment was unbearably sticky, even at night, as the sun beamed through our top floor windows all day, and the A/C window unit Laura and I had ineptly "installed" barely functioned. Laura's invitation for dinner in an air-conditioned restaurant sounded ideal before my early bedtime. Plus, I was ecstatic she thought I was cool enough to hang out with. My plans for a low-key night stopped there.

Somehow, we ended up at the Pink Elephant Club in the Meatpacking District (where in Elizabeth's day they slaughtered and stored livestock), but a century later the cavernous space had transformed into trendy nightclub. We cradled a Methuselah-sized bottle of Belvedere in a velvet booth with a tech tycoon (or, so he told us). Laura had given me a second piece of her ID and apparently it worked like a charm. It was the first time I saw someone "do drugs," and Laura explained that was why everyone's eyes looked like toonies (the Canadian two-dollar coin). Alcohol was enough of a mind-altering substance for us so we steered clear. New York nightlife was like shooting out of a cannonball into a feral jungle, and by 2 a.m., it was time to exit the revolving door of debauchery. I paper-mâchéd the side of a cab with puke on the way home.

When I woke up with a mild headache (the era of horrible hangovers had yet to infiltrate my teenage body), I was left with the aftertaste of vodka cranberry and three thoughts: I hope I apologized to that cab driver, I'm never drinking again, and I'm going to be late. *What the hell was I thinking going to a nightclub before my first day of work?*

With no time to spare, I brushed my teeth, took a cold shower, threw on the red skirt suit that the organized, responsible version of myself had laid out earlier in the week, and sprinted out the door—wet hair and all. I bargained I could still stop for coffee if I forewent blow-drying.

The woman in front of me at Starbucks looked like a modern-day Elizabeth Arden—or was I still drunk and hallucinating? She wore a pink wrap dress, rose-scented perfume, and just the right amount of blush to highlight her cheekbones. Her ethereal essence emanated perfection, like little doves helped her to get dressed in the morning. I didn't know her, but I overwhelmingly wanted to be like her. Seeing an Elizabeth doppelgänger felt like a positive omen after a rushed start to the morning. The woman ordered a grande iced coffee, and on impulse, I ordered the same, though I'd never had iced coffee before. Wasn't coffee supposed to be hot? My mom microwaved the remnants when it got cold, so I was confused as to why anyone would buy it like that.

Sipping my decidedly gross cold coffee, I weaved through throngs of heel-clad fashionistas and investment bankers in the sweltering summer heat of lower Manhattan. Melting into the pavement, the bricks, and the buildings, I became one with the choreographed chaos.

The city was not for the claustrophobic. I would soon learn how to live among the masses, breathing in unison, flowing through the streets like veins. It was as though our collective oxygen supplied the energy to keep the city alive, activating its lungs.

Thankful for the tacky tourist compass and laminated map my mom had put in my suitcase, I navigated north. My pink Nokia 6100 mobile phone that I'd had since high school didn't have GPS. "Now remember, New York's a numerical grid. Avenues run vertical and streets are horizontal," my mom had prepped me. A helpful tip, only when I *finally arrived* at the numerical grid. Until then, everything below Bowery and East 1st seemingly started with *W: Whitehall, Water, William, and Wall Street,* in what felt like a never-ending game of Snakes and Ladders.

My aunt had advised I take the subway, given it was about an hour's walk from the Financial District to Union Square, where the Elizabeth Arden head office was located. However, I decided to get my bearings aboveground before tackling that cosmopolitan coal mine.

As I strolled along, I sensed I was walking on top of a subterraneous labyrinth; one ruled by rats in conductor hats that made Manhattan's aboveground chaos seem calm. I knew I would have to brave the subway eventually, but in Elizabeth's day, she'd walked everywhere in the city, so I opted to stay above the surface.

New York emitted a sense of familiarity from having seen it through the filtered lens of movies and the confines of books. *You've Got Mail* and *Breakfast at Tiffany's* were among my favorites. In real life, looking up at the looming skyscrapers, I saw it with fresh eyes. Being there for the first time was like meeting someone you've heard a lot about, maybe lightly stalked on the internet, but in person, they're intensely more vibrant. I'd never seen such tall buildings before. Their physical majesty seemed to symbolize that the only way to grow was up. On the ground, the frenetic energy was electric.

I felt the omnipresent ghosts of the Twin Towers as I passed the construction site that now occupied their place. I was twelve when I watched the footage of their fall on TV, seven years prior, and couldn't help take a moment's pause despite the commotion surrounding me. It struck me then that Elizabeth also never saw a Manhattan skyline with Twin Towers. Somehow, we had both ended up on the bookends of this chapter in the city's history.

I kept walking, dabbing beads of perspiration, from alcohol and humidity, with the back of a soggy napkin. Shivers shot through my fingers from the ice at the bottom of the cup, a welcomed relief. I tried to make eye contact and smile at the parade of passersby, but no one looked up. Maybe they were trying not to trip over their stilettos. A man in a suit stopped abruptly ahead of me to untangle his earphones. I bumped hard into the back of his sweat-stained jacket. "SORRY! Pardon me," I said reflexively. "Canadian, eh," he said over his shoulder before picking up the pace again. Duly noted: I would have to curb the accent and apologies if I wanted to be taken for a real New Yorker. I glanced at the time on my Nokia. I had to pick up the pace if I wanted to arrive by 8:00 a.m. sharp.

After an endless game of human checkers, I arrived at the south side of Union Square. I stood on the corner in front of a Virgin Records Megastore, a giant digital clock hung above it with a string of random numbers changing by the second.

Across the street, there were men playing chess on concrete tables. Over the summer, I came to recognize their faces as they sat with the same paramount concentration day in, day out. The game looked like serious business, as though world domination was at stake. Beyond them was a lush little park. Nannies pushed lavish strollers with stylish children propped up inside, like a porcelain doll convention.

On the west side of Union Square, I weaved through a farmers' market; freshly cut lavender, sweet-smelling jars of honey, oven-baked bread and homemade raspberry pie wafted through the air as my eyes feasted on the psychedelic produce: ruby-red rhubarb with leafy tops, golden kernels of corn hugged by lime green husks, and piles of plums in rich violet skins.

In consultation with my laminated map, I finally found my way to 200 Park Avenue South. I looked up at the massive glass door—disappointed it wasn't painted red, like the famous Arden logo. Later, I learned the landmark entrance on Fifth Avenue remained red, but the corporate offices had moved to Union Square.

I scanned the plaques on the marble wall beside the grand entrance until I found what I was looking for: ELIZABETH ARDEN, etched indelibly in gold. At last, I was in the right place. A stampede of suits pushed past me and disappeared into the corporate stratosphere. I darted to the side of the building to avoid being trampled further. I reached into the depths of my purse and shoved a stick of men's Old Spice deodorant into my armpits (the scent reminded me of my boyfriend) and swallowed a handful of spearmint Tic Tacs to dilute my iced-coffee breath. Finally, I switched my filthy commuting flip-flops for a pair of office-appropriate pumps. I whipped around and hoped none of my future coworkers had spotted me in this unglamorous grooming ritual.

I strolled back to face the (non-red) door. Suddenly, I felt very small, like a shrinking Alice in Wonderland. "This is it," I whispered to myself. I took a deep breath, exhaled sharply, and walked through the doors into the lobby.

"Morning, miss, who ya here for?" boomed the elderly doorman, glancing up from the sports section of the *New York Post*. His embossed name tag told me his name was Joe.

"I'm interning here. It's my first day!" I couldn't help myself. My voice sounded so much squeakier than the mature maven I envisioned myself to be. *I should research where Elizabeth got those enunciation lessons and see if they'd take me on.*

"Knew you were fresh. You've got rookie written all over ya, kid," said Joe.

Definitely not the seasoned New Yorker vibe I was going for.

"I am here to work for Elizabeth Arden," I tried again, lengthening the words as though they were an elastic band. I read in one of my dad's *Economist* magazines that stretching syllables thickened your vocal cords, like adding starch to a recipe, to make you sound more powerful.

"Ooh the big leagues, huh? Seventh floor, slugg-ah," Joe teased, in what I later learned was a heavy Bronx accent.

The elevator dinged, and the pack of people in the lobby stood erect with lethargic alertness. Their faces melded together like a Picasso painting with no distinctive features. I looked at my watch: 7:54 a.m. *Six minutes to spare.* Joining the ranks of the communal blur, I jostled my way into an air pocket of the elevator. My enthusiasm momentarily dulled by their ominous presence; a corporate cult dressed in black that stared blankly ahead on the monotonous ride upward.

***

I spilled out of the elevator onto the seventh floor. A giant red lacquer wall snaked along the lobby, where there was a reception desk, glass coffee table, and plump chairs in the shape of lips. I had envisioned gilded pinks, antique chandeliers, and Parisian carpets like Elizabeth's era, but it was distinctly modern: minimalistic clean lines with bright red pops of furniture.

Framed ads of Catherine Zeta-Jones, the company's current spokeswoman, hung from the walls. In one image, she was draped over the top of a red door holding a bottle of Arden's signature *Red Door* fragrance, seemingly naked, save for red gloves and the spritz of perfume. Through my research, I had become enamored with old Arden ads. Elizabeth had never used celebrities in her campaigns, as she said, "Elizabeth Arden is the only famous face and name that should be associated with the brand." Instead, her ads featured delicate watercolors and nameless models, which I collected and pasted into a scrapbook (until I discovered Pinterest). The lack of diversity depicted in the early years was grossly evident. "Blonde, blue-eyed" beauty and "creamy, pale skin" was revered.

My curiosity got the better of me, so before my internship, I went to the library and took out every book I could find on the beauty industry in the 1900s. It was in *Enterprising Women: 250 Years of American Business* by Virginia Drachman where I learned about Annie Turnbo Malone and Madame C.J. Walker, pioneers of the black beauty business. Madame Walker became the first female self-made millionaire in recorded history! As Drachman wrote in *Enterprising Women*, "Not only were Malone and Walker a testimony to the vitality of the beauty industry, they stood as proof that the era of the 'self-made man' included women, white and black."

By the time I joined Arden in 2008, the company had long woken up to inclusive and diverse depictions of beauty, but more work would need to be done before systemic racism was eradicated. Ten years before I arrived, the *New York Times* ran a headline on July 16, 1999, "Elizabeth Arden Campaign Strives for the Unconventional." The article applauded the company for their avant-garde EMBRACE YOURSELF ad campaign, where they featured unretouched, journalistic-style photos of "real women" of various ages and ethnicities. My favorite tagline was: "My best feature is my big, beautiful, sexy brain." In 2009, the company hired Lerato Moloi as the first black spokeswoman for the brand. Nigerian model Adeola Ariyo would succeed her and Yoo In-young would become the first Korean woman to act as Arden's exclusive global model in 2013.

Back in the lobby, I stared down at my horrendously chipped hot pink nails. I'd never had a salon manicure before and had painted them myself. Nervously, I picked away at the jagged edges of a hangnail until I was too far down the road of no return and ripped it off like a Band-Aid. Blood oozed from my thumb. I popped it into my mouth to stop the bleeding. My first foray into adulthood and I was already sucking my thumb like a giant baby.

The five other interns, all in their early twenties, were from across the United States. They thought I was from Ontario, a small city in Ohio, until I said Canada and, for some reason, their expressions turned to pity, like I had revealed my losing hand in poker.

"I figured the ratio of males to females would rule in my favor," said Jack Thomas—the only male intern had two first names (why was I not surprised?). His tailored suit looked expensive, but his shaggy hair and doughy face made him look young, like a boy trying to be a man. "That's a *loud* color," said one of the female interns, in reference to my all-red ensemble. Two of the other girls and Jack snickered. Everyone else was wearing black or gray. My face turned as red as my blazer. I had never minded being different, but standing there, all I wanted was to blend in.

The internship coordinator skittered into the room; a scattered, squat man with an affinity for slide decks and Dr Pepper. He gave us a tour of the office, which encompassed three floors, and then introduced us to our respective teams.

By the twenty-first century, Arden was a full-scale beauty business, with products sold in over ninety countries and estimated annual global retail sales in excess of $1 billion. "Cosmetics," I learned, was an umbrella term for anything that "enhanced one's appearance," so the cosmetic company was divided into three pillars: skincare, color (the industry term for makeup), and fragrance. I was designated to the Global Color Marketing department.

Betty Baker was my boss (alliteration and all). She was polished and sophisticated, as though she had sprung from the womb a fully formed adult. Betty wore red lipstick, winged eyeliner, and blanket of blush, which nicely juxtaposed her jet-black bob. She wore a different pair of glasses to match her outfit every day. They suited her so much I forgot the fashionable frames weren't a permanent part of her face. Once, she took them off to rub her eyes during a meeting and it was like seeing someone remove a freckle or a birthmark.

Reportedly, Elizabeth wouldn't hire anyone who wore glasses in an interview (despite being nearsighted herself), insisting they were "aging and we're in the youth and beauty business, dear." A lot had changed since the 1900s, and by proudly sporting her specs, Betty subtly dismantled one of the many dichotomies about femininity for me, as I thought they made her look both brainy *and* beautiful.

As a boss, Betty was stern and serious, but I became aware that, like Elizabeth, it was a curated professional front, a shield of protective armor to keep her personal life private, which I respected. The rest of the Global Color Marketing team was comprised of Natalie, a waifish brunette with a smattering of cute freckles, and Jada, who had a halo of gorgeous curls and gray-cashmere eyes. Their ages were hard to place in a city like New York, which suffered from Peter Pan syndrome; everyone acted "grown-up," but no one aged.

I needed to impress Betty, Natalie, and Jada if I wanted to be hired back at Arden in subsequent years. Intern spots were scarce, but full-time positions were even harder to come by. I couldn't afford a misstep if I was serious about working my way up in the company.

My first day flew by in a glossy haze of newness: new names, new desk, new coffee machine, new log-in passwords, and new expectations.

The fragrance, skincare, and color marketing departments were on one floor in an open cubicle layout, with executive offices flanking the perimeter overlooking Union Square Park. My biggest highlight of the day was when Natalie brought me to the stationery supply closet: endless shelves of pens, pencils, highlighters, rulers, stickers, notepads, folders, and envelopes embossed with the Arden red door logo. It smelled like the inside of a freshly bound book, pages hot off the press, ink not yet dried. My internship offer letter had originated from a stack of paper on a shelf in that room; a small full-circle moment I recorded later that night in my red journal.

On the way back to my desk, carrying the school supply haul of my dreams, Natalie introduced me to an elderly gentleman named James "Jimmy" Campanella, the resident "Godfather" of the company; rumor had it he was a retired kingpin. Jimmy's sharkskin gray suits matched his slicked strands, and a cigar wouldn't have looked out of place perched in his breast pocket. He had the second-largest office beside the CEO, but I never knew what his actual job was—only that he was beloved and seemed to have been at Arden since the beginning. You could never find him when you actually needed to speak with him; he just magically appeared like the fairy godfather he was. He wasn't fussed with hierarchy or interoffice politics and easily transitioned from chatting with senior management to helping a lowly intern, like me, change an ink cartridge.

"Great getup!" Jimmy said, upon introduction.

"Thank you. Not too *loud* for the office?" I asked, sensing he was an honest critic.

"God, no. Red's your color, kid," he responded sincerely.

From day one, we formed a special bond. Jimmy always looked out for me, and I forever had a soft spot for him.

At the end of my first day, I was relieved to slide my sore-heeled feet back into flip-flops. On my walk home, I opened a U.S. bank account to deposit my paychecks. I walked out of TD Bank, turning the shiny credit card in my hands, silently acknowledging how, unlike Elizabeth, I hadn't needed a man's permission to obtain it.

Later that night, from my bed overlooking the BMW bridges, I lay on my stomach and recapped the day's events in my red journal: "Dear Liz, what a DAY! It started off a bit stressful (and sweaty)…but I LOVE NEW YORK already. I went out in the Meatpacking District last night (which, I know, you would have *not* approved of), but I won't make it a habit. It was fun getting to explore the city with Laura (she's the best), but work is my #1 priority…bedtime! Need my beauty sleep ⊠ Until next time, Lou xo"

I wanted to shadow Elizabeth's success, but there was something about the city that bewildered my sense of self. I had always followed my formula (*Plan Ahead* + *Work Hard* = *Achieve Goals*), but I slowly started to feel other aspects of my budding identity trying to break free. There must have been a part of Elizabeth, too, that yearned to veer off the structured path. How had she handled this splintering of selves?

The intensity of my arrival in Manhattan did not leave me for hours, weeks, even months. Everything was a revelation: unfurling, presenting itself to me. The quivering sense of newness was refreshing. New York, on the other hand, was indifferent to me. I was in love, and it barely knew I existed.

Chapter 4

Paint the Town Red

New York

1912–1915

NEW YORK TIMES

May 5, 1912

SUFFRAGE ARMY OF 10,000 WOMEN OUT ON PARADE

As the late afternoon shadows were beginning to slant across the green of Washington Square, a ripple of anticipation and muffled cheers from spectators erupted as the suffragettes assembled in the cross streets on foot, as flower-bedecked carriages and Joan of Arcs on horseback trotted smartly underneath the Washington Arch

Ten thousand strong marched up Fifth Avenue to Carnegie Hall at sundown yesterday in a parade which New York has never seen. 4,000 spectators watched from the steps of the new Public Library as women young and old, rich and poor, banded in sisterhood dressed in simple white, wearing VOTES FOR WOMEN sashes and 39-cent straw hats with ribbons.

There were women whose faces bore traces of a life of hard labor, young girls lovely of face and fashionably gowned, and women who smiled in preoccupied ways as though they had just put the roast into the oven, whipped off their aprons and hurried out to be in the parade—many plainly worried at leaving their household cares for so long.

POLICE PROTECTION INEFFICENT AS ROWDIES RUSHED THE LINES

Onlookers jeered as they would at a circus parade without any thought as to the political significance the event held for women. There was hardly a moment when you could not hear gibes, cat-calls and hisses.

Women were constantly rushed by flying wedges of rowdies without any policemen in sight to check them. Crowds from the sidewalks surged into the street and blocked the progress of the parade.

The men watching gave no signs of encouragement, yet women waved banners, handkerchiefs and scarfs from every window on Fifth Avenue.

Walking in a suffrage parade requires moral courage and every worn marcher at Carnegie Hall must have murmured to herself with deep satisfaction: "It was entirely worth the while." Women's fight for suffrage is transforming her from a doll into a human being.

Elizabeth watched the suffrage parade from her office window at 509 Fifth Avenue on May 4, 1912. She was a staunch supporter of women's rights, but dismayed to read about the backlash from the march in the next day's newspaper. By daring to enter the world of commerce, "a man's domain," Elizabeth had already disrupted the social order, and feared an overtly political stance could bury her growing empire.

Many women who had marched were fired by their employers. The *New York Times* reported on Miss Aimee Hutchinson, a twenty-one-year-old teacher who lost her job when the school's principal discovered her participation in the suffrage parade. He called her into his office and said, "The women's suffrage movement is hatred of mankind, and you are not a good example to the students."

However, six months later, on November 9, 1912, Elizabeth could no longer stand idly by in silence. Shuttering the salon for the day, she took to the streets and joined twenty thousand women, double the size of the previous parade, and advocated for the right to vote. The most striking sight was the bold red color on the women's lips, as they vibrantly spoke their truth.

Elizabeth weaved among the masses handing out her Venetian Lip Paste and Venetian Arden Lip Pencil in deep red—the original "lip kit." In history, it is often the slightest gestures that become revolutionary. The red lip kits were small, yet mighty weapons—a red pout in place of a middle finger against the patriarchy. Red lips were still considered illicit and immoral, so the women wore them in unison as a rebellious emblem of emancipation. Makeup was no longer a sign of sin but of sovereignty.

Elizabeth narrowly avoided arrest as women were handcuffed and jailed for "disrupting the peace" and "obstructing the sidewalk"—but most daringly, she risked the reputation of her business. There was a rumbling undercurrent of antisuffragists who feared destabilization and destruction of the political, economic, and social stratosphere should women be granted autonomy over their minds and bodies. The *National Association Opposed to Woman Suffrage* argued "women lacked the mental capacity to be informed on political issues" and were "too busy taking care of her husband, children, and the home to have time to devote to anything else." As a single businesswoman, Elizabeth was an easy target for negative press. The media painted suffragettes, especially "spinsters," as bitter, frigid, and angry man-haters. Major news outlets, including the *New York Times*, warned against the "reign of terror" that would ensue if gender roles were reimagined and to stay away from "fiendish" women who supported this first-wave of feminism.

Elizabeth's first foray into the political arena, although controversial, solidified her standing with likeminded women who shared her worldviews. Her burgeoning beauty business was one of the few industries where women had equal-opportunity employment. Elizabeth, as female founder and CEO, made it possible for women to imagine themselves climbing the corporate ladder into leadership roles. The patriarchal nature of academic institutions and corporations fostered the perception that women were somehow less qualified and incompetent; meanwhile it was the laws and systems (created by men) that denied women the opportunities to excel.

The women's suffrage movement, born and bred underground, had finally burst through the trapdoor and onto the national agenda. I felt a deep sense of gratitude for women like Elizabeth, who fought on my behalf decades before I was born. Because of their strength and sacrifice, the doors of opportunity were flung open for the next generation of women; mine just so happened to be red.

In the months following the suffrage parade, makeup began gaining mainstream acceptance. Women slowly started to claim their independence, decorating their faces as *they* saw fit in both private and public spaces. In a 1913 article entitled "The Art of Making Up" it advocated that "a little judicious makeup hurts no one, but it pays to go to a professional of good taste and study the secrets of touching up the face to make the most of one's good points. If you handle colors gently, eyes will brighten and crow's feet become less evident. Dab the lips slightly with rouge, but do not make your mouth look like raw beef."

Over a century before blogs became a part of our cultural zeitgeist, Elizabeth's beauty booklet, "The Quest of the Beautiful," had gained a cult-like following. The advent of the printing press had fostered the emerging medium, and she updated the pamphlet regularly with tips about the latest anti-aging techniques and lotions and potions that would "prolong the spirit of youth." After the suffrage parade, she started to introduce makeup products into her Venetian skincare line. Through customer salon visits, product mail order and word-of-mouth at department store beauty counters, Elizabeth created a community of brand loyalists. She continued her strong advertising crusade and was strategic in using images and ad copy that were instantly identifiable with the Arden brand. "Repetition makes reputation, and reputation makes customers," Elizabeth said. Her ingénue approach to business offered a level of approachability in direct-to-consumer marketing that large, impersonal corporations in the early twentieth century failed to provide. Women felt as though Elizabeth spoke directly to them, sharing beauty secrets as friends would over tea at a ladies' luncheon.

Fashion magazines began to overtake the beauty pamphlet in popularity, as they had the advertising money for mass distribution. *Vogue* first circulated in America in 1892 as a men's magazine, but after Condé Nast acquired it in 1909, he switched the magazine's focus to upper-class society women, transforming *Vogue* into the fashion bible known today. Elizabeth had foreseen the power of print and press with her beauty booklet and was eager to take advantage of the women's magazine industry in its infancy.

Since 1910, *Vogue* editors in chief have always been female, and in 1914, Edna Woolman Chase succeeded Marie Harrison, where she would reign as editor in chief for over fifty years. Edna was the same age as Elizabeth, and the two enterprising women began their formative careers in Manhattan at the same time. The pair worked their way up from the bottom, Edna in the mailroom, Elizabeth as a bookkeeper, to become leaders in their fields—both were later awarded the Legion of Honor in France, as recognition of their contributions to the fashion and beauty industry. Some sources believe Edna and Elizabeth first met at Martha Washington's Hotel For Women, a boarding house in Manhattan, though even if they did pass each other in the hall, neither woman was interested in making friends—both were purely focused on their corporate ambitions. Years later, Edna's obituary confirmed their shared philosophies: "Edna hardly seemed to have a personal life. She made her career her only happiness."

The most likely account of Edna and Elizabeth's first meeting was shortly after Edna was appointed editor in chief, in 1914, when she made history by putting on the first fashion show in the United States. Parisian workrooms were closed to Americans during World War I, so Edna asked leading seamstresses in New York to create designs for presentation under the sponsorship of *Vogue* to a group of society women. To make up the models, Edna called upon the leading beauty salon, Arden's Salon d'Oro on Fifth Avenue. Edna and Elizabeth hit it off immediately, as Edna believed "beauty was not an adornment added for decoration, but a quality essential to the expression of the best." After the success of the fashion show, Edna began regularly including Arden advertisements in *Vogue*. Beauty products were becoming a popular accessory to fashion and a small way to boost spirits during the war. Elizabeth's first *Vogue* feature was a full-page, black-and-white ad with the copy: "Don't wear a passé complexion this season and match your makeup to your costume the Arden way!" She highlighted her Venetian range of skincare and makeup for women to "look their best even during the hard season of war-time," which added "lines of tension and fatigue." The continuous coverage in *Vogue* helped to further catapult Arden as *the* name in beauty.

Edna and Elizabeth met regularly for lunch, where conversation almost always turned to shop talk. Their friendship circle grew over the years to include a select group of businesswomen. Over an informal luncheon, Edna, Elizabeth, Eleanor Roosevelt, a few other women conceived of the idea for Fashion Group International (FGI), to publicize and propel the careers of women in the fashion and beauty industry. FGI was officially incorporated in 1930 and still exists today. Edna and Elizabeth's friendship endured a lifetime, but as two strong-willed women, they would occasionally lock horns along the way.

By 1915, Elizabeth had finally moved out of the back room in her office and into a small apartment at 321 West 94th Street on the west side of Central Park. The added brand exposure from *Vogue* had increased foot traffic at Salon d'Oro so much that she needed more space. When 509 Fifth Avenue was marked for demolition that year, Elizabeth moved her Salon d'Oro up the street to 673 Fifth Avenue, amicably parting ways with the Ogilvie sisters, who found a spot at 505 Fifth Avenue. The timing of the move couldn't have been more fortuitous as European beauty culturist Helena Rubinstein had just opened her first American beauty salon at 15 East 49th to great fanfare—and much to Elizabeth's chagrin, with a big announcement and glowing review in *Vogue*:

A FAMOUS EUROPEAN "HOUSE OF BEAUTY"
ANNOUNCES THE OPENING OF ITS DOORS IN NEW YORK

Madame Helena Rubinstein, a scientific beauty culturist whose Maison de Beauté Valaze in London and Paris are well-known landmarks to the ladies of European high society, announces the opening of her American Maison de Beauté Valaze at No. 15 East 49th Street. Radiating the spirit of beauty, Madame Rubinstein's knowledge is now at the disposal of the women of New York City.

Elizabeth was furious Edna had allowed direct competition to infiltrate the pages of *her* territory—and demanded a double-page feature on Salon d'Oro's move, while not-so-subtly reinforcing her position at the top of the beauty culturist food chain.

ELIZABETH ARDEN ANNOUNCES MOVE TO 673 FIFTH AVENUE

This announcement will occasion no surprise as it has long been an "open secret" that my present Arden Salon d'Oro at 509 Fifth Avenue was fast becoming inadequate to meet the demands of a rapidly growing clientele, the LARGEST OF ITS KIND IN NEW YORK. I therefore take this opportunity to announce the move of Salon d'Oro to 673 Fifth Avenue. As the leading expert in scientific treatments, staff has been increased and thoroughly trained in my Venetian methods. New equipment has also been installed. My interior decorator's efforts have been highly successful from every point of art and utility. You are invited to view the new Salon d'Oro as soon as it is opened. I am confident you will judge it a worthy successor to the old.

In 1915, three years after Elizabeth handed out red lip kits in the suffrage parade, Maurice Levy created a cylindrical metal twist-up tube that ameliorated lipstick application. The invention prevented women from getting rouge paste all over their fingers and made it easy to pop the tube into their purse on-the-go. Elizabeth immediately switched her Venetian Lip Paste, in shades Star and Carnival, from a pot to refillable cream formats in gold metal tubes. Red lips were becoming a sign of the times.

Upon her five-year mark in Manhattan, Elizabeth Arden—the person *and* the company—began to merge into a single entity. As Elizabeth's business transformed into a brand, the line blurred between who she truly was and who she was trying to portray. Elizabeth had perfected her public persona, but self-doubt simmered beneath the extraverted surface.

- LOU -

Prior to the summer of 2008, I'd only worn lipstick once for a high school dance. I looked like a clown and fervently tried to wipe it off, but the skin around my mouth stayed stained for the whole night, like a scarlet letter of my failed attempt at femininity.

Now that I was interning in the beauty industry, I felt compelled to experiment with makeup again. Elizabeth had helped turn red lipstick into a symbol of women's liberation, so maybe a swipe of cherry on the lips could tease out my own confidence? At least getting familiar with the products, testing them on myself, would help me to become a better makeup marketer.

Getting free samples was an unexpected perk of the job. My boss, Betty, gave me endless eyeshadow, blush, foundation, and lipstick testers to bring home, in various textures and formats: matte, shiny, liquid, liquid-to-matte, ultra-pigmented, lightly tinted, cream, powder, metallic, and velvety finishes—in every hue of the rainbow.

One morning, I decided to rock a red Arden lipstick shade called Poppy Cream to work. Notorious B.I.G. was blasting through my headphones as I stepped mindlessly into the elevator. I felt a tap on my shoulder and turned to face Mr. Beattie. The music was aggressively audible as I struggled to turn off my pink iPod.

"Hello, Louise. How's the internship going so far?" he asked.

"Hi, hell...hello, Mr. Beattie," I fumbled. "I'm really enjoying it. Learning a lot," I replied, slowly regaining my speech. I had forgotten how commanding his presence was. I wondered if there were pheromones people emitted once they reached the pinnacle of success. He was the same as when we first met, but now that I knew he was the CEO, I suddenly withered under the weight of my own timidity.

"Thank you again for this incredible opportunity," I word-vomited.

"Don't thank me; you got yourself here. I've been hearing good things about your work from Betty," he said. *The king of beauty was keeping tabs on me?!*

Before he exited the elevator, he turned and said, "Keep making us proud."

In that instant, I thought of the "us" as him and Elizabeth. I wanted to keep showing up in a way that honored both of their legacies at Arden. In response, I smiled so wide my cheeks ached even after the muscles relaxed. Mr. Beattie gave me a strange head tilt before veering into his office and closing the door.

On the way to my desk, I made a pit-stop at the restroom where I caught a glimpse of myself in the mirror. Every one of my teeth was covered in Poppy Cream red lipstick. Not only that, it was somehow smudged sideways up my cheeks, like a devil Cheshire cat. I cringed at the thought of the big Joker grin I had just flashed Mr. Beattie. My only interaction with the CEO that summer, and I bared my bloodthirsty gums like a vulture. I prayed he wouldn't tell Betty that her intern didn't even know how to apply beauty products properly—I pictured my internship application being rejected the next year; denied with a big red stamp: *NOT ARDEN MATERIAL.*

After that embarrassing snafu, I asked Natalie and Jada to give me a few tutorials on the art of makeup application. They patiently obliged and took me on a "field trip" to the Red Door spa where an Arden treatment girl taught me some tips and tricks—everything from a winged cat eye to keeping lipstick off my teeth (form an "O" with your lips, put your index finger through the "O," and slowly pull it out, also, lip liner can act as an anchor to prevent the color from budging). Reading was my preferred method of learning, so I stocked up on step-by-step pamphlets used for beauty advisor trainings at department stores and studied industry terms and techniques like it was for a final exam:

- FIFO = First In First Out

- DC = Discontinued

- AIO = All-in-One products

- GWP = Gift With Purchase

- COGs = Cost of Goods

- BAs = Beauty Advisors (sales reps at the beauty counters in department stores)

- ELF = Eyes, Lips, Face

- FNDT = Foundation

- Foil(ed) = Process of mixing eye shadow with water/liquid for a more pigmented effect

- HE = High-End, Prestige product

- DS = Drugstore, Mass Product

- MMU = Mineral Makeup

- HGP = Holy Grail Product

As an intern, I was privy to only part of the process for bringing a new product—and corresponding campaign—from conception to completion. We had a designated project manager who kept us on a strict budget, timeline, and schedule: creative brainstorming, research and development (R&D), cost of goods (COGs) assessment, product testing, sales projections, through to packaging design, prototyping, copywriting, and advertising strategy for each SKU (stock-keeping unit) that launched in-store.

With the long lead times, I learned the industry couldn't just be *on* trend; it had to be *ahead* of trends. Throughout my time with the company, I attended "trend projection labs." They were workshops put on by a theatrical woman, draped in fabrics and rattling bangles, who I wouldn't have been surprised to see moonlighting as a fortune teller in the West Village. This fashion clairvoyant gave us PowerPoint presentations on what were predicted to be the hottest *future* fads— then part of our job in marketing was to integrate her predictions into our product packaging and ad campaigns. I imagined her consulting tea leaves and a crystal ball, but I never understood how she knew chevrons were in and polka dots were out. As woo-woo as it was, the process seemed to work, as if by wizardry. There were a lot of moving parts, but it was thrilling to get a behind-the-scenes look into the inner workings of the fashion and beauty industry.

A highlight for me that summer was naming two lip glosses in the Elizabeth Arden permanent collection: Berrylicious and Pink Pout. It started with a team meeting where Betty, Natalie, Jada, and I were given the new formulas from the in-house chemist. We each brainstormed a list of options before voting on the final names. When both of mine were chosen, it was a small feat, but I got a taste of what it must have felt like for Elizabeth to come up with clever shade names and quippy ad copy. When I later saw Berrylicious and Pink Pout displayed in-store at the Arden counter, I beamed with pride. The fact that they had transferred from the tip of my pen to a product on shelf gave me an unexplained rush. It was the first time I saw my words in print, and, I hoped, not the last.

By midsummer, I felt like I was starting to master the art of makeup marketing *and* its application. I still had a lot to learn, but my previous ineptitude was slowly transforming into aptitude. It wasn't a dramatic *Devil Wears Prada* makeover montage where I transformed from drab to fab—but the more knowledge I gained, the more self-confidence I developed.

One day, after I'd been sent to pick up Starbucks coffees, Betty invited me into a meeting with *Vogue*. My real-time thoughts were: BE COOL. ACT CASUAL. DON'T SPILL ON ANNA WINTOUR. As I entered the conference room, I was relieved to see Anna Wintour, the editor in chief of *Vogue*, was not in attendance that day. The rest of the *Vogue* team was unrecognizable to me, but had an audible air of authority. They paid me no attention as I divvied up their coffee orders (sans spillage) before I took my seat, feeling like I'd just graduated from the kiddie table to join the adults at Christmas dinner.

The meeting was to review the Arden holiday campaign in *Vogue's* winter issue. I picked up snippets of information, like getting a "front-of-book, double-page spread and back-cover placement" was coveted magazine real estate. It was summer, so talk of frosted fonts and snow-flake packaging seemed out of place in July, but marketing campaigns were meticulously planned, often over a year, in advance. Mini Arden lip glosses, packaged like hanging ornaments, would also be given out to over fifty-thousand *Vogue* subscribers on their mailing list.

Fearful of saying something stupid, I stayed silent, took notes, and refilled my water glass one too many times from the jug on the table. Suddenly, I had to pee, like stuck-in-traffic-on-a-long-road-trip-go-ing-to-burst. I tried to cross my legs under the table, but my bladder had switched on the urgent valve, and all I could think about was the mortification of peeing my pants in front of the fashion industry's high priestesses.

I didn't want to be rude, so instinctively, I raised my hand like I was in kindergarten. Betty hadn't been looking in my direction, but the motion caught her eye.

"Sorry to interrupt, but may I use the ladies' room?" I asked. The room fell silent.

"You don't have to ask. Just go," Betty said, dumbfounded.

Hot flames engulfed my face as I bolted for the door.

And so it went: whenever I felt like I was starting to get the hang of things in the concrete jungle, I would lose my grip on one of the monkey bars and have to claw my way back again.

Chapter 5

Mr. Elizabeth Arden

Paris, London, and New York
1912–1920

It was the summer of 1912 when Elizabeth first set sail for Europe. She was nervous as the "unsinkable" *RMS Titanic*, the world's largest ship, hit an iceberg and sank to the bottom of the North Atlantic, killing over fifteen hundred passengers, only a few months prior in April 1912. But with her flagpole firmly planted in Manhattan, Elizabeth was eager to conduct market research abroad to expand her growing empire. Europeans were trendsetters in the beauty industry, having experienced the ebb and flow of cosmetics far longer than in North American history, so she wanted to observe the latest trends and techniques used by beauty culturists across the pond. Elizabeth boarded the ship at Pier 54 and sailed the reverse route of the *Titanic*, traveling from New York to Southampton, but not before counting every lifeboat aboard the vessel for peace of mind.

Pre-war Europe was brimming with sophistication, affluence, and creativity—everything Elizabeth aspired to be. She fell in love with the carefree, joie de vivre lifestyle of the elegant Parisians and ladies of London. Their liberalism also likely elicited a pang of jealousy, for deep down, she longed to be untethered from customary expectations, as they were.

Elizabeth visited beauty salons, taking notes and product samples, just as she had done in the early days during her field research for Mrs. Adair. While women in New York had only just begun wearing light powders and red lips in public, Elizabeth noticed European women wore full eye makeup, with artful application of eye shadow, liner, and mascara—a triple threat concept that she brought back to test out at her Manhattan salon.

On the SS *Olympic* return voyage out of Southampton, Elizabeth caught the eye of a Manhattan banker named Thomas "Tommy" Jenkins Lewis. It was love at first sight for Tommy. Elizabeth was not easily won over by male suitors, but with idle time to mix and mingle, she dined and danced with Tommy every evening on the weeklong cruise as their shipboard romance ensued.

Tommy was so taken with Elizabeth that he proposed marriage the night before they docked in New York. Elizabeth was flattered. In their short time together, Tommy had made her feel beautiful, heard, and seen—something she hadn't yet experienced from a man at age thirty-four. She knew it would "look good" for business to return home with a fiancé, as married women were given more credibility as they aged, but she feared the loss of autonomy. Being a wife came with a strict set of societal rules and meant giving up control over her personal and professional affairs. Elizabeth yearned to love freely and be loved in return, but she knew the world was not set up for her to have both a career and a companion. After a moment's consideration, Elizabeth rejected Tommy's proposal.

They disembarked the following morning, but even after bidding each other adieu, Tommy refused to accept no as the final answer. He doggedly pursued Elizabeth for the next few years until she finally acquiesced. Whether it was Tommy's persistence or Elizabeth's realization that the legalized union would grant her American citizenship, three years after their maritime meet-cute, Elizabeth agreed to take Tommy's hand marriage—on the condition she could keep her company and with the understanding that she would never be a traditional housewife. Her business was her baby.

***

Elizabeth and Tommy married on November 29, 1915, at the ivy-covered Church of Transfiguration ("The Church Around the Corner") at Fifth Avenue and 29th Street. No family or friends were in attendance except for Lanie, Elizabeth's first employee, to sign the marriage certificate as a witness. Following the ceremony, Elizabeth returned to work until 8 p.m. that evening before joining her new husband for a small reception at the St. Regis Hotel, a convenient two-minute walk from the office. Elizabeth was thirty-seven years old, which would have been considered ancient for a first-time bride; however, she had lied (or rather, refused to reveal) her real age to everyone, including Tommy. At age forty, he assumed his blushing bride was in her late twenties.

On her wedding day, Elizabeth dressed simply in a crisp black skirt suit with a fox fur shawl draped around her shoulders. In lieu of a veil, she wore her hair bobbed under a cloche hat. The dark ensemble was an uncharacteristic choice given Elizabeth's wardrobe was full of bold reds and pinks. Black certainly bucked traditional bridal white; perhaps symbolically mourning the death of her independence. The occasion was noted in the *New York Times* with a small announcement in the society pages. In a renegade move, Elizabeth did not adopt her husband's surname:

MARRIED

LEWIS–GRAHAM: On Nov. 29, 1915, Florence Nightingale Graham wed Thomas Jenkins Lewis at the Church of the Transfiguration ("The Little Church Around the Corner") where the Reverend George C. Houghton officiated.

There was no honeymoon. From the get-go, the marriage seemed to be one of convenience rather than romance. But with a husband by her side, Elizabeth's reputation swelled among Manhattan's elite. In society circles, they were referred to as "the Lewises," and began receiving regular invitations to charity galas, dinner parties, operas, and ballets. "Outside of work, dancing is my greatest pleasure," said Elizabeth, who joined the ragtime movement and loved learning the foxtrot and one-step with her new husband as she attempted to balance work and play in the city. The rise in her personal profile helped increase the flow of wealthy society women to the Arden salon, as they wanted to learn the beautifying techniques that had caught the eye of an eligible financier. Elizabeth had no real friends, but acquired many acquaintances.

A new problem soon arose, as gradually, people became suspicious of a wife who continued to choose work over building a home life. In cocktail conversations, it was assumed Tommy owned and operated the beauty business, but when they discovered it was Elizabeth, she was counseled to relinquish control so she could focus on her husband and having children. Although Elizabeth was the true breadwinner, banks only dealt with the "the man of the house," so her growing fortune appeared to be Tommy's. Elizabeth's desires were seen as secondary, just as she feared.

In those days, it was rare for a man to be attracted to such an ambitious, career-driven woman, but Tommy relished having a success-ful wife, so long as she did the hard work behind the scenes while he publicly took credit. Corporate success made men more desirable part-ners, but for women, it was the opposite. Elizabeth realized she would have to play the part of doting, pie-baking wife while her husband puffed up like a pastry from praise on the business she had *actually* built from scratch. To the outside world, "the Lewises" presented as a picture-perfect couple, their social stock soaring, but in truth, the seams were starting to unravel.

A few months into married life, Tommy was sent overseas to fight in World War I (WWI). For most newlyweds, a war-torn separation would have been devastating. For Elizabeth, a long-distance husband secretly suited her. Left to her own devices, she could maintain her independence and resume running the company without interference. As Woodhead wrote in War Paint, Elizabeth was "superficially the brave war wife, but beneath the façade, she was relieved the war had postponed married life."

- LOU -

My boyfriend Logan flew to New York for a visit as my internship neared completion. I hadn't realized how much I missed him until I saw him stepping out of the cab, running a hand through his soft brown hair like a teenage heartthrob in a Mary-Kate and Ashley straight-to-VHS tape. My first loves, Logan and Manhattan, were meeting for the first time. Until the two of them, nothing had ever made me feel so significant.

Throughout the muddy waters of adolescence, Logan was my beacon in the bog. We had grown up spending our summers together in a small cottage community in Quebec, where our parents, grand-parents, and great-grandparents had done the same, but I only *really* noticed Logan when I was fifteen.

It was golden hour, the summer sun in slow descent amid a sherbet sky, as I arrived at a cottage party and saw him standing on the deck. Logan and I knew of each other, but that night, I noticed details I'd previously ignored. Tanned from months spent outdoors, Logan was cute and clean-cut with a perpetual boyish charm. He had a button nose and the longest lashes I'd ever seen on a boy, splaying like spider legs when he laughed. Logan was self-assured for a sixteen-year-old; observant, but not shy. When he felt comfortable, he came in at just the right moment in conversation with a witty one-liner or clever remark. His antenna was always up, collecting information. This sensibility appealed to me the most, his ability to read situations and people with ease.

Someone handed me a can of Pabst Blue Ribbon, and I took a few sips for liquid courage. People were talking about celebrity crushes when a girl asked mine. My face turned as pink as the sweater and matching hair ribbon I was wearing. Looking down at the wood grain on the deck, I mumbled, "Um, I don't know, can't think of anyone."

Luckily, the host of the party turned up Big Shiny Tunes 2 on the boom box, and everyone dispersed except for Logan and me. "So, no celeb crushes, eh?" he asked, turning toward me. I couldn't believe he was actually speaking to me. Logan was a year older, a lifetime at that age, and categorically much cooler. Unable to look him in the eye, I said, loud enough for him to hear and for me to be mortified, "No… but I think you're pretty cute." The words came from an unknown part of me I did not yet recognize. "Thanks, you're pretty cute too. I like the pink ribbon," he said, grinning. We had nothing else to say after that, so we took a simultaneous swig from our beers. Mine was empty, but I pretended to anyway.

A few weeks later Logan invited me to stay at his house on a group trip into the city before summer ended and everyone went back to their hometowns for the rest of the year. There was always a period of adjustment transitioning from cottage life to city life. Wearing clothes instead of a bathing suit felt strange; finding sand in the sheets was no longer standard; and slipping on socks felt foreign on my sticky pine-gum feet—but being with Logan outside of our safe summer haven was the wildest feeling of all.

On a tour of his family home, I stared at a series of Logan's school portraits from kindergarten through eleventh grade. It has always fascinated me to see photos of people growing up. Everyone changes gradually as they age, almost invisibly, but the transformation is highlighted in hyperspeed through year-by-year snapshots.

That night, after eating dinner with Logan's family, we went to a pre-party at one of his friend's houses before meeting up with our cottage group at a dive bar that supposedly let in underage kids with bad fake IDs. "Going out," to me, had previously meant trips to the local library, so I was out of my element. I slammed shots of Captain Morgan's spiced rum until the pirate on the bottle raised his eye patch and winked at me. All I recall about the drive to the bar is the wave of nausea rising up in my stomach like a rogue wave and how badly I did not want to throw up in front of the boy I liked.

We were still in line when, wordlessly, I ran behind the building and vomited. I didn't see Logan come around the corner, but I felt his hand on my back and the loose ponytail he tied with the hair elastic from my wrist. Rather than recoil in revulsion, he knelt beside me as my upchuck reflux kicked into high gear again. Tears of shame poured down my cheeks. Logan praised me for matriculating a fully formed carrot, as though I was a magician who had performed a particularly dazzling act. "But I watched you chew your food at dinner! You couldn't have swallowed that carrot whole," he said. *He'd watched me chew!* It was revoltingly romantic.

We never made it inside the bar and returned to his parents' house. His mom had made up a bed for me in the basement where Logan brought me a large glass of water, a Gatorade, and an Advil. He lay down on top of the covers beside me, and we talked until the sun came up. I was in a delirious state of embarrassment from the night's events, coupled with the euphoria of his presence. As the sun started to rise, Logan asked if I would go to prom with him. *Prom?* It was August. That was almost a year away and a "real world" event outside of our summer utopia. "How do you know you'll still want me to be your date by then?" I asked. "I just know," he said. After a few seconds of silence, "So, is that a yes?" he asked. "It's a yes," I said.

He kissed my forehead, tucked me under the blanket, and went back upstairs. It wasn't the prom proposal itself, so much as the trust Logan had in his feelings about me, about us, that no matter what happened in between, he was confident his future self would pick me in the end. A warm sensation flooded my veins; my skin tingled; my heart fluttered. I know now they were the early symptoms of love.

Having a boyfriend who lived beyond my suburban bubble was like discovering a portal to the outside world. I didn't have to hide any versions of myself. He liked me for me, quirks included. We never had the "are you my boyfriend/girlfriend?" formality as is pivotal for most teenagers. Our relationship progressed organically. We just belonged to each other, as though it had always been and always would be that way.

Over the years, I came to despise the terms "young love" and "first love." Logan and I were young when we fell in love, but those labels diluted the intensity of what I came to know as mature emotions and real feelings wise beyond our years. Age may have conveyed the raw purity of our youthful dalliance but failed to capture the full extent of its power. "First love" was too finite. "First" insinuated there was a numerical order, a rite of passage, a phase that you moved through. It also gave love a foreboding quality, as something that entered your life and then exited. The idea of making a mark on another human heart, only to have it erased and retraced, as if it never existed, terrified me. My love for Logan required no qualifier because I couldn't imagine life without him. I did not yet understand how seldom love came into one's life and how difficult it was to lose.

I later came to think of first love like the first snow. The freshness enters our lives virtuously, bringing the purest kind of joy and a silent power that invigorates the senses—but once love (and snow) melts, no traces remain except for the crisp memory.

***

New York had rather emptied when Logan came to visit as many people escaped upstate or to The Hamptons on long weekends. I remember apologizing, as though the city was my child and it had gone selectively mute at a dinner party. The stillness made it feel as though Manhattan was underperforming, purposely hiding its spectacular tricks. I wanted Logan to be impressed by the city's chaotic charm, the way I was.

After I gushed about the BMW bridges from my living room, I swept him up in a whirlwind weekend itinerary: walking the Brooklyn

Bridge, strolling through SoHo, seeing a Broadway play, exploring Times Square at night, a picnic in Central Park, people-watching in Washington Square Park, and sipping coffee at The Grey Dog in Union Square. Logan's visit shifted my focus from thinking about myself to anticipating someone else's needs. *Was he having fun? Was he happy?* When I was with Logan, nothing else mattered.

After Logan left, the rest of summer moved as if in fast-forward. Time had seemed infinite and unchanging when I was young, but as my first internship faded into fall, I began to understand time was an illusion. Time *seemingly* sped up as I got older, but in reality, it was the same; only my perception of time had changed. In the years to come, I would wonder the same thing about myself: was I changing or was my perception of self merely an illusion?

Whenever I thought about my trajectory to career domination— intern to full-time employee to CEO—I likened it to a fairy tale: lowly peasant becomes lady-in-waiting and ultimately the queen of the castle. But I failed to take into account the Shakespearean importance of love in one's life. In retrospect, neither did Elizabeth. We saw corporate and romantic success as two separate storybooks—and only one had a heroic ending.

I was torn between the intensity of my love for Logan and the ambitious goals I had set for myself in New York. At the time, I looked to Elizabeth's life as a road map, and all signs pointed to a solo journey. She had built her queendom *before* marrying Tommy, from 1908 to 1915, by focusing on work, not relationships. If solitude provided the soil for her success, did that mean I had to turn inward to grow? How did anyone devote equal time and energy into nourishing both a fulfilling relationship and career?

I was on the precipice of a decade of transitions, but with the future still foggy, I clung to the familiar comforts of the past.

Chapter 6

The Pinktriarchy

New York
1915–1920, 1929–1930

As WWI raged on, and with her new husband stationed across the Atlantic, business erupted for Elizabeth. With men on the battlefields, women stepped in to take over the corporate roles they were previously barred from. Despite the new frontier, women remained grossly undervalued and underpaid in these positions.

Elizabeth was a champion of the notion of "for women, by women," and set to task pioneering what she thought of as "the pinktriarchy." She hired predominantly females for both service and managerial roles, allowing for growth opportunities and financial benefits that their male counterparts would have received at other companies. She believed femininity in business was an asset, not a hindrance. While the "Mad Men" on Madison Avenue viewed women's gossip at the agency as frivolous chatter, Elizabeth saw it as word-of-mouth marketing and welcomed female recruits. To her, pink was powerful.

Although red would forever be synonymous with the Arden brand, pink practically oozed from Elizabeth's pores. From her wardrobe to her office to her signature rosy lips, she all but lived inside a pocket of pink bubblegum. Pink peonies and blush roses filled both her office and apartment. "There was nothing more cheering to Elizabeth than the scent of fresh pink flowers," an employee said. Eventually there would be over fifty distinct shades of Arden pink lipsticks in the portfolio.

Elizabeth favored pink skirt suits, even requesting to be buried in one, and made her treatment girl uniforms pink with matching silk moiré ribbons for their hair. She wanted her favorite hue to be reclaimed from soft and diminutive to strong and authoritative. As her fame and fortune grew, Elizabeth became an iron-fisted ruler; Miranda Priestly in Elle Woods clothing.

Given there were so few industries where women were respected, let alone at the helm, Elizabeth protected her brand with the ferocity of a lioness over her cub. She advocated for female employment; however, she showed no mercy to employees based on gender. Elizabeth began to be known for making staff cry with her "tyrannical and mercurial" outbursts. The world wasn't used to women in power. If she were male, Elizabeth's leadership style would have been expected and respected.

During this time, "Elizabeth was the leading force at the top of the emerging beauty business in New York," wrote Woodhead in War Paint. While she was ineligible to fight overseas, Elizabeth indulged her inner Florence Nightingale and contributed to the war effort by visiting hospitals with creams to soothe burns, reduce scarring, and provide cosmetic coverage for patients who returned from war with facial or bodily disfigurement, to help boost their self-esteem.

With business booming, Elizabeth could no longer keep up production operations by herself in the homemade laboratory at the back of her office. She sent over cosmetic samples to Stillwell & Gladding Inc, an independent testing lab in Manhattan, to see if someone could mass produce her formulas and was introduced to Axel Fabian Swanson, a Swedish-born chemist. She was so thrilled with Mr. Swanson's reproductions and recommendations for new products that he joined Arden full time. It would be her second greatest hire (after Lanie) as Mr. Swanson remained a dedicated employee for the rest of his life. He expanded Elizabeth's Venetian line during the war by adding these SKUs:

- *Venetian Amoretta Cream*: "a protective cream to help adhere powder to the skin"

- *Venetian Lille Lotion*: "a medicinal liquid powder that is good for the skin while offering sun protection"

- *Venetian Orange Skin Food*: "deep tissue builder of unusual potency and high nutritive value to rebuild worn tissues and activate glands"

- *Venetian Beauty Sachets:* "antiseptic healing lotion to quickly relieve irritations caused by acne, poison ivy, or other skin eruptions"

- *Venetian Crème Glacier*: "paraffin wax treatment for beautifying hands and arms"

- *Venetian Snowdrift*: "your new favorite talcum powder" (an early dry shampoo)

- *Venetian Eyelash Grower*: "for thick, lustrous growth, glossiness and length"

- *Venetian Eye Sha-Do*: "simulates eye shadows to perfection; used on the lids to lend mystery to the eyes"

- *Venetian Enamel*: "slightly pink, translucent nail enamel"

Hiring Mr. Swanson allowed Elizabeth to expand her product lineup, and also her brick-and-mortar stand-alone. Her New York salon had proven so profitable that even amid the First World War, Elizabeth swiftly opened salons in Washington, Boston, San Francisco, Palm Beach, Detroit, and Rhode Island. It was one of the first times in history where women were able to earn their own money and spend it as they pleased—a little self-care and pampering at an Arden salon was one of those ways.

In 1918, Elizabeth shook up the traditional role of the "traveling salesmen" by training and deploying the first-ever troupe of "traveling sales*women*" (dressed in all pink, of course) to showcase her products by giving "head-to-toe makeovers" and skincare treatments across the country at department stores during the dawn of the beauty counter.

Elizabeth wrote a sequel to her coveted beauty booklet, "The Quest of the Beautiful," called "Your Masterpiece: Yourself," which included her new "Elizabeth Arden Home Course" that detailed ways (with accompanying illustrations) women could "cultivate the habit of beauty to perfect their figure as well as their face" in the comfort of their own home during the war. An excerpt from Elizabeth's ad copy at the time remarked on the wartime climate:

Dinners and dances will be tendered to our departing heroes this season and every woman will wish to look her loveliest when she says goodbye, so she may be remembered at her best. To keep fresh and charming in spite of newfound work and worries, extra precautions must be taken, and this can be so agreeably achieved by an occasional Muscle-Strapping Treatment at my Arden Salons. I understand regular visits may not be possible in wartime, so you can follow my methods in your own home with my Elizabeth Arden Home Course.

***

WWI officially ended with an armistice agreement on November 11, 1918, but it took several months for Tommy to return home to New York City. He was weary but unharmed when he showed up at Elizabeth's apartment on 321 West 94th Street in 1919. The "newly-weds" had been separated for four years, but Elizabeth welcomed her husband, a relative stranger, with open arms.

With men home from war, women were required to return to work in the home so men could resume their positions. Tommy was in need of a job, so Elizabeth hired him to be the general manager of Arden's growing international wholesale division. She made it clear to her husband that he was still an employee, not an equal partner, and he did not receive any shares. At work, Elizabeth continued to go by Miss Arden. It was still extremely taboo for a woman to refuse her husband's last name, but then again, it was also unheard of for a man to work for his wife. Elizabeth gave Tommy his own sales office at 212 East 52nd

Street so she could continue working without his interference above the salon at 673 Fifth Avenue. "My dear, never forget one little point; it's my business, you just work here," she said.

Upon their reunion, Elizabeth was no longer able to elude the question of "when will you have babies?" in their Manhattan social circles. She was forty-one when Tommy returned home from war, but many believed her to be a decade younger (she never corrected them), so fertility wasn't thought to be an issue. "Someday, should we be so blessed," Elizabeth offered as a vague response to close the conversation. The truth was, she wasn't sure she wanted children, but women couldn't freely admit this. Marriage and children were purportedly the fulfillment of every female's purpose. To Elizabeth, the birth of her business was achievement enough—and she was taught it wasn't possible to have both. Deep down, Elizabeth also knew that bringing a child into the mix with Tommy wasn't a good idea. She could handle a subpar husband, for she knew she was a subpar wife, but her gut told her he couldn't be trusted.

After the war, New York rolled fervently into the roaring twenties. The name 'Elizabeth Arden' and her Fifth Avenue salon were popular enough among Manhattan's elite that Tommy and Elizabeth began rubbing elbows with the kind of people young Florence on the farm had only read about in books, like the Morgans, Astors, and Vanderbilts. Their busy social calendar kept the reunited couple so preoccupied that they were able to ignore the burgeoning dissonance between them. It was easier to pretend everything was perfect on the surface, rather than unearth their true feelings.

Their affluent new couple friends introduced "the Lewises" to the New York nightlife of supper clubs and speakeasies as Prohibition loomed. 21 Club in Midtown became one of Elizabeth's favorite haunts (where I would later celebrate my twenty-first birthday). In addition to "the speaks," they loved Broadway shows, vaudeville, the Tiller Girls, and the Ziegfeld Follies. One thing Elizabeth and Tommy had in common was their affinity for beautiful women. Elizabeth had made beautification her trade, while Tommy was a fanatical admirer. It was a tireless social parade, but Elizabeth networked at every event and benefit gala to promote her business (which people still assumed was owned by Tommy). Elizabeth didn't drink a lot of alcohol at the time, as "it's too drying for the skin," she said, but Tommy began drinking heavily. He began showing up late to work and cured his hangovers with a "hair of the dog" at the office. By late afternoon he was intoxicated again and ready for another night out on the town.

Despite Tommy's increased partying, to his credit, he was a formidable salesman. His pre-war banking background and international contacts proved their weight in gold as he succeeded in establishing the Arden wholesale business in every prestige department store across America, South America, Australia, and the first Canadian subsidiary in Toronto in 1929.

Tommy's focus on the wholesale division freed Elizabeth up to work on the big picture strategy for the salon and to create new products. She also began developing a newfound friendship. In 1926, at the behest of Edna Woolman Chase, editor in chief of *Vogue*, and Henry Sell, editor in chief of *Harper's Bazaar* and their mutual advertising acquaintance, Elizabeth was invited to Elisabeth "Bessie" Marbury's Sunday tea, a luncheon at Bessie's home attended by the most celebrated people in Manhattan. The qualification to secure an invite to a Marbury tea, even as a plus-one, was that the guest had to "be somebody."

Born and raised in one of the oldest and most affluent families in nineteenth-century New York, the Marbury name helped Bessie establish her foothold as the world's leading (and only) female theater and literary agent. She represented playwrights such as Oscar Wilde and George Bernard Shaw and had a pivotal role in the creation of the "book musical"—later known as the "Broadway play." From the outset, Elizabeth and Bessie appeared to be polar opposites, both physically—Bessie was thick and stocky, while Elizabeth was fit and petite—and personality-wise—Bessie was loud and blunt, while Elizabeth was soft-spoken and sweet (not at the office, but in polite society)—and yet they were immediately drawn to one another.

Bessie and her longtime lover, Elsie de Wolfe, were the most famed lesbian power couple of the Victorian age. Lesbianism was illegal at this time, so they never publicly defined their relationship but were openly accepted as lovers since their late-teens within their close circle of friends. In the 1920s, the *New York Times* described Bessie and Elsie as "the most widely known women in New York social life." Elsie was named the best-dressed woman in the world and acclaimed for being America's first interior decorator. Her clients (who were also the couple's closest friends) included J.P. Morgan's daughter Anne Morgan, Amy Vanderbilt, and the Duke and Duchess of Windsor. Bessie, Elsie, and Anne Morgan had previously bought and restored the interiors of Villa Trianon in Versailles, France, where it was rumored that Elsie had an affair on Bessie with Anne, but they continued living in a ménage à trois and were known as the "triangle of Versailles." The tryst threatened to destroy the reputation of the Morgan dynasty, but somehow, the three women weathered the rumor mill and moved back to Manhattan, living next door to each other in Sutton Place. The Colony Club, New York's first female social club, was the brainchild of Bessie and Elsie, which they spearheaded together from their home at 13 Sutton Place.

At the Marbury Sunday tea, Henry Sell and Edna Woolman Chase filled Elizabeth in on recent developments of Bessie and Elsie's love story. After thirty years of living together as a couple, Elsie had suddenly announced her wedding in the newspaper to Sir Charles Hendl, a British diplomat, and that she would be moving with him to France. Bessie was enraged, both by the news itself and the way she found out with everyone else in the paper. The marriage was platonic for both Elsie and Sir Charles Hendl (who was also gay), part of the ruse to keep up their public façades as straight members of high society. They had separate apartments in Paris and appeared together only at social functions, but Bessie was completely gutted.

When Elizabeth met Bessie at Sunday tea, she was estranged from Elsie who had recently left for France. The fast friendship that developed between Elizabeth and Bessie following the Marbury luncheon caused whispers about whether the cosmetic queen was a closeted lesbian herself. They dined, danced, and had sleepovers at each other's apartments like any close girlfriends would, but they continued to raise eyebrows as Elizabeth was seen out-and-about more and more with Bessie than her own husband. Coming out as gay in the 1920s was considered treasonous and guaranteed a public beheading of the business and reputation Elizabeth had worked so hard to build. Society was eager to demonize independent women who didn't *need* or *want* a man. Questions surrounding Elizabeth's sexuality still remain shrouded in mystery today. Regardless of the context, Elizabeth and Bessie's relationship was fostered on mutual admiration. Bessie lived her life authentically, and Elizabeth revered fearless women who forged their own paths. She was also dazzled by Bessie's ancestry and ease within societal circles. Bessie saw Elizabeth for who she was behind the smoke-screen of success.

However, several months into their budding camaraderie, Elsie set sail from France to reconcile with Bessie, who she missed dearly. Back in Manhattan, Bessie, who had loved Elsie since adolescence, welcomed her with open arms and they settled back into their love nest at Sutton Place. Elsie remained Lady Hendl by law, but lived as lovers with Bessie for the rest of their lives. Upon Elsie's return, Elizabeth and Bessie remained friends, but their close companionship cooled.

Elizabeth preoccupied herself with her cosmetics empire and the influx of competitors infiltrating the field. Dorothy Gray, who had worked as an Arden treatment girl for less than a year, quit after learning Elizabeth's trade secrets and opened her own beauty salon, financed by her father, at 734 Fifth Avenue—just down the street from Arden's Salon d'Oro. Dorothy boasted that she was trained by Elizabeth and advertised knock-off Arden products at discounted prices.

Elizabeth was outraged and immediately took out full-page ads in *Vogue* asking women to "beware of imitations" and stating "no one but me knows the formulas." Elizabeth referred to Dorothy as "that pest," while she continued to churn out poorly made replicas. Dorothy launched Orange Skin Tonic (a duplicate of Elizabeth's Orange Skin Food) and a carbon copy of Arden's exclusive travel cosmetic case. Elizabeth let her ingenuity speak for itself by releasing new products and creative campaigns faster than Dorothy could copy the old ones. Unable to keep up, Dorothy sold her shop to Lehn & Fink in 1927, less than a year after opening, and moved out of Manhattan. Elizabeth never heard of Dorothy Gray again.

Elizabeth's biggest beauty competitor, by far, was Helena Rubinstein. Ever since the Polish-born beauty guru had set up shop in Manhattan, in 1915, the makeup mavens had developed a competitive oligopoly, both vying for the largest piece of the pie.

In late 1928, Elizabeth was reportedly offered $15 million by the Lehman Brothers, a global financial firm based in New York, to sell her business. Tommy urged his wife to take the offer, but Elizabeth's identity was so interwoven with the company that she couldn't fathom giving it away. She feared taking the company public would erase her autonomy and her entire existence. "You're a real sap, you know that," said Tommy, to his wife after she turned down the offer. He couldn't believe she'd walked away from being a millionaire, fifteen times over.

A couple months later, Helena Rubinstein sold her American business to the Lehman Brothers and floated shares on the stock market. From the outside, it looked like Tommy was right and his wife had forfeited a major growth opportunity.

And then, in October 1929, the stock market crashed. In a panic sell-off, Wall Street triggered the start of the Great Depression. The Lehman Brothers and Helena Rubinstein lost hundreds of thousands of dollars, but managed to survive the collapse. (A century later, the Great Recession hit in 2008 when I was an Arden intern; the housing bubble burst and the subprime mortgage crisis would force the Lehman Brothers to declare bankruptcy). Unbeknownst to Elizabeth, her decision had been a fortuitous and foreshadowing move all in one.

While Elizabeth devoted herself to expanding her empire, it soon became clear to everyone except for her that Tommy had a wandering eye. Tommy was a relentless flirt with Arden treatment girls when his wife was out of sight, but his coquetries extended to chorus girls and cocktail waitresses. "He became a philandering man-about-town, and in his escapades, he had a most unlikely companion…" wrote Lewis and Woodsworth in *Miss Elizabeth Arden*, "…his wife's brother."

Elizabeth and her brother, William Graham, had fallen out of contact after she paid back his loan to start her own salon, but after the Wall Street Crash of 1929, William had fallen on hard times. He asked his sister for a job to support his wife and three young daughters: Beatrice (Beattie), Virginia (Ginnie), and Patricia (Pattie). Without question, Elizabeth gave her brother a position working for her husband in the wholesale division. Her nieces touched a maternal nerve and she treated Beattie, Ginnie, and Pattie as if they were her own.

Tommy and William hit it off and soon became wingmen. Tommy began cavorting with pretty young women all over Manhattan—wining-and-dining them with reckless abandon; charging expensive dinners, bar tabs, lavish gifts, and hotel rooms to his wife's corporate account. William also had multiple mistresses, and the two men covered for each other. When Lanie, Elizabeth's longtime bookkeeper, mentioned the enormous expense report, Tommy waved it off as part of the price salesmen pay to entice buyers and drum up business. The war may have been over, but with Tommy and Elizabeth back under the same roof, cracks began to show in their "war paint."

Elizabeth was still in the dark about Tommy's philandering ways when she asked him to help her lease (a wife still required her husband's signature) the ground floor and five upper floors of the gorgeous Aeolian Building at 691 Fifth Avenue. While Tommy was checking out women, Elizabeth had been checking out real estate. Once she got the keys, Elizabeth spent several months reconfiguring and designing her ultimate dream salon with top interior designers including Rue Winterbotham Carpenter (who was referred to in the press as Mrs. John Alden Carpenter; married women were only identified in relation to their husbands) and Nicolai Remisoff (as a man, he required no qualifier from the media). Bessie's girlfriend, Elsie de Wolfe, also contributed her highly sought-after expertise on the décor. By the time the salon was ready for its unveiling, it was Bessie and Elsie, not Tommy, who were on hand to witness one of Elizabeth's proudest moments—the grand opening of the first Elizabeth Arden Red Door.

Arden's Salon d'Oro, a few blocks away at 673 Fifth Avenue, had been a great success for over fifteen years, but a new decade called for a new signature salon. On a brisk, bright sunny day in January 1930, Elizabeth cut the ribbon in front of her gleaming, oversized red door in a monumental move that would transcend history.

The New York Times, January 1930

SALON FOR BEAUTY: Elizabeth Arden Opens Red Door at 691 Fifth Avenue

Elizabeth Arden opened her new flagship beauty salon at 691 Fifth Avenue, decorated by Nicolai Remisoff and Mrs. John Alden Carpenter. It has a note of classic severity and yet a modernistic feeling is presented by the cut glass walls, jade green panels, and feathered chandeliers. On the five upper floors, each room has a unique individual style.

The Aeolian building, home of Elizabeth's new multi-floor salon, was designed by Warren & Wetmore, the same architects behind Grand Central Station. 691 Fifth Avenue was formerly the home of William G. Rockefeller until his death in 1922. The Goulds, a wealthy real estate family, purchased the property and leased it to the Aeolian Company, one of the largest and most successful piano companies in the world. In 1927, George Gould's daughter, Celia Gould Milne, purchased the building for her personal portfolio, for $3 million, and agreed to lease six floors to Elizabeth Arden.

Paul Goldberger, a reporter for the *New York Times*, described the Aeolian building as "a lyrical gem, the city's most inventive merging of modern commercial design with French and neoclassic architectural detail—a good reminder that New York architecture can be exuberant and fanciful, yet discreet and well-mannered." While unintentional, Mr. Goldberger's description of the building, also adhered to its historic tenant, Ms. Elizabeth Arden. According to the *New York City Guide* that opening year, the new Arden Red Door Spa was "the most luxurious beauty salon in the country." After the grand opening, the Aeolian building soon changed titles and became universally known as the Elizabeth Arden building.

Framed by a marble façade, the alluring, bright red entrance would catapult the Arden brand into a household name and became Elizabeth's famous insignia. Elizabeth chose the color red for a few specific reasons. In ancient traditions, painting a door red was a welcoming symbol to weary travelers in search of a safe haven. Red was also a popular color in Chinese culture symbolizing luck, happiness, and power. Elizabeth resonated with these customs and chose to paint her door red, a bold move at the time, as she wanted everyone to feel free when they walked through her door. At the opening she said, "You're in another world when you come through the red door of Elizabeth Arden. And the world is based on one exclusive object—you."

Behind the red door, Elizabeth and I would feel untouchable, like flames in a fire, but beyond it, we were vulnerable, at risk of being burned. The red door was a border between our two selves: who we truly were and who proclaimed to be.

- LOU -

With my time in the city coming to a close, there was still one Manhattan monument I had not yet seen. After work one evening, instead of beelining downtown, I turned at the corner of Union Square to walk uptown. I don't know if it was the anticipation of impending change or the warm breeze that swirled sweetly around my legs, but in that moment, I was fully aware of being blissfully content. Usually, happy moments only crystallized upon later reflection, but that particular night, I felt it in real time as happiness seeped into my bones and stayed a while.

I walked until I came to the corner of 54th and faced 691 Fifth Avenue. I stood in front of the historic Elizabeth Arden building for a meditative amount of time, appreciating its architectural beauty. The rounded terracotta edges and intricate garland carvings were elements they just didn't make anymore. The twenty-first century rewarded productivity and efficiency; beautification required patience and dedication to detail. In our fast-paced technological age, it seemed we had forgotten the beauty of slowing down.

Staring up at the oversized red door, for some reason, I became overcome with emotion. Tears rimmed my eyes as I soaked in the ornate stone crowning with ELIZABETH ARDEN in giant gilded lettering. Standing there, where Elizabeth had been before me, I felt rooted in time. Entranced by this portal to the past, I stood still in the present and wondered what the future held. The setting sun had created a shadow across the building, like a finger stroking the cheek of its external façade. I stepped from the shade into a patch of light and felt a serene sense of calm as I walked home with the sinking summer sun.

***

I returned to London, Ontario for my second year of university and turned nineteen with a renewed sense of self. My last week in New York, Betty (my boss) had asked if I would like to return as an intern on her team the following summer. I answered a gunshot "YES!" like it was a marriage proposal. My first baby step into adulthood was complete; the next goal was to secure two more internships until I graduated and could apply for a full-time job at Arden. My career ambitions consumed me. Everything was progressing accordingly: *Plan Ahead + Work Hard = Achieve Goals*. I charged ahead on Elizabeth's path, never pausing to self-reflect or consider other avenues to success.

A push-and-pull pattern developed as I alternated between two realities and two selves over the next few years. When I was at school, I longed to return to the magical realm of Arden, and by the end of my internships, I was homesick for everything I had left behind in Canada. Life only existed between those two spheres, a sheltered way of thinking that reflected my naiveté up until that point, but I would soon discover the world was so much bigger. My identity fractured as I struggled to assimilate, and I would eventually question my true place in the mosaic of life, but at the time, I was enjoying the wild ride.

***

New York hadn't noticed my absence in the eight months I was back at school in Canada, but I had desperately missed the city's magnetism and inexplicable aura that made you feel as though anything was achievable. The sights, sounds, and colors of the city still intoxicated me during my second summer as an Arden intern. I attempted to commit everything to memory in my "Dear Liz" red journal recaps, but there was no substitute for the unprocessed reel of reality. My time in Manhattan from 2008–2010, ages eighteen to twenty, was so visceral in the moment that rereading about my experience in notebooks, even now, feels like a cheap projection of the past. I worried that without documentation, the memories would fade, and it would be like none of it had happened at all.

Journaling allowed me to write uncensored. The words were for an audience of one; as the only reader, both the interesting and mundane parts of my day were reflected on the page. In that sense, the red journals would become the most accurate representation of my personal history. My "Dear Liz" entries also opened up a doorway of connection to Elizabeth, taking what I learned from her life and applying the lessons to my own. Writing protected both of our memories from the erosion of time.

During my second internship, in 2009, online diaries, known as "blogs" (abbreviated from web log), were gaining popularity as a form of personal storytelling. It was the golden years of blogging, before they became a bona fide business with sponsored ads and a fraught quest for "followers." I didn't know anyone who had a blog, but it seemed like a great tool to share stories with family and friends, like a mass group email. My type A personality loved the tidy, shopkeeping aspect of online journaling, with its organizational features, colorful fonts, and ability to embed photos.

Digital diaries were similar to the written diaries I had been keeping, except with the added dimension of an audience. Writing online offered an external validation of my experiences that private journaling did not. Blogging affirmed my existence; on the Internet, I was seen.

To start a blog, I first needed a name. I came across the word **"maven," an old Yiddish term meaning** "expert or connoisseur." The dictionary definition indicated that no one could become a maven overnight; it required an accumulation of knowledge *over time*. I liked the word, as it acknowledged it would take *time* for me to master all the city had to offer. I also had a penchant for alliteration, so the blog brainchild "Manhattan Maven" was born.

```
Manhattan Maven

Escapades of a New York City Intern

Blog Launch: May 1, 2009

HELLO, NEW YORK!!!!!!!
```

I'm so excited to be working as a marketing intern at Elizabeth Arden for my second summer. Friends and family have asked me to share details of my escapades and I want to remember them when I'm old and gray, so I thought I would start a blog!

MANHATTAN MAVEN is meant to document my NYC experiences and observations as they happen.

XOXO

–   Manhattan Maven

My blog escapades soon included details of trendy restaurants, celebrity sightings, and glamorous events I was able to attend through work. "Manhattan Maven" was the cooler, chicer, more cosmopolitan version of *me*. Online, I was glossier than the matte version of myself in real life. I assumed no one would want to hear about my simmering self-doubt or the boring bits of my day, so I portrayed my digital life through rose-colored glasses.

"Manhattan Maven" became my adopted alter ego, like "Elizabeth Arden" was to Florence Nightingale Graham. I didn't know it then, but this detachment from our true selves was a defense mechanism; hiding behind another name provided a barrier, like a shield of armor, from the harsh judgments and criticisms of society. At first, there was a freedom in assuming an alias, but the longer I hid behind the façade, the more I found myself in a tug-of-war between my dual identities.

***

At work, part of my tasks that summer involved creating content for Arden's newly launched Facebook page (the "like" button was invented later that year) and writing articles about new beauty trends for the company website and internal newsletter. Social media was a big evolution from Elizabeth's handwritten beauty booklets, and at the time, a new frontier for many of my senior counterparts. Before digital marketing, online promotions for most companies were limited to banner ads, which didn't drive a lot of traffic or sales, and it was hard to track ROI (return on investment)—so when I first started as an Arden intern, in-store promotions and magazine print ads reigned supreme. Many senior executives didn't think social networking sites would last or impact the beauty business, so initially, little attention was paid to its marketing capabilities.

In 2009, Facebook wasn't foreign to me (it launched in 2004), so I was able to leverage my millennial expertise to help create a corporate page and show my team how to upload content and write captions. Writing never felt like "work," so getting the opportunity to set myself apart and add value in this way boosted my corporate confidence.

Laura had moved to London, England that year, so I was assigned a shared room in an NYU housing unit called Carlyle Court, located above the Coffee Shop, a hip café by-day turned late-night bar in Union Square (featured often in HBO's *Sex and the City*). Carlyle Court was less than a minute's walk to the Arden office at the north end of Union Square Park. Great commute, but the divide between work and play became nonexistent. I would have stayed squirreled away in that small square radius for the entire summer had it not been for my new roommate.

Kristin Tice Studeman was twenty-one and hailed from the San Francisco Bay Area. She studied at the University of Southern California's Annenberg School of Journalism during the year and was an editorial intern at *Interview* magazine that summer. Kristin wore her golden locks in messy, beachy waves and had crystal blue eyes that looked as if tiny diamonds were embedded in the irises. She was warm, outgoing, and effortlessly cool with an infectious laugh.

Like Laura, Kristin would become a lifelong friend. Although fostering female friendships was not of the utmost importance to Elizabeth early in her career, the relationships she developed with Edna Woolman Chase and Bessie Marbury also endured a lifetime. I, too, was discovering how influential female friendships were to my developing sense of self.

As a "second year" intern, I had a better handle on the routinized work grind, but outside of office hours, I started to succumb more to the vices of the city. Kristin and I drank cheap rosé out of paper cups in our dorm room, stuffed our keys and lipstick into tiny, unpractical purses, and breezed through the summer streets of Manhattan with alcohol and the sanguinity of youth pulsing through our veins. I documented many of my escapades with Kristin that summer on my Manhattan Maven blog: movie nights in Bryant Park, sunbathing in Sheep's Meadow, fancy dinners at Butter, buckets of beer at the Frying Pan, perusing the shelves at the Strand Book Store, Shake Shack burgers, Tory Burch sample sales, and sipping cocktails beside famous actors and musicians at MercBar (as though sitting next to Jake Gyllenhaal was a regular occurrence).

Kristin introduced me to the concept of "the slash generation," whereby our careers—and moreover our identities—didn't have to be singularly defined. It was a new-age notion that made me melancholic for the previous generations of women, like Elizabeth, who weren't afforded a multitude of options. As I aged, I was becoming more attuned to the nuances of history; how far women had come and how far we still had to go to achieve true parity. Maybe Elizabeth would have loved to be a part of "the slash generation" (CEO/mother?), but in her era, divergence wasn't an option; she had to choose between fame and fortune or a family life. Slowly and subconsciously, I was awakening to new ideas about what it meant to "have it all" as a woman in the world.

***

My second summer in the city flashed by faster than the first. Before I knew it, I was hired back for my last internship at Arden in May 2010. Although it was my third summer, I was still tantalized by the possibilities that prospered between the sun-scorched streets and the skyscrapers. The stakes were high to secure a job after graduation and make the move from Canada to New York permanently. I had no backup plan if I failed to get hired full-time. Manhattan was my dream city, and Arden was my dream company. It was my only one-way ticket to success.

During my final internship in 2010, NYU assigned me a single room in Lafayette Hall, just below Canal Street in Chinatown. Laura was still in London and Kristin was living in her own apartment, working for *Women's Wear Daily*. It was my first taste of true independence, without roommates, and I relished in it. Outside of work, I spent a lot of time by myself and discovered I quite enjoyed being alone with my thoughts. I never tired of people-watching and nearly every night for dinner, I ate takeout glass noodles from Republic on a bench in Washington Square Park while jotting observations in my red journal. There were tourists taking photos by the fountain, NYU summer students studying on the grass, a man playing the piano under the Arc de Triomphe replica, hippies holding signs that said FREE HUGS, acrobatic street performers doing backflips, and a homeless man with a permanent flock of pigeons perched on his head. I wondered, if I were to observe myself, where I would fit into the composite of characters surrounding me.

At Arden, competition for full time roles was fierce. There was a large cohort of eligible interns and external candidates vying for one open position in the marketing department. With less social interaction, except for my nightly Skype calls with Logan, I was laser-focused on excelling at work and getting hired at the end of my internship. I applied the FILO method (a term I learned in business school) and made sure I was the "first in, last out" of the office, arriving early enough to turn on the lights and staying late enough to turn them off.

My nerves were amplified, as there was a survivalist feeling among the interns who were all about to graduate and shared the scarcity mentality.

Jack Thomas had also returned to intern at Arden that summer, but he had already accepted a sales job in Boston, so other than his cocky attitude and snide remarks toward me, he wasn't a worry. Jack and I worked on different floors in different departments, so I managed to avoid him mostly, until one day, I returned from a meeting to find him sitting in my chair, legs propped up on my desk like he owned the cubicle.

"Can I help you with something?" I asked.

"You're coming with me to the Yankees game tonight," Jack said, in a statement rather than a question.

"I have a boyfriend," I reminded him.

"Well, I only have two tickets, so maybe he can come next time," he responded, cheekily.

"Thanks for the offer, but no thank you," I affirmed.

"Your loss," he said, shooting up out of my chair and walking away abruptly.

Was I mistaken, or had he looked disappointed? Jack's reaction took me by surprise, as it revealed a hint of humanity behind his outward bravado. He was always so snarky that I had assumed it was his true personality, but I realized he, too, had curated a persona. The macho mask he donned was a form of self-preservation, his version of "war paint" against his inner insecurities. It wasn't just Elizabeth and I who had come to New York and were trying on a new identity to see how it suited us.

***

"I am leaving the company…" my boss, Betty, began.

"NO! Where are you going?" I blurted, cutting her off.

"Estée Lauder offered me a role I couldn't refuse," she concluded.

I was a few weeks away from my final intern evaluation and full-time job interviews loomed when Betty pulled me into her office and told me she was leaving the company. I had been banking on Betty's vote of confidence, having watched me work over three years, to vouch for me in the application process. My disappointment was twofold: selfishly, I worried there was no chance of getting the marketing role at Arden without Betty (which, in hindsight, showed how much my self-confidence relied on external validation), but I was also upset for Elizabeth, as though Betty leaving to work for a competitor was a personal betrayal that affected both of us like secondhand smoke.

I documented my displeasure to "Dear Liz" in a red journal entry, which continued to hold space for the raw reality of my true self—but I kept any semblance of stress or self-doubt hidden from my Manhattan Maven blog, which had amassed a loyal following over three years. I felt beholden to my online audience to keep posts positive with pretty photos, while the truth behind the scenes was becoming far more blemished.

Chapter 7

The Great Unknown

New York
1933–1934

After the grand opening of Elizabeth's first signature red door in 1930, the Great Depression deepened, and Tommy suggested they close some of the subsidiary salons. Elizabeth refused, instead increasing treatment options for the "budget-conscious" and switching her business focus from skincare to cosmetics. In tough times, "a swipe of color is cheering," she said, and was proven right, as lipstick sales soared. Unfortunately, they weren't enough to keep her bank balance afloat. By the end of the Great Depression, Elizabeth's North American fortune mimicked the state of the economy, and she was $500,000 in the red.

A bright spot, despite the economic downtown, was reuniting with her younger sister, Gladys, whom she once had been a mother figure to in their early years on the farm. Gladys was trying to escape a bad marriage to her alcoholic and abusive husband, John Baraba, the father of her baby, John Jr., when she reached out to Elizabeth for help.

Elizabeth helped Gladys and the baby, John Jr., flee Canada and moved them into her Manhattan apartment. The rekindling of their sisterly bond was mutually beneficial, as Gladys filled the void of loneliness left by Tommy, as his indiscretions were becoming less discreet. Elizabeth frequently returned home from working late at the office to find their bed empty. She would crawl in next to Gladys and lay awake until she heard the turn of the key in the lock as the sun came up.

Elizabeth gave Gladys a job as a trainer for the all-female team of saleswomen who traveled to department stores across the country to demonstrate Arden facial massage techniques and showcase products at the beauty counters. She would have gladly mopped the salon floors; anything to earn her own money and provide for her young son. Physically, Gladys resembled her older sister so much they were often mistaken for twins, but many employees later remarked Gladys exuded an exuberance and warmth that immediately differentiated them. Elizabeth had grown colder and more reserved over the years. Gladys was intelligent, hardworking, and excelled at her job. She soon earned the financial freedom to officially file for divorce from her estranged husband.

Gladys was introduced to her sister's best friend, Bessie, before Elizabeth left on a weeklong trip to the Marbury estate, Lakeside Farm, in Maine, where she rode horses, read in the garden, and sipped iced tea with Bessie, Elsie, and Anne Morgan. It was the first real vacation Elizabeth had allowed herself in a long time, and to her surprise, she found she quite enjoyed relaxing. Elizabeth had never known such genuine kindness and deep friendship as she had developed with Bessie. Theirs was a true and lasting bond.

"How was Maine with Bessie and the girls?" Gladys asked, upon her return.

"I pick good women, but not sure I have the same luck with men," said Elizabeth, who noted Tommy's absence at the apartment when she got home from Maine. Lakeside Farm soon became Elizabeth's favorite escape, away from her problems and the airs of Manhattan society that she both loved and loathed in equal measure.

Two years later, in 1932, Elizabeth could no longer ignore her husband was an adulterous cad, as members of her staff began reporting numerous incidents of infidelity. She hired a private detective who confirmed the allegations. Elizabeth learned Tommy was having an affair with one of her treatment girls, Mildred Beam, and that she was footing the bill for the expansive list of hotels, dinners, and extravagant gifts he lavished on her. Heartbroken and humiliated, she soon learned that wasn't the worst of it.

The detective discovered Tommy had secretly been going behind Elizabeth's back to meet with lawyers, business associates, and bankers to try and cut his wife out and take over control of the company. Tommy had become increasingly dissatisfied in his role as employee, and the public emasculation of being referred to as "Mr. Elizabeth Arden" had gotten to him. It was still a man's world in the 1930s and Tommy assumed that as a husband, it was his God-given right to take full ownership of his wife's company. This information infuriated Elizabeth more than if he had a million mistresses in Manhattan. After seventeen years of marriage, Elizabeth kicked Tommy out, tossing his belongings onto the sidewalk, and filed for immediate divorce citing "mental cruelty." The *New York Times* reported in 1932:

ELIZABETH ARDEN SUES! DIVORCE ACTION AGAINST THOMAS JENKINS LEWIS

Testimony was heard before Superior Court Justice Herbert T. Powers late yesterday in an uncontested divorce libel filed by Mrs. Florence Lewis of New York. Mrs. Lewis is nationally known as Elizabeth Arden, proprietor of a beauty preparations concern. Mrs. Lewis told of alleged mental cruelty by the husband, Thomas J. Lewis, over a long period of time.

It was a landmark divorce—not only was it rare for a woman to file the papers, it was also unheard of for her to be the breadwinner. With Bessie's help, Elizabeth hired celebrity attorney and vice president of MGM, J. Robert Rubin, to represent her. Rubin ensured Tommy only received a settlement of one hundred dollars, which, even in the 1930s, was considered a pittance from his successful spouse. One hundred dollars was less than the cost of a full day at her salon. Tommy was also forbidden to work in the cosmetics industry for five years from the date of their divorce. Elizabeth had given all she could to Tommy, and he had blindsided her by trying to take all of it and more. For that, she would never forgive nor forget.

Elizabeth was also furious with her brother, William, who had lied to her for years. Not only was he privy to the philandering, but he took Tommy's side in the divorce proceedings. William was fired from the wholesale division and Elizabeth never spoke to her brother again. She did, however, continue her relationship with his three daughters, Beattie, Ginnie, and Pattie, whom she had developed a motherly affinity for and would later employ at the company.

Throughout the early days of the divorce proceedings, Bessie was a constant source of comfort and support to Elizabeth. But then, Bessie committed the ultimate act of betrayal: she died. Bessie was heavyset, but showed no signs of illness when she died of a heart attack at home in Sutton Place. Elizabeth was devastated, but jumped into action and helped plan her funeral at St. Patrick's Cathedral in New York, which had an impressive turnout of the most important American dignitaries, leaders, and artists. One person was noticeably absent from the funeral despite being the prime beneficiary of Bessie's will: Elsie de Wolfe. Elizabeth had loved Bessie so unconditionally that she was willing to take a backseat when Elsie came back into the picture, but she couldn't understand why Elsie missed the funeral of her longtime girlfriend. Despite all of the fun times the three shared at Lakeside Farm in Maine, Elizabeth never spoke to Elsie again.

The mid-1930s were a tough time for Elizabeth. She mourned the loss of her closest friend, the demise of her marriage, and the downturn in the economy. Grit began to pepper Elizabeth's glamorous view of the world. Behind her brave façade, she was distraught. As a result, Elizabeth shifted her affections away from people and toward horses, her childhood love, for they had never let her down.

On the bright side, Elizabeth still had Gladys by her side, and she was reflecting a lot about her first trip to Europe in the summer of 1912, over a decade prior. While Elizabeth reigned supreme at the top of the beauty empire in North America in the 1930s, she daydreamed about the luxurious salons she had toured in Paris and London, and how incredible it would be for her growing global brand to establish European subsidiaries. Elizabeth had been swept up in the cultural awakening after WWI, but it was finally time to set her sights on Europe.

- LOU -

As I approached the end of my final internship, the reality of entering the "real world" hit me. For twenty years, it felt like I was wading in the shallow end of the pool. Interning at Arden was akin to dipping my toe in the deep end, but officially joining the corporate world felt like jumping into the ocean and losing sight of the horizon. Any shred of confidence I thought I had developed over the past three years vanished. I was dismayed to discover my shield of armor was as thin as tinfoil; I still relied on the validation of others, their approval of my abilities, to dictate my self-worth.

At the end of the summer, the full-time job interviews were held in a large conference room and I was given a two-hour time slot. The morning of the interview, I had to change the outfit I'd chosen for a long-sleeved, high-necked dress (think: Little House on the Prairie) just to cover the red hives I'd developed all over my body from nerves. I remember walking into the conference room, seeing an intimidating number of people sitting around the table, pens poised to take notes on my answers, and immediately feeling the sweat start dripping from my forehead.

Unbeknownst to me, before Betty left Arden, she had given a letter of recommendation to the human resources department to keep on file for my interview. I only learned of the letter after the fact, but whatever she wrote seemingly helped my case, as a few weeks later, after of the candidates were interviewed, I was offered a full-time position as Marketing Coordinator on the Global Fragrance team in New York, effective immediately upon graduation. Arden had just secured a licensing deal to develop a line of perfumes for a girl who was my age and about to win *Billboard's* Woman of the Year, Taylor Swift. Part of the reason I was hired was because the company wanted someone with beauty industry experience that also understood Taylor's millennial demographic.

On the last day of my final internship, Natalie and Jada (who had been promoted to Betty's position) surprised me with a "Goodbye/Congratulations" celebration by decorating my cubicle. We toasted with sparkling cider in plastic cups (although I could legally drink in Canada, I was still a few weeks shy of twenty-one) and their departing words brought me to tears. When I returned to pack up my desk, there was a beautiful bouquet of red roses. On an Arden–embossed notecard, in scrawling, scratchy handwriting, it said: "Red's your color, kid." There was no signature, but I knew they were from Jimmy. Three years later and he still remembered that nervous girl in the "loud" red outfit on her first day in the big city.

With my box of belongings and bouquet of red flowers, I took one last look around. I would be back in eight months after I graduated, but never again as an intern. When I returned, it would be…forever?

I pushed the elevator button. Staring blankly ahead, dressed all in black, I stepped inside and rode down to the lobby. I pushed through the doors into the warm summer air, feeling as though I had finally traversed the elusive threshold into adulthood.

On my way home, I walked through Union Square Park and passed by a man holding a sign that said: "ASK ME ABOUT THE CLOCK." Usually, I avoided small talk with strangers, but there was a small group of earnest-looking people around him, and for some reason, I felt compelled to stop. The man pointed to the ever-changing numbers on the southeast corner of Union Square, the same digital scroll that had fascinated me on my first walk to Arden, three years prior. The numbers continued to change rapidly above what had been a Virgin Megastore on the first day of my internship in 2008 but had since been replaced by Forever 21.

"It's a commissioned art piece called Metronome, a modern hourglass," the man explained. "The numbers count down in hours, minutes, and seconds, until midnight, with time flowing from left to right *and* right to left. You'll see the numbers move fastest in the middle, just like the grains of sand in an hourglass. It's meant to represent the intangibility of time." His words would repeat in my mind like a scratched record: "The intangibility of time." I couldn't help but think how poetically prophetic and accurate that was.

Before I had left Canada, I knew little about life beyond the border, but that's the thing about bubbles; you never know you're in one until they burst. Manhattan had been my big bang. I had grown accustomed to the routine of school, the linear movement from one level to the next, the years divided neatly into semesters and summers, in parallel to my peers—but life took on many deviations once we were released from that continuous track into the real world. The promise of my future self had sustained me throughout high school and university, but it was much easier to "Plan Ahead + Work Hard = Achieve Goals" when the goalposts—graduation and getting a job—had been so clear. I had achieved those two goals…now what?

***

In my last year of university, Logan and I broke up. The seasons were in transition, as was I. There was a chill in the fall air as I walked along a winding path to where Logan sat on a bench in the park across from our student houses. We had made the decision to break up the night before, but were meeting to talk about it once the heaviness of reality sank in.

The strange part was that I loved Logan with every fiber of my being, so I had done the only thing I could think of to preserve what we had: I ended it. As irrational as it sounded, I thought I was saving us.

Back then, I believed (as Elizabeth illustrated) that isolation and independence were paramount to success. I recognized how attached I

105

became to people I loved, like barnacles to a boat, and how I submerged my sense of self below the surface to accommodate the needs of others. When Logan hurt, I hurt. When he was happy, I was happy. It was intoxicating while I was in it, but the deeper we dove into our relationship, the more I worried I would let too much of myself get swept away before I even had a chance to figure out who I was.

The majority of the real estate in my head and my heart was devoted exclusively to him. My thoughts, actions, and choices were consumed by our twosome, and I needed to see what I was capable of accomplishing on my own.

More than anything, I wanted to avoid going down the clichéd path of becoming one of those young couples who later resent each other for not following their individual dreams. As our joint lives diverged, I thought a clean break, time to figure out who we were independently before stitching ourselves back together as a couple was a healthy, mature decision. My hope was that we would emerge after several months with a solid foundation of our fully formed selves, ready to tackle the next phase of adulthood as an even stronger team. I failed to anticipate, however, that the short-term wound might callous over so completely, it would be impossible to repair in the long-run.

In hindsight, I see the selfishness in my actions and how I let love become a casualty of my ambition, just like Elizabeth. Single-minded to a fault, I was too inexperienced in the ways of the world to realize that I could have had *both* a fulfilling relationship and career. But back then, I naively believed in the notion that if it were meant to be, we would find our way back to each other.

Strangely, I also thought I had not worked hard enough to deserve that kind of deep love. *Plan Ahead + Work Hard = Achieve Goals.* Hard work reaped rewards. Hard work equated success. My relationship with Logan had blossomed so naturally, I felt unworthy of its rewards. Loving him had been so easy, I thought I'd somehow taken a short-cut and needed to work hard, as I did with everything else in life, to prove I deserved it. I didn't recognize it then, but my mercurial mind undermined the things I loved most. Years later, I would come to see the familiar pattern: as soon as I felt safe and secure, the impulse for destabilization was forthcoming. Only then, I would ask myself: *why, when I was at my happiest, did I self-sabotage?*

Back on the bench in the park, I sat beside Logan. His eyes were red, his soft cheeks tearstained. My own tears trembled beneath the surface and broke free in a steady stream. We sat there in silence until he said, "I just know I'll be that old man sitting on a bench, like this one someday, still talking about the girl that got away." For once, I had no words.

***

Several months later, Logan and I made plans to see each other before I moved to New York "forever," as I told my family. "For the foreseeable future," they quipped, not wanting to believe my move away from them was a permanent one. Truth be told, I tried not to let myself think about it either.

With only a couple weeks left before I was set to leave, I got a call from human resources (HR) at Elizabeth Arden. My immediate instinct was that I was about to be fired; it had all seemed too good to be true anyway. However, I was *not* expecting what HR did have to say.

"Hi, Louise, I know you are prepared to move to New York, but we have an exciting last-minute opportunity at our European headquarters in Geneva, Switzerland, and we think you would be the perfect candidate. I will detail all of this in writing, but it is a one-year position, working in marketing across all three pillars: skincare, color, and fragrance, and you would return to our New York office afterward as planned. Geneva will give you an opportunity to practice your French."

Shit, or rather "merde." Apparently, Arden had noted the mention of my high school bilingual certification on my resumé. Little did they know I could recall only a few French phrases and they were mostly profanity.

"On top of your salary, we will cover your accommodation and a weekly food allowance. I know this is a lot to take in, so think it over on the weekend and let us know your decision by Monday," the woman in HR concluded.

I hung up and my mind went into panic mode. *SWITZERLAND?! GENEVA?! WHAT ABOUT NEW YORK?!* I knew Manhattan. Manhattan knew me. Geneva and I knew nothing about each other.

Although Logan and I weren't officially dating, we still kept in touch, the line of reconciliation always within reach. There was no textbook for love (trust me, I tried to find one); it didn't just turn off like a faucet, so we were navigating the tricky waters of figuring ourselves out while still caring deeply for one another. Logan and I met off-campus at Coffee Culture for our preplanned goodbye, but after my call with HR, I wanted to ask his advice on what he thought I should do. Our rapport was so natural, so comforting, that after we downed two mugs of drip coffee, we continued walking and talking until the moon replaced the sun. It was dusk when we sat on swings in a nearby playground and mulled over the pros and cons of Switzerland versus New York. Long after the stars came out, Logan and I continued swinging back and forth, pumping our legs like little kids. We fell into a comfortable silence as we soared toward the sky before falling back down to earth. The temperature had cooled after the sun went down, but I was flushed with warmth.

"Do you think we should, maybe, get back together?" I blurted. "I…I really miss you," I said, looking at my scuffed sneakers, embarrassed by my bluntness. I felt fifteen again, pink ribbon in my hair standing on the cottage porch, telling him I thought he was cute.

"I think that might be challenging with an ocean between us," he said.

Logan was right. How could I ask him to rekindle our relationship when we both knew I was leaving again for an indefinite amount of time? *For the foreseeable future.*

"But yeah…I miss you too, Lou," he said sincerely, and then we slipped into another soothing hush, steadily pumping our feet in tandem.

A breeze rustled past my face. I looked over at Logan on the swing, legs dangling, the moon bouncing off his rosy cheeks. In that instant, I couldn't help but feel like I'd be that old woman sitting on a swing someday, still talking about the guy that got away.

Insomnia struck that night, and my mind flashed back to the Metronome clock in Union Square. I reached for my red journal on the nightstand, flipped back a few pages, and underneath where I had written "the intangibility of time," I added, "the intangibility of love," and I couldn't help but think how poetically prophetic and accurate that was. Eventually, I drifted off to sleep. When I woke, my sights were set on Switzerland.

Part II
MAVEN

Europe: Paris, London, Geneva

"It is remarkable what a woman can accomplish with just a little ambition."

—Elizabeth Arden

Chapter 8

Across the Atlantic

Paris
1930s

For wealthy travelers in the 1930s, sailing to Europe was a sign of status. The cost of a seven-day ocean voyage was about $159 for first-class passengers, including luxurious sleeper cabins, meals, and alcohol. Elizabeth afforded herself the extravagance.

Steamships were built for luxury, and first-class quarters were on par with the finest hotels in the world, filled with opulent ballrooms and state-of-the-art dining parlors. Following the tragedy of the *RMS Titanic* in 1912, people were more wary of the industrial sea marvels, yet with commercial air travel still two decades away, steamers were the only way to cross the Atlantic from America.

With no air conditioning, the humidity in the cabins could be stifling, so Elizabeth preferred to spend her time above deck, reading a language book, desperately trying to teach herself French. "Elizabeth experienced one of her few failures in life and never learned to speak the language properly, but it was not for want of trying," wrote Alfred Lewis, in *Miss Elizabeth Arden*.

Elizabeth left Manhattan, reportedly on the *SS New York*, and disembarked in Cherbourg, France, before the ship continued onward to Southampton, England. From the small port of Cherbourg, Elizabeth traveled by train for three hours to arrive at her final destination: Paris.

France's "belle époque" (the beautiful age) was eclipsed by "les années folles" (the crazy years). It was a period of rich creative and cultural collaborations. The French franc had dropped drastically, making it an attractive and affordable place for American artists, writers, and thinkers to visit. Artists, singers, dancers, poets, and writers gravitated to Paris and met in cafés like Le Jockey, Le Dôme, and La Coupole. Ever the romantic, Elizabeth was enamored by the broad, unhurried boulevards, charming café society, and nonchalant airs of the chic Parisians.

She stayed at the Ritz Hotel in Place Vendôme, the most expensive hotel in Paris, where the cost of a room was a whopping nine dollars a night. Upon arrival at the Ritz, Elizabeth poured a hot bath with her Venetian Rose Bath Salts (she never traveled without them) and indulged in a facial with her skincare line to unwind after the long trip.

In Europe, Elizabeth abandoned her healthy diet and allowed herself to gorge on wine, cheese, meats, and bread. She dined at Café de Paris, where "unescorted women" were not allowed after 9 p.m., but Elizabeth greased the palms of the waitstaff to seat her at one of the discreet back tables, typically reserved for single male diners meeting their mistresses, and sipped champagne until the wee hours, watching with a pang of jealousy as glitzy couples danced to the nightly live jazz band. Elizabeth loved dancing, but as an "unescorted" woman, she was unable to partake.

Nighttime in the City of Lights was Elizabeth's favorite, as she could be uninhibited and let her carefully curated guard down for a few, blissful hours. After a late supper, Elizabeth would traipse through Paris where she watched a barely clad Josephine Baker dance the Lindy Hop Charleston at the Folies Bergère and a twenty-year-old Edith Piaf sing, in what would become her signature "little black dress," at Le Gerny nightclub off the Champs-Elysées.

Daytime in Paris, Elizabeth toured retail spaces, visited competitive salons, had afternoon tea at Angelina's Tea Room, perused the bookshelves at Shakespeare & Company, and picked fresh flowers from Marché aux Fleurs, the oldest and largest flower market in Paris, to make her hotel room feel like home during her Parisian sojourn. Early evening, she would retreat to the Ritz Bar in the hotel lobby for boozing and schmoozing. The art worlds of New York and Paris often collided so it was through mutual acquaintances that Elizabeth was introduced at the Ritz Bar to fellow creatives: famed French writers, Gertrude Stein, her girlfriend Alice Toklas, Colette, Simone de Beauvoir, James Joyce, Ezra Pound, Marcel Proust, Zelda and F. Scott Fitzgerald, and Ernest Hemingway, who came to Paris as a foreign correspondent for the *Toronto Star,* a Canadian newspaper.

Throughout les années folles, the Ritz Bar was a favorite haunt of the "Lost Generation," a term coined by Gertrude Stein for expatriate writers and creatives living in Paris. Ernest Hemingway popularized the term in his novel, *The Sun Also Rises*: "You are all a lost generation." F. Scott Fitzgerald set his famous short story, *Babylon Revisited*, at the Ritz, loosely based on his years spent parked at the bar. Elizabeth happily joined the Lost Generation during her time in Paris where creativity flowed as much as the alcohol.

Elizabeth became fast friends with Zelda Fitzgerald, an American socialite, artist, and writer—although her husband's literary celebrity often overshadowed her talented accolades. "Beautiful, sharply smart, and funny, Zelda embodied Scott Fitzgerald's fantasy of the golden girl wife," wrote *Interview* magazine. Elizabeth and Zelda had both grown up poor in small farm towns with big career dreams; sharing a zesty hatred for the way society undervalued feminine potential. They made their way to New York City, Zelda at nineteen from Alabama, Elizabeth at twenty-nine from Canada, in search of something greater for themselves. Although Elizabeth was twenty-two years older than Zelda (born in 1878 and 1900, respectively), their friends assumed they were the same age as Elizabeth looked and purported to be decades younger. Unbeknownst to one another, the two women also struggled with maintaining their flawless façades. In her diary, Zelda wrote about feeling like she was always *performing the role* of an exceptional woman and *playing the part* of a picture-perfect society wife. Elizabeth related wholeheartedly to those sentiments, if only she had known.

The golden age in Europe was far more free-spirited and cultur-ally advanced than North America. F. Scott Fitzgerald foreshadowed in a letter to a friend: "In twenty years, New York will have the culture of Paris." Elizabeth took note of how liberated Gertrude Stein and Alice Toklas were, openly kissing and holding hands in public, whereas her dear friend Bessie Marbury and Elsie de Wolfe had to keep their displays of affection behind closed doors. Gertrude reminded Elizabeth of Bessie and was enamored by her commanding presence and boisterous self-confidence. "Einstein was the creative philosophic mind of the century, and I am the creative literary mind," Gertrude proudly self-declared.

At one of Gertrude and Alice's lively parlor parties in their pied-à-terre (apartment) on 27 rue de Fleurus, Elizabeth was introduced to Sylvia Beach, the charming founder and owner of the Paris bookstore, Shakespeare & Co, and her girlfriend Adrienne Monnier. Sylvia was an American-born bookseller, publisher, and staunch supporter of aspiring authors, giving James Joyce and Ernest Hemingway their big breaks. She edited, financed, and published the classic novel *Ulysses* by James Joyce in 1922 after it was rejected by every other publishing house. She also published and sold copies of Hemingway's first book, creatively titled *Three Stories and Ten Poems*, in 1923. In his book *A Moveable Feast*, Hemingway credited Sylvia's enduring kindness: "No one I ever knew was nicer to me."

There was speculation among the Lost Generation that Elizabeth fancied Sylvia, but she respected her relationship with Adrienne and continued to suppress her latent lesbianism. While Elizabeth's sexuality remained shrouded in mystery, there was no doubt that she enjoyed fostering close bonds with like-minded, entrepreneurial women like Bessie Marbury, Gertrude Stein, Zelda Fitzgerald, and Sylvia Beach.

Years later, during the "fall of Paris" in 1941, Sylvia was forced to shutter Shakespeare & Co., but she cleverly painted over the sign and kept her books hidden in the vacant fourth-floor apartment above the bookshop to avoid having them destroyed by the Nazis. She was taken to an internment camp but released after six months, where she lived with Adrienne above the bookstore on Rue de l'Odéon (the original location) until the war ended in 1944. Shakespeare & Co. stayed closed until 1951 when George Whitman reopened it. His daughter, whom he named Sylvia Beach Whitman after the shop's founder, still runs Shakespeare & Co. today at 37 Rue de la Bûcherie.

***

Near the end of Elizabeth's Parisian portion of her Europe trip, a woman by the name of Gabrielle "Coco" Chanel, "the belle of the Parisian social elite," according to the BBC, had just returned from vacationing in Côte d'Azur with her lover, the grand duke Dimtri Pavlovich. Coco was well known in French fashion circles and had opened a popular boutique at 31 Rue Cambon in 1918. While on holiday, Coco enlisted the expertise of master perfumer Mr. Ernest Beaux to help her expand into beauty. At the time, traditional scents worn by "respectable women" only used the essence of a single garden flower. Fragrances with mixed notes and animal musks were thought to be too sexually provocative, but Coco recognized the changing times and wanted to create a signature fragrance for the liberated spirit of the New Woman. The perfumed, Mr. Beaux, presented Coco with ten tiny glass vials of various scent compositions. She chose the fifth vial—a mixture of jasmine, rose, sandalwood, and vanilla—and decided to keep the name simple. "I present my dress collections on the fifth of May, the fifth month of the year, and so we will let sample number five keep the name it has already. It will bring good luck," Coco said to Mr. Beaux, about what would become her signature fragrance, Chanel No. 5. The perfume's bottle design was inspired by Coco's previous longtime lover, Arthur "Boy" Capel, who had died in a car accident on his way to visit her, so she modeled Chanel No. 5 after Boy's whiskey decanter. Like Elizabeth, Coco was innovative in taking things traditionally thought of as "masculine" and infusing them with femininity.

Elizabeth and Coco would have first met at the Ritz Hotel in Paris, where Elizabeth was staying and Coco lived (*today, guests can still stay in Coco's unchanged, black-and-white, 2,024 square-foot suite on the second floor of the hotel for twenty thousand euros per night*). The ladies bumped elbows again at their favorite lunch spot, Angelina's Tea Room on Rue de Rivoli, known for their Mont Blanc pastries and chocolat chaud. Opened in 1903, Angelina's was exquisitely designed with romantic high ceilings, marbled tables, and gold-accented mirrors. It was the place to be seen for aristocrats and celebrities. As legend has it, Coco tested the market for Chanel No. 5 by spritzing the perfume around her table at Angelina's, and women stopped in their tracks on the way to the powder room to ask about the amazing scent. Chanel No. 5 was a runaway hit (*to this day, one bottle is sold every thirty seconds worldwide*). Elizabeth watched the success of Chanel No. 5 with eagle-eyed precision, like sharpshooter Annie Oakley in the Wild West. By then, she had a stronghold in skincare and cosmetics but recognized the profit potential of adding fragrance as the third and final pillar to her brand portfolio. It would take another few years before Elizabeth successfully broke into the fragrance market, but she was inspired by Coco, another powerhouse businesswoman dominating Europe in les années folles.

While Elizabeth mixed business with pleasure in Paris, she was eager to travel onward to London. She wanted to open salons across Europe, but to do so, she needed help to divide and conquer. Elizabeth sent for her sister Gladys to sail from Manhattan to take over expansion plans in France while Elizabeth traveled onward to England. There was no one else she trusted. Although Elizabeth never mastered French, Gladys was completely fluent, having taught herself the language when she lived in Canada. Gladys had never been to Europe, but it was love at first sight for the youngest Graham sister when she disembarked with her young son, John Jr., in tow.

Paris was even more beautiful than Elizabeth had described in her letters. Gladys was so enamored by the City of Lights that she decided never to return to Manhattan, choosing to live permanently in Paris for the rest of her life. Elizabeth hired a French nanny to care for John Jr. so Gladys could take on the challenge of expanding the Arden brand throughout France for the next few years.

The brilliant Gladys got to work establishing distribution for Arden products across the country. With her darling Canadian-French accent and natural business acumen, she charmed Raul Mayer, the head of Galeries Lafayette, the most luxurious department store in France, to do a trial run of Arden products. The exquisite, delicate packaging sold out so fast, he gave Arden a dedicated beauty counter in Galeries Lafayette.

Outside of the city of Paris, Gladys traveled from Provence to Alsace, across the countryside to train local women to stock and sell Arden products, just as she had done with the traveling troupe of saleswomen across the United States. Word-of-mouth spread about the efficacy of the scientific formulas and the pretty yet simple packaging appealed to French women's sensibilities that skincare and cosmetics were enhancement tools to bring out their natural beauty. Products were selling out so fast, Gladys had to wire the Arden headquarters in Manhattan to double the stock shipments—but soon, this replenishment method became problematic, as sea travel was slow and salon shelves sat empty for long stretches.

Gladys astutely opened a one-room factory in Neuilly, a suburb of Paris, and hired a chemist to reproduce the formulas. Elizabeth was thrilled Gladys had found a solution to eliminate shipping and lower production costs. Once the wholesale division was running smoothly, Elizabeth was eager for Gladys to help open a Red Door spa in Place Vendôme, near The Ritz and Angelina's. The Red Door Spas had become signature showrooms that elevated the brand. Elizabeth envisioned having Arden Red Doors in every country in the world. "In a sense, they were proof of her existence. When she looked up at the engraved name, Elizabeth Arden, over the red doors, she knew she was entering a haven in which she would be forever safe and somebody of substance," wrote Lewis and Woodworth in *Miss Elizabeth Arden.*

Elizabeth scouted and secured the retail location while Gladys hired and trained two Parisian treatment girls. They opened the first European salon at 255 Rue Saint-Honoré. Zelda Fitzgerald was one of the Paris salon's first and most loyal customers. Her day planner was uncovered years later and indicated near-daily appointments at "Le Salon d'Elizabeth Arden." When Zelda and F. Scott Fitzgerald posed for a feature in *Hearst's International Magazine,* Zelda was quoted as saying she had to put on "her Elizabeth Arden face" for the editorial.

With Gladys handling the business affairs in France, Elizabeth set off to conquer a new frontier: England. For the first leg of the two-day journey, she hopped on the Orient Express train from Paris to Calais, then boarded the cross-channel ferry from Calais to Dover, England, before taking the South Eastern Railway from Dover to arrive in London.

When Elizabeth and Gladys were growing up on the farm in Canada, they never could have imagined the faraway places and adventures they would experience someday, growing up into strong, independent women traveling through Europe together. Gladys and Elizabeth's relationship reminded me of the deep bond I shared with my sisters (Grace and Meredith). As the older siblings, our younger sisters looked up to us. I empathized with the enormous pressure Elizabeth put on herself to keep up the pretense that everything was perfect for Gladys, who relied on her emotionally and financially. Even in front of family, we kept up the pretense of perfection. However, Elizabeth and I failed to remember that most often the best way to show others the path to success is by fully exhibiting our failures.

- LOU -

Flying into Switzerland, I kept my nose pressed to the window, as though the tip could touch the top of the Alps. It was late summer

2011, but the snow-capped mountains were impartial to the seasons. As we flew above Geneva, clouds stippled the cobalt sky and gave way to rich, earthy land. Pea-green pastures, antique gold fields, and emerald forests formed a patchwork quilt of rural beauty.

With alpine views that forever hugged the horizon, it felt as though I had entered a three-dimensional postcard. Speechless from the sheer beauty of the Swiss landscape, I soaked in the azure waters of Lake Geneva (customarily called Lac Léman). The crescent-shaped lake snaked along the shores of the Swiss Riviera, and half belonged to France, whose borders crisscrossed through the neighboring Jura Mountains. The Swiss city of Geneva wrapped around the southern tip of Lac Léman, where among approximately 195,000 people, I would soon call home.

In Switzerland, over 75 percent of people spoke German, while the remaining 25 percent spoke French. I was Geneva was in Romandy, the French-speaking part of Switzerland, as my German skills were *nicht existent*. My French skills were so rusty I had spent the plane ride reading a French-English pocket dictionary and writing down useful phrases in my new Moleskine notebook (red, of course). I hadn't written to "Dear Liz" for nearly a year, since my last summer in Manhattan, but as I was entering full-time employment at her company in a new country, rekindling our one-way correspondence provided comfort, like cuddling a stuffed animal or talking to my imaginary best friend.

Geneva was a melting pot of nationalities. Similar to Manhattan, the majority of the population came from somewhere else. With its historic stronghold in the banking industry and home to the United Nations, Red Cross, and the World Health Organization, Geneva was a global hub for financiers and diplomats. The expat community was extensive as many multinational corporations set up shop in the small city due to its centrality to the rest of Europe and attractive tax breaks. With its chic boutiques, quaint restaurants, cobblestoned streets, and breathtaking alpine views, the quality of life was luxe and the cost of living high.

Looking out over Geneva from my window seat in the plane, I recognized the fleeting luxury of my current life. I was twenty-one, with a dream job in a dream place, but a large part of me still felt like a fraud. I didn't know there was a name for it then, but throughout my time in Switzerland, I was plagued by impostor syndrome, which the dictionary defined as feelings of inadequacy, chronic self-doubt, and a persistent sense of intellectual fraudulence despite past proof of competence.

I couldn't shake the feeling that Arden had overestimated my abilities. I had "faked it 'til I made it" during my three internships in Manhattan and now it felt like I had somehow tricked them into giving me a full-time position—in Switzerland, no less. I didn't know how I was going to maintain the façade of the assertive, ambitious businesswoman everyone now believed me to be—and that I perpetuated on my blog.

"It's only twelve months. You're only here for twelve months," I repeated to myself. In that moment, it made sense why new parents refer to their kids' ages in months, as opposed to years. I never understood why new parents said their toddler was "twenty-four months" instead of "she's two," but breaking time down from years into months shrank it into manageable components.

When the plane landed at Cointrin Airport, the dawn of the day lingered. While the remaining hours until nightfall were pregnant with potential, I hailed a taxi (luckily it was the same word in French and English) to the Crowne Plaza Hotel. Arden was amazingly covering my rent while I lived in Geneva, but it was up to me to find the apartment. In the meantime, they were putting me up at a hotel. After I checked into my room and ate the tiny Toblerone chocolate on my pillow, I fell into a deep sleep until the next morning.

My mom and youngest sister, Meredith, who was on summer break from high school, met me in Geneva the following day (the company had arranged my flights, so they flew separately). They kindly agreed to transport extra luggage (my own personal Sherpas) and help me find a place to live. Arden gave me a monthly rental budget of approximately three thousand Swiss francs, the equivalent of almost $4,000 Canadian dollars, which I thought was astronomical for a single, furnished apartment. *I'll be living like European royalty with marble accents and a sweeping terrace!* However, I soon discovered what my travel books meant by Geneva being "one of the most expensive cities in the world to live in." The Swiss rental agency swiftly brought me back to reality, as they told me three thousand francs would yield the most bare-boned accommodation on their real estate roster. By then, I was used to sleeping in a shoebox-sized dorm, so I didn't care, any place to call my own was thrilling.

The man who rented me the apartment had a gray Groucho Marx moustache, chain-smoked hand-rolled cigarettes from a tobacco tin tucked in his breast pocket, and spoke thick, heavily accented French. When I received the keys, he referred to my new humble abode as a "pied-à-terre," which fit nicely into my romantic notions about European life.

My mom, Meredith, and I shared a double bed in the hotel for nearly two weeks, as the cost of an additional room was insanely expensive, just enough time to submit the paperwork for the pied-à-terre and move in. There was no time for reflection, only action. Almost all of the rental cars in Europe were stick shift, which I had no experience driving, and at twenty-one I wasn't even old enough to rent, so I was grateful my mom agreed to navigate the narrow stone streets in our baby blue Peugeot to transport the luggage from the hotel to my new Swiss home.

After two weeks together, my mom and Meredith flew back to Toronto. None of us liked to over exhibit our emotions, but our embraces lingered, fraught with the onset of melancholy. Meredith and I hugged first, and then my mom pulled me in tight.

"I love you, Lou. I'm so proud of you," she said as her voice cracked, a telltale sign of the tears to come.

"I love you too, Mom. Thank you for everything," I said, forcing my tone into nonchalance, attempting to suppress my own waterworks.

Looking back, I don't know who needed that hug more: her or me.

After they left, fat tears rolled down my cheeks. I was so grateful to be there, but caught in a moment of self-pity for what I'd left behind and the foreignness of the future. After I collected myself, I cracked open my red journal:

```
Dear Liz,

    I have officially moved to Switzerland to work for
YOU! My family just left and I miss them already. Not
sure when I'll see them next so maybe that's why I
cried, even though I'm excited to be here. Now that
I'm no longer in New York, I also need a new alias
for my blog. I'm thinking Matterhorn Maven to keep
with the alliteration. I can't wait to explore more
of Switzerland and Paris & London to re-trace some of
your European adventures. Time to unpack and make this
place feel like home!

Love,

Lou
```

I reincarnated my blog from *Manhattan* to *Matterhorn Maven*. The return of my inner rhetoric with Liz (through journaling) and outer rhetoric with the world (through blogging) brought back my dual selves: my raw, messy, stumbling self and a picture-perfect curated version that was slowly trying to fuse on top of my true identity, like an invisible full-body cast. Switzerland was a clean slate. I could be anyone I wanted to be; the problem was figuring out who that was.

The tiny, sparsely furnished apartment on Rue Cornavin was in a walk-up building above a boulangerie and a block away from the Jet d'Eau on Lac Léman, Geneva's world-renowned *pièce de résistance*. The train station, Gare Cornavin, was conveniently located on the same street as my apartment, so the ease of escape was enticing. At a moment's notice, I could hop on a train to Paris for the weekend and be strolling along La Seine within three hours.

Europeans seemed so sensual and sophisticated. They embodied minimalism, from their furniture to their style of dress to their approach to life. Everything was uncomplicated and simple, the way nature intended it to be. In Switzerland, I could already tell the cultural emphasis was on disconnecting from technology and reconnecting with nature. It was hard not to drool over the great outdoors when the glistening lakes and *Sound of Music* hillsides called your name at every turn. The only contradiction to the holistic, healthy lifestyle I observed was smoking. I had never been a fan of "hacking darts" (as the "cool kids" said back home), but it was still commonplace throughout Europe in 2011. Smoking in public spaces had been banned in Ontario since 2006, so it took me (and my lungs) some getting used to. "Non, merçi," became my go-to answer whenever I was offered my daily dose of cigarettes on a coffee break at work.

On a whim, I decided *not* to get a cell phone because the cost of the international plan was steep, I didn't have any friends or family to text locally, and the Geneva office operated by email, they called cell phones "une nuisance." Also, I wanted to test myself to see if I could assimilate to the breezy, bohemian way of life where no one relied on phones for entertainment or escapism. My pied-à-terre came with a vintage television set (complete with antenna) that had only one fuzzy French channel, so, like the telephone, it, too, remained an unused vice. Skype, email, my blog, and old-fashioned snail mail seemed like sufficient mediums to keep in touch with people back home. The only issue was that the internet connection at my apartment was so shoddy it took over an hour to load. The Starbucks down the street became my go-to for Wi-Fi, but I quickly learned that even American corporations in Switzerland still ran on Swiss time, meaning Starbucks closed early (well before I got home from work during the week) and had limited weekend hours (everything was closed on Sundays). My Saturday morning ritual became siphoning Wi-Fi at various coffee shops throughout Geneva during their small window of open hours.

I learned how to set up a Swiss bank account (which made me feel like a badass mobster offshoring), find "le laundromat" to wash clothes, and "l'epicérie" to buy groceries. There were no big-box grocery stores in Geneva, mainly little markets. It was customary to pick up only a few fresh items—fruit, vegetables, bread, cheese (and wine)—nothing more and nothing less than what was needed. Food was humble and homemade.

Before Switzerland, the kitchen intimidated me. Growing up, I was spoiled by my mom's home cooking and survived off cafeteria food at school and takeout during my internships. My only specialty was boxed President's Choice White Cheddar Mac & Cheese, which didn't count as "pasta" on the continent that created carbs. Living on my own in Geneva, the experience of shopping and preparing a meal became therapeutic: a simple nightly ritual to be savored.

When I got home from work, I dropped the needle on one of the dusty records left by the owner, usually Edith Piaf, Ella Fitzgerald, or Billie Holiday, and took my time slicing a still-warm baguette, delicately layering it with Gruyère cheese (delivered that day from the neighboring town of the same name). I considered each vegetable as I washed and chopped it for a salad, and I learned to slowly savor a glass (or two) of red wine with dinner. In university, there was no "cherishing" the experience; the point of drinking was to guzzle as much as possible until you became a human wine bottle, but in my new Swiss life, there was no need to hurry to get to where I was going.

Chapter 9

London Calling

London
1930s

Upon arrival in London, Elizabeth stayed at Claridge's Hotel in the posh Mayfair area. Claridge's was a favorite among the city's elite, including European royalty, and epitomized art deco glamour with its handsome red brick exterior, crystal chandeliers, and Victorian fireplaces. The hotel indulged Elizabeth's penchant for the high life and afforded her ample opportunities to consort with the who's who of London. Just as in Paris, Elizabeth explored the city mostly on foot, from Bond Street to Oxford to Piccadilly. She tried to convince shopkeepers to stock Arden products—hoping her reputation in America and France would precede her—but by the end of her first week in London, she failed to land a single order.

Dismayed but undeterred, Elizabeth regrouped and focused her efforts on Knightsbridge, the home of Harrods, London's finest department store. She leveraged her department store connections in New York and scored a meeting with Edward "Teddy" Haslam, the head of Harrods "drug department," which would turn out to be a fruitful and fateful encounter. Teddy was sharp-witted and a smart strategist. Elizabeth liked him instantly. He was a tall, stately British gentleman, who liked Elizabeth's feisty, won't-take-no-for-an-answer attitude, but wisely warned her that the English were apprehensive about new American products. Yardley and Floris were popular beauty brands in the UK at the time, and the Brits typically stuck with what they knew, liked, and trusted. Teddy advised Elizabeth to build her reputation by training English saleswomen to sell the line through local merchants in England's outer regions (similar to Gladys' approach in the French countryside). According to Teddy, small-town shopkeepers were "less snobby" than in Central London and apt to test diverse ranges, so long as the formulas worked. If women saw results and were impressed, word-of-mouth would reach London, where department stores would have no choice but to stock Arden products. Elizabeth was confident British women would be on board once the product was in their hands.

Teddy's advice was astute, and although the market takeover tactic was similar to how Gladys conquered France, England did not embrace the Arden brand as quickly or as easily as their French neighbors. It was a slow climb to convince the Brits to convert to an American brand, but once women were hooked on the formulas, Elizabeth's British business started skyrocketing.

The next step in solidifying the Arden stronghold in the UK was opening a Red Door Spa in London, but Elizabeth needed to find someone as capable as Gladys to manage and oversee the business once she returned to New York. There was only one person for the job: Teddy. Elizabeth had a knack for reading people and trusted his instincts implicitly, not to mention his advice was the reason for her London success.

Initially, Teddy refused. He was wary of leaving his longstanding position at Harrods, but Elizabeth made a monetary offer he couldn't refuse. Elizabeth and Teddy set sail for Manhattan, where she personally trained him in the "Arden way" of overseeing the staff, salon, and wholesale business. After six months of training, Elizabeth and Teddy returned to London to prepare for the opening of her first London Red Door. Elizabeth trained the English treatment girls herself before leaving Teddy in charge to run the operation. Elizabeth took out a full-page ad in the *London Times* to announce her arrival:

WHO IS ELIZABETH ARDEN?
Is she a painter, sculptor, musician, or a writer? The name may be vaguely familiar, linked with memories of beauty.

```
It is a lovely, haunting name.
You may have heard it in New York, in Paris, or
simply on the lips of friends.
Elizabeth Arden is a creator—a creator of beauty.
She teaches women that they themselves
are masterpieces.
Elizabeth has come to London to establish, in
person, at 25 Old Bond Street, a salon that will
be an inspiration to all women.
It is worth your while to make acquaintance
without delay.
```

When the first London location was officially opened at 25 Old Bond Street—where it would remain for over half a century—there was a line down the block. Teddy proved to be steadfastly loyal, working for Elizabeth for the rest of his life, and despite being on the payroll, became one of her dearest friends.

In quick succession, Elizabeth went on to open Red Door Spas in Monaco, Rome, Berlin, Madrid, Milan, and Cannes. The famous chef Julia Child was a frequent Red Door client in Cannes, as she always made the trip after visiting friends in Lausanne and Montreux, Switzerland. Julia's husband Paul called her excursions "getting Ardenized." Suffice it to say, by the time she had turned into an adjective, Elizabeth had successfully expanded her growing empire across Europe. With her professional life on an upward trajectory, Elizabeth returned to New York to pick up the pieces of where she left off after her personal life had imploded with the death of Bessie and divorce from Tommy.

Back in her Manhattan office, Elizabeth couldn't get the success of Coco's Chanel No. 5 perfume out of her mind and became obsessed with the idea of adding fragrance to her beauty portfolio. She sent a letter to her sister in Paris, home of the world's leading perfumeries, to find a winning scent. Gladys sourced six unique scents at a fashion house called Babani, which was looking for an exclusive distributor for their fragrances. She mailed them to Elizabeth in New York, who couldn't pick a preference, so she decided to launch with all six. Babani was a well-known fashion house in Europe (Actress Katharine Hepburn had gotten married in a Babani dress), so Elizabeth leveraged the brand-familiarity and called the fragrance line: "Babani, exclusively imported by Elizabeth Arden." She crafted a campaign around the six scents, wanting women to have a choice in what she coined as "a wardrobe of perfumes" to fit their mood or the occasion, cleverly linking the language of fashion with fragrance, and marketing the scents as accessories to a woman's outfit. There was initial buzz about the Babani launch, but the fashion house wasn't popular enough in North America to sustain sales of Arden's "wardrobe of perfumes." It was Elizabeth's first big professional failure, one that could have punctured her perfect public façade, but she quietly discontinued the six scents, and somehow, the media left her corporate reputation unscathed.

It would be another couple of years before Elizabeth finally found success in fragrances. Gladys discovered an irresistible scent at Fragonard, a French perfume house, and sent it to Elizabeth in 1936. The mixture was a unique blend of fresh-cut florals, including lavender and orange flower, with spicy hints of clove and nutmeg. Elizabeth loved the juxtaposition and snapped up the scent. She named the fragrance Blue Grass, a whimsical nod to the rolling hills where horses, forever her favorite animal, roamed wild and free. The male department store executives at Bonwit Teller and Stern Brothers in New York advised Elizabeth to choose a different name, predicting "Blue Grass" would result in another fragrance failure, as they said no respectable woman would buy a beauty product associated with smelly horses and stables.

Elizabeth ignored the *neigh*-sayers and proceeded with the launch for Blue Grass. She crafted luxurious glass bottles in baby blue and cream boxes that included the fragrance, an eau de toilette, dusting powder, bath essence, and scented soap cloths for traveling. Elizabeth's intuition was right as the launch turned out to be a smashing success—both the scent and the packaging actually appealed to society women who dreamed of escaping to the countryside, the wind blowing through their hair as they galloped through a field of wildflowers. Blue Grass dominated the fragrance market for over thirty years; not bad for a predicted flop.

Elizabeth's patience and persistence to integrate perfume into her portfolio paid off—a trait I strove to emulate at the start of my corporate career a century later. By the time I arrived at Arden in 2008, fragrances were the largest part of the company's profits. After the successful launch of Blue Grass in 1936, over seventy-two new fragrances were created under the Arden brand, and the company also owned and developed over two hundred celebrity and designer fragrances by the mid-2000s. In 1989, the year I was born, Elizabeth Arden launched what would become the company's signature fragrance: Red Door.

Overall, Elizabeth's expansion into Europe was considered a stellar success, largely due to the dedicated and loyal work of Gladys and Teddy, who continued to flawlessly manage affairs across the pond after Elizabeth returned to Manhattan. But Europe was about to enter into another world war that threatened to leave unprecedented amounts of devastation and destruction in its wake.

- LOU -

"C'est quoi un 'coffee *TOGO*'?" the woman at the boulangerie asked earlier that morning.

"A coffee TO GO," I repeated, slowly spacing out the words, hoping she would understand my English enunciation.

The woman peered at me from behind the counter with a blank expression.

"Umm, I mean UN CAFÉ AVEC milk, si'l vous plaît. I would like to take it AVEC MOI...DEHORS," I tried again, fumbling with my rusty French while pointing outside and simulating walking movements. There was a reason no one ever wanted me on their team for charades.

"Café au lait? Bien," she responded, in no mood to hear any more of my pathetic attempts to order.

"Eh voila," she said fifteen minutes later, as she placed a doll-sized mug and saucer on the counter in front of me. I pinched the tiny handle, tilted my head back, and gulped down the coffee in one swift sip. I hadn't really needed to *sample* the coffee, but it was nice of her to let me taste it, like wine at a fancy restaurant.

"Six francs, si'l vous plaît," she said.

Oh my God. The doll-sized sample *was* the coffee "to go" I had ordered, and it had cost me over eight Canadian dollars. I quickly learned I would require a ratio of about ten Swiss-sized coffees to equal one North American-sized cup. The concept of coffee in a takeaway cup "to go" was also baffling in Europe. Coffee was something to sit and savor, not rush out the door.

It was my first day of work in Geneva. After the coffee confusion, I was now at risk of being late. The rain pelted sideways and turned my blow-dried hair into a slip-n-slide as I struggled to open my umbrella. In my groggy state earlier that morning, I had mistakenly used body-wash as shampoo, so with or without the downpour, my hair never stood a chance. I had also stubbornly insisted on wearing my new black pumps. Rain boots would have been much more appropriate, but my first-day-at-a-new-job-in-a-new-city vanity prevailed. My purse strap slid off my shoulder, contorting my body into unintended calisthenics.

I stood nervously in the lobby upon arrival, flushed with nerves yet chilled to the bone from the elements. It felt like the first day of kindergarten: scared to meet my new teachers, worried my peers wouldn't like me, and missing my mom—except now the stakes were *slightly* higher than getting a gold star for construction paper scribbles, and there were no midday naps.

Smoothing my damp hair to one side, I sat in one of the two stiff waiting room chairs of the Elizabeth Arden European headquarters. There was no reception desk, just a long hallway with a multitude of locked doors. It reminded me of an insane asylum or the ever-expanding hallway in *Willy Wonka and the Chocolate Factory.*

A poised, statuesque woman, who conjured images of Mrs. Claus, wearing wire-rimmed glasses and a wool knit sweater, emerged from an office and walked toward me.

"La-weeze! Desolé, je suis Dominique. I forgot you were coming," she said in a mix of French and English.

A wave of nausea suddenly arose in my stomach. *I had just moved halfway across the world and they had forgotten I was coming?* Ignoring the avalanche of fresh fears in my head, I stood up, extended my hand, and forced out my brightest "Bonjour!"

Before I realized what was happening, Dominique was kissing my cheeks three times in alternating succession. My outstretched hand bent awkwardly between our stomachs as I dodged a make-out session with Santa's wife. Eventually, I learned the artful dance of the standard Swiss greeting: three kisses, from left cheek to right to left, but not before I nearly locked lips with every employee.

Dominique handed me an electronic badge, which was my access key to the building, elevator, bathroom, and doors to each department. Dominique sternly warned that I must keep the badge with me "TOUJOURS" (AT ALL TIMES), as without it, I would get locked out going from my desk to the bathroom. I was surprised at how tight security was at the Geneva office, but it also made me feel important, just as my first day in Manhattan, like I was a part of something bigger than myself.

Badge in hand, Dominique brought me to the floor where the marketing, sales, and the creative teams sat in an open concept layout. From what I had read about Geneva being one of the chicest, wealthiest, and most stylish cities, I was initially surprised at the dingy décor of the European HQ. From carpet to cubicles, everything was a muted, dull gray. If it weren't for the fluorescent lights poking out from the popcorn ceiling tiles, the office would have felt as gloomy indoors as it was outside. With only the audible hum of the fan, a sneeze would have sent shock waves throughout the hushed atmosphere. Quiet never bothered me; I preferred to keep office chitchat to a minimum while I ticked tasks off of my to-do list, but there was an eerie quality to the silence that first day. Soon, I came to respect the unfussy style of the Geneva head office. The Swiss didn't put on any pretenses when it came to how the office *looked*, as they were more focused on how the office *performed*.

After visually soaking in my new workplace, Dominique introduced me to my new team: Giovanni, Vivienne, and Noémie. Giovanni was our boss as the marketing director for Europe.

Giovanni and Vivienne stood to greet me as soon as Dominique brought me over to the marketing department. Noémie remained seated. She didn't look at me until Giovanni turned to her and said, "Noémie, this is Louise, the newest member of our team."

"Bonjour, Noémie!" I said.

"We say salut, not bonjour," Noémie muttered, side-eyeing me before returning to her typing.

"Salut is casual and friendly. Bonjour is more formal, but don't worry, we say both," Vivienne interjected warmly.

In Geneva, Noémie and I were marketing coordinators who reported to Vivienne, (marketing manager) who reported to Giovanni (marketing director). However, with such a small team, Noémie and I had direct exposure to Giovanni and often presented to him at our weekly team meetings. Vivienne was a sweet, petite French-Chinese woman who had grown up in Paris. She was reasonable, reliable, and like most people in the Geneva office, was impressively fluent in four languages. I liked her immediately. Noémie was thirty, the same age as Vivienne, with the same position as me. I didn't know it yet, but that would become a point of contention. Noémie, born in Germany but raised in Switzerland, had a hard-edged jawline and a model physique. Her outer beauty masked a sinister undertone that would reveal itself with time.

The marketing team was nimble and responsible for all three pillars: skincare, cosmetics, and fragrances. Originally from Sicily, Giovanni spoke fluent Italian, French, English, and German. All of the men at the Geneva office were impeccably dressed, from designer shoes to custom-lined suit jackets, and Giovanni was no exception. He wore black, thick-framed glasses, and with his clean-shaven complexion, he reminded me of Jude Law in *The Holiday*. He even commuted to work on a motorcycle. With a degree in chemical engineering and years of marketing experience at CPG companies, Giovanni was a shrewd, no-nonsense businessman who had been poached by Arden to help grow the European business (much like how Elizabeth had enticed Teddy Haslam). While sometimes stern, Giovanni was kind-hearted and cracked the occasional bad pun to those on his team who worked hard and earned his respect.

The differences between being an intern and working full time for the company were revealed to me in the coming weeks and months. My internships at Arden had felt similar to school semesters, with a fixed tenure, breaks in between, and a goal of "graduating" at a point of completion—whereas the horizon of working life was infinite. As an intern, I learned how to take direction and complete smaller, project-based tasks, like a student completing assignments for a teacher, but in a full-time role, the scope of work was broader and required more strategic, big-picture understanding of the multistage marketing process. Initially, the prospect of being a full-time employee was daunting, but soon I felt untethered. The job allowed me to be an independent decision-maker and gave me a sense of autonomy over my abilities, not to mention being a permanent employee was a reminder that I was inching closer on my corporate climb to CEO and becoming Elizabeth 2.0.

Men outnumbered women at the Geneva office, which was a stark contrast to the female-dominated New York office, although the entire European business operation was headed by Elisabetta Richards. Giovanni, and the rest of the male directors, reported to Elisabetta. For some reason, it gave me great comfort knowing a powerful woman was at the helm in Geneva. Elizabeth would have been proud to know her European legacy was in good hands—they even shared the same name (Elisabetta was the Italian variation).

Before Dominique could bring me to Elisabetta's office to meet her, she bolted into the hallway to introduce herself and gave me the standard three kisses on alternating cheeks before ending with a big bear hug. Her sincere warmth reminded me of my mom and melted away any trace of Noémie's cold demeanor toward me moments earlier. Elisabetta was Italian-American, a genetic combination that fostered exuberance. Before I met Elisabetta, I had always assumed "speaking loudly and passionately" was a negative quality attributed to women to demean our emotional range. As a result, I'd naturally assumed a passive stance in meetings and the boardroom, not wanting my passioned opinions to be mistaken for the negatively connoted "too emotional," "too aggressive," or simply "too much." But Elisabetta was one of the smartest people I had ever met, with a high level of emotional intelligence. She was shrewd *and* sentimental, commanding *and* charming, professional *and* passionate; one never negated the other.

After meeting Elisabetta, Antonio was another memorable mention from my first day on the job. He was a Spanish art director on the creative team, by far the liveliest bunch on the floor, and a dead ringer for Zorro, minus the mask and his last name wasn't Banderas. Antonio refused to call me anything other than Lou Lou. He greeted me upon arrival and departure from the office with "Saluttt, Lou Louuu" in his singsong voice. It reminded me of how my family called me "Lou." Hearing it every day was like a hug from home.

The next few weeks flew by as I transitioned to Swiss time and ever so slowly settled into my new life in Geneva as Matterhorn Maven, but not without some turbulence.

Matterhorn Maven
Escapades of a Swiss Miss

Blog Post: September 2011

Salut!

Matterhorn Maven is the sequel to **Manhattan Maven**. It's the continuation of my journey, as I leave the interning world behind and embark on my next adventure as a full-time employee, working my way up the corporate ladder.

The Matterhorn is one of the highest peaks and most iconic symbols in the Swiss Alps. Fun fact: The triangular shape of the Matterhorn is believed to have inspired Theodore Tobler's Toblerone chocolate bar! Please excuse the cliché factor, but I like to think of the Matterhorn as a metaphor for the mountain I'm trying to climb to reach my goals.

À la prochaine!

- Matterhorn Maven

On the blog, I continued to only show my shiniest self—a one-dimensional corporate climbing world traveler. I didn't yet understand how identifying with that idealized version was a form of self-rejection. It subconsciously reinforced that who I was *behind* the screen wasn't good enough.

Arden had never sent an employee to Switzerland before, so my impostor syndrome flared like a fire-breathing dragon. To quell my mounting self-doubt, I threw myself into adapting to my new role and assimilating to the culture. The Geneva office was the centralized hub for the European affiliates (referred to as "markets") across all three axes: fragrance, skincare, and color. The markets I was responsible for were the France, England, Ireland, Scotland, Spain, Italy, Germany, and "the Nordics" (Finland, Denmark, Sweden, and Norway). In essence, I was "the boss" of these markets as their teams reported into the Geneva HQ, but I felt like a fraud flexing my authority over people who were my parents' age and had worked in the beauty industry longer than I was alive. I had heard my voice on an answering machine before, so for the first few conference calls with the markets, I pictured the teams in London, Paris, Stockholm, Milan, and Barcelona staring at each other in confusion, wondering why a kid on helium was trying to tell them what to do. Luckily, no one knew I was only twenty-one, so I was able to keep up the ruse that I was their equal in both age and experience.

Unlike Elizabeth, who always wanted to appear younger, I desperately wanted to seem older—as with age came experience, and with experience came credibility. In the workplace, I thought youthfulness could be mistaken for incompetence, so I didn't want to give anyone a reason to think I wasn't smart enough to handle the responsibility bestowed upon me. Determined to excel, I planned my presentations and drafted reports with a surgeon's precision to ensure my output and work ethic showed no signs of ageism. In Geneva, it wasn't that I continued to withhold my age on purpose (just as Elizabeth had); no one ever asked.

"Know your numbers," was advice I'd read Elizabeth adhered to in meetings and when presenting to key stakeholders, as she said "numbers never lie and you can't argue with facts." Even though I was more right-brain dominant, Elizabeth was bang on. "Knowing my numbers" and backing up my ideas with financial and statistical analysis played a crucial part in establishing my credibility as a leader.

I was lucky that English was the chosen universal business language (as it was the most commonly known second language among the markets); otherwise, I would have struggled to communicate strategies with confidence. I felt embarrassed that while my European counterparts were fluent in multiple languages, I was only proficient in one. It reminded me just how big the world was and how much there was to learn.

As the weeks went on, Vivienne, Giovanni, and most importantly, Elisabetta, seemed pleased with my performance thus far; only Noémie maintained her distance. The more I tried to befriend her by bringing her an espresso or asking to eat le déjeuner (lunch) together, the more her disdain seemed to grow.

One day, Vivienne asked me to help Noémie finish a presentation. I could tell Vivienne was exasperated, as the delayed PowerPoint was making Vivienne look bad to her boss, Giovanni. Noémie did not like being told what to do, especially by me, so I had a feeling my "helping" was not going to go over well.

"I don't know why Vivienne asked you to help me, but I can finish this myself," Noémie said when I sat down beside her in an empty conference room.

"Vivienne asked us to work together on this. What am I supposed to tell her?" I asked, still dumbfounded as to why Noémie hated me so much.

"Ce n'est pas mon problème," she said coldly.

This wasn't elementary school; I couldn't go tattling to the teacher that a classmate refused to play with me. I decided if Noémie didn't want to be a team player, that was *her* problem. An hour later, I had finished my version of the presentation we were asked to complete, saved it onto the team computer server, and went back to my desk to make headway on my own work. After lunch, I heard Vivienne thank Noémie for sending her the presentation. I was just happy our joint assignment was over, and Noémie could continue ignoring me. At the end of the workday, Vivienne emailed the markets with Noémie, Giovanni, and me in copy:

Dear all,

Please find attached the beautiful presentation for our Red Door Limited Edition fragrance this holiday season that Noémie completed.

Let us know if you have any questions upon review.

Regards,

Vivienne

I opened the attachment. It was the PowerPoint I had made that morning. Noémie looked over at me smugly. She had gone into my files on the global server and passed the presentation off to Vivienne as her own. My blood began to boil. WWED? Elizabeth had always handled conflict by letting actions speak louder than words. Taking a page out of Elizabeth's book, I said nothing and closed down my computer for the day. On my walk home, I stopped at "Mac Dough" (McDonald's) and treated myself to an underrated Swiss delicacy: the Toblerone McFlurry. Eating my feelings never tasted so good.

Chapter 10

Pomp and Circumstance
Paris, London, and Maine
1931-1937

Elizabeth toggled between Paris, London, and New York for the better part of the 1920s to mid-1930s. In a show of confidence, but also to avoid paying French taxes, Elizabeth signed over the Arden business in France to Gladys. She hoped her sister would eventually return to live with her in New York where they could grow old together, but as fate would have it, Gladys fell in love.

Gladys had made the Arden business such a success in France (and spoke the language fluently) that she was quickly indoctrinated into Parisian high-society. Elizabeth and Gladys attended a bal masqué (masquerade ball) at the Château de Versailles where Gladys was charmed by Vicomte (Count) Henri de Maublanc. They fell madly for one another and, to Elizabeth's surprise, married after a rapid romance. Marrying into the aristocracy made her Viscountess (Countess) Gladys de Maublanc.

Elizabeth was admittedly weary of love after Tommy's bitter betrayal, but tried to warm to the Count for her sister's sake. His first impression at Versailles hadn't won her over. Elizabeth found the Count's flattery insincere, as though he spouted Shakespeare sonnets to many women, and was aggrieved to see how quickly his emotions could turn cold. She watched him whisper sweet nothings into Gladys' ear at the masquerade ball and a split-second later bark at waitstaff for more hors d'oeuvres and champagne.

Gladys' son, John Jr., moved in with his mother and the Count at Place Vendôme, until he turned thirteen. As a teenager, John Jr.

requested to live with his estranged father in North America, whom he hadn't seen since he was a baby. Gladys had sacrificed so much to escape the abusive relationship and provide John Jr. with a better life, that she never expected her only son would later leave her. Gladys' heartbreak was stymied only by the love of the Count, but Elizabeth's suspicions about him grew more concerning after she learned he was showing signs of support for the rising German regime as the second world war began to brew.

***

By the mid-1930s, Elizabeth's professional life was well-intact but her personal life was still in shambles following her divorce and Bessie's death. However, she was shocked to learn that in her will Bessie had left Lakeside Farm in Maine to Elizabeth, the only asset not bequeathed to Elsie, who (after missing Bessie's funeral) was living back at Villa Trianon in Versailles, France, allegedly with Anne Morgan.

Lakeside Farm was Elizabeth's favorite reprieve away from the chaos of the city. She shed tears of gratitude at Bessie's enduring thoughtfulness in leaving it to her. The neighboring property was up for sale, so Elizabeth bought it to create a sprawling twelve-hundred-acre resort, with the intention of fulfilling Bessie's lifelong wish to create an oasis for women where they could be uninhibited and free from the heavy constraints placed upon them by society.

Elizabeth spent as much time as she could in Maine trying to recreate what were the most joyous times of her life with Bessie. Parallel rows of pine trees lined the long driveway up to the grand compound, which had a gorgeous view of Long Pond. While Elizabeth sat on the porch sipping her daily cup of hot water with lemon ("for proper digestion, dear"), a grand vision for the Maine estate came to her: a health and beauty camp for women—in what would become America's first destination spa.

Gentlemen's clubs were wildly popular, so why shouldn't women have a place of their own? She pictured an upscale "gentlewomen's club" combined with the charmed glamour of European health centers. The idea of a women's luxury resort also fit Bessie's dream for a place where women were free to unmask, discover new layers of their identities, indulge in self-care, and escape the demands of daily life.

Ever the word weaver, Elizabeth named the resort Maine Chance Farm, a play on words from something Bessie used to say to her: "You've got an eye for the main chance," a phrase to describe someone who was ambitious and continuously seeking opportunities to succeed and advance oneself.

Creating a reprieve where women would be surrounded and supported by other women was a revolutionary concept in the 1930s, as women were not encouraged to pursue their own pleasures. Elizabeth spent over $200,000 to transform Maine Chance into the first destination spa. The project became a form of personal therapy to stave off her loneliness. Elizabeth enlisted the interior designers of her New York Red Door Spa, Nicolai Remisoff and Rue Carpenter, to spin their magic. Nicolai took over design of the main house where he added signature touches of old-world elegance with mirrored walls and Chinoiserie wallpaper with a mix of modern elements. Rue was responsible for designing the surrounding buildings: horse stables and riding trails, groundskeepers' quarters, lush flower gardens, a greenhouse with fruit and vegetables, swimming pool, sunbathing patio, over a dozen guest-houses, treatment rooms, steam rooms, exercise and yoga pavilion, meditation and reading room, bowling alley, tennis court, croquet lawn, boathouse, and indoor/outdoor dining facilities.

Elizabeth firmly believed that diet and exercise played vital roles in achieving holistic beauty: "The inside of the body must be nurtured as much as the outside." She hired natural food chef Gayelord Hauser to design a menu that was "delicious, yet highly nutritious," she said. Elizabeth was ahead of her time in advocating for whole foods, rich in Vitamin B, and advising against the consumption of refined sugar. At

Maine Chance Farm she insisted on preparing foods that were fresh, organic, and grown on the property.

Elizabeth wanted the clientele to feel as pampered as they did at her Red Door Spas, and her genius was in marrying beauty treatments, nourishing foods, and exercise routines with an environment of unparalleled luxury. Women, so often in those days, rarely believed they deserved to feel good about themselves, as was fundamental to patriarchal power, so Elizabeth was determined to create a place where women felt empowered and were catered to—like men. *It made me wonder if Elizabeth, who had looked after herself and others since childhood, wished someone would take care of her too?*

Elizabeth was an early adopter of yoga and the long-term benefits of movement on the body and mind. Unsuspecting employees would often walk into Elizabeth's office and find her doing her daily headstand for increased circulation. Stretching, dancing, and eurhythmic exercise not only helped the immune system, Elizabeth advocated, but also staved off bouts of depression. In today's modern age, many of Elizabeth's theories and practices fall under the umbrella of self-care, but in the 1930s, there was no such term, and mental health was seldom discussed. She was one of the earliest visionaries of the holistic approach to health, beauty, and lifestyle—*and* its link to improved psychological well-being. Foremost, Elizabeth truly believed beauty began within, and she served to highlight the underlying philosophy that women deserved time and solitude to reflect, grow, and flourish to become the best version of themselves.

Maine Chance guests were provided with silk white robes and soft fluffy slippers to wear throughout their stay. Daily itineraries were typed on pink pulp paper and spritzed with Arden perfume (*long before Elle Woods*). Breakfast was served in bed, on a tray with embroidered linen, fine bone china, and a rose from the garden, as Elizabeth said, "Flowers start the day off on a cheery note." Typical activities at Maine Chance included yoga, dance, hula hoop–based exercises, massages, facials, swimming, boating, tennis, croquet, bowling, reading, writing, and meditating. Elizabeth's greatest form of stress relief was horseback riding so she spent many hours in the stables tending to the horses at Maine Chance. Deep-conditioning scalp treatments and an Ardena bath, which encased the body in melted paraffin wax "to reach down to the very roots of your nerves to free them from tenseness and fatigue," explained the brochure, were offered every afternoon, and hair was set twice a week.

In the evenings, a makeup artist was available to apply Arden cosmetics, and women changed into their most ravishing gowns and sparkling jewels to socialize and play bridge in the parlor. Elizabeth believed fashion was a form of self-expression and wanted to ensure the ladies were granted the opportunity to play dress-up as they pleased, without being under the objectifying eye of the male gaze.

Vegetable juice "mocktails" were provided at happy hour—as alcohol was "much too drying for the skin," said Elizabeth, who drank on occasion but wanted to ensure her clients left Maine Chance with strengthened immunity. Although it was becoming more in vogue for women of café society to smoke with their long opera-length cigarette holders, Elizabeth hated smoking ("It's wrinkle-causing"), so that vice was also prohibited at Maine Chance and in her Red Door Spas. At work, staff scrambled to stub out their smokes if they caught sight of their boss arriving at the building. One of the treatment girls in Manhattan panicked when she heard Elizabeth was coming, quickly stubbed her cigarette out in a desk drawer, and forgot about it until plumes of smoke poured out and the building was evacuated until the fire department arrived. Elizabeth fired the poor girl on the spot.

In the summer of 1934, Elizabeth held a soft opening for Maine Chance. The event was akin to the lavish parties described in *The Great Gatsby*, with twinkle lights strung throughout the manicured lawns, an accordionist, and champagne fountains. Attendees included beauty journalists and notable names such as First Lady Eleanor Roosevelt, Mamie Eisenhower, Ava Gardner, and Judy Garland.

By 1935, Maine Chance's rural retreat was a highly coveted indulgence with society women who sought a reprieve from the relenting pace of city life. Maine Chance Farm was only opened in the summer, from May to September (*the length of my internships at Arden*), and guests forked over nearly $500 for a weeklong stay—an extravagant sum at the time, but after the elaborate renovations and extensive upkeep of the immaculate property, the fees barely covered the overhead. For the first few years, Maine Chance didn't turn a profit, but the project had lifted Elizabeth's spirits during a challenging personal phase of her life, and she was content to share her favorite place with other like-minded women while honoring Bessie's memory. The destination spa also turned out to be a formidable marketing tool—attracting the nouveau riche and Hollywood stars while adding an aspirational element to the Arden brand. Women of more modest means who were dazzled by articles they read about Maine Chance in magazines, but couldn't afford to visit, instead connected to the magic of the Arden brand by attending the Red Door Spa or buying a lipstick at a department store beauty counter.

A few years after Maine Chance's grand debut, Elizabeth returned to Paris in 1937 for the opening gala of her new Red Door Spa at 2 Rue de la Paix in Place Vendôme, a square in the 1st arrondissement, north of the Tuileries Gardens and east of the Église de la Madeleine where Gladys and the Count lived. The first Parisian Red Door Spa at 255 Saint-Honoré had done so well that they needed more space. 2 Rue de la Paix was the epitome of French luxury with ornate crown molding and gilded accents, and a short commute from Gladys house to the salon. On that visit, Elizabeth tried to persuade Gladys to move back to Manhattan for a while, as rumblings of an impending war in Europe were escalating—but Gladys was in love and refused to leave her husband, insisting the Count would protect and take care of her.

Before returning to New York, Elizabeth stopped over in London to visit with Teddy Haslam who continued to oversee Arden's English branch. Elizabeth and Teddy had grown close and they corresponded regularly on both business and personal affairs.

The talk of the town in 1937 was the historic coronation of King George VI and Queen Elizabeth (the Queen Mother). In the wake of the abdication crisis, public sentiment was warm toward the British royal family. Princess Elizabeth was eleven years old at the time, but sixteen years later, at the age of twenty-seven, she would be crowned. The success of the London Red Door Spa had caught the attention of the Queen Mother who became an Arden loyalist and as years went on a "treasured friend," said Elizabeth. Born in 1900, the Queen Mother was twenty-two years younger than Elizabeth, but many assumed they were the same age. In this pre-WWII era, Elizabeth could slip over to the Palace for tea and return home for supper unphotographed and unbothered by the press.

When Princess Elizabeth became Queen Elizabeth II in 1953, she not only inherited the crown but her mother's devotion to Elizabeth Arden—the woman *and* her beauty products. Queen Elizabeth II developed her own friendship with Elizabeth, despite the forty-eight-year age gap. She also granted Arden a Royal Warrant, the brand equivalent of being knighted—an official recognition of products that are beloved by the royal households. Companies that are bestowed with the Royal Warrant can put the royal coat of arms on their packaging so it is instantly recognizable that the brand has the monarchy's stamp of approval. Only twenty-one health and beauty brands in history have been decreed with the Queen's Royal Warrant—an honor Arden holds to this day.

Queen Elizabeth II adored all Arden skincare and cosmetic products, but her most-worn lipstick shade has always been Arden's Beautiful Color in the shade Pink Sensation. Queen Elizabeth II later introduced the brand to her daughter-in-law, Princess Diana, who loved experimenting with makeup, and shocked the world with electric blue eyeliner (Arden's High Drama Liner in Midnight Dream) and heavy coats of deep navy mascara (Arden's Beautiful Color Lash Enhancing

Mascara in Ocean Blue). The queen's grandchildren, Diana's sons, also became avid Arden fans. Prince Harry later famously packed a tube of Arden's Eight Hour Cream to protect his skin during an expedition to the South Pole in 2013. To this day, Eight Hour Cream remains one of the most iconic, best-selling beauty products in the world. In the UK, a tube of Eight Hour Cream is sold every two minutes.

The British love affair with Arden was facilitated by Teddy Haslam's early strategic expertise, but the brand gained even more popularity following the 1937 coronation. The Queen Mother discreetly wore Arden makeup, however as a deeply religious ceremony the use of cosmetics was not publicly broadcast for fear it was against God's will to alter one's natural state. Elizabeth wrote the copy for a gorgeous, delicate black-and-white watercolor ad to commemorate the monumental occasion in history:

Flutter of banners in the May sunshine.

Fanfare of trumpets at the Royal Exchange.

A gilt coach moving slowly towards the Abbey between ranks of scarlet and gold—amid the cheers of thousands.

England's Coronation will remain forever the most splendid event of 1937; and the beautiful women who will have added to its elegance are Elizabeth Arden's clients.

On May 12, 1937, Elizabeth and Teddy gave the treatment girls the day off and popped a bottle of champagne in the London Red Door Spa as they turned on the radio to tune into the historic coronation. Elizabeth was fifty-nine years old and opted to avoid joining the large crowds in the streets. They listened, mesmerized, as the fairytale procession passed Big Ben along the royal route and then for the entire four-hour ceremony, which was broadcasted directly from Westminster Abbey—a historic moment, and one of the first live news events heard worldwide.

The pomp and circumstance that surrounded the royal coronation and Maine Chance Farm's grand opening during the mid-1930s were bright spots for Elizabeth in the onset of a decade clouded by darkness. From the outside, Elizabeth continued to maintain her manicured exterior, but everything was about to be thrown into disarray as World War II erupted in Europe.

- LOU -

While Elizabeth was hobnobbing with the Queen Mother and launching the first world-class destination spa, I was missing my mother and attempting to assimilate to life in a world-class destination city.

After a few months in Europe, I had grown fond of my Genevan pied-à-terre. The furnishings were sparse and outdated, yet cozy. I hesitated to fill the small space with too much clutter, as my stay in Switzerland was supposed to be temporary. The largest item I brought from Canada were my skis, which gave the apartment a Swiss ski chalet feel as I propped them against the wall. The bedroom and living room were one and the same, with a small adjoining bathroom. My bed took up most of the square footage in the studio, but a tiny couch, coffee table, and antique wooden dresser somehow fit like a game of Tetris. The curtains were a 1970s shade of fluorescent orange and matched the rug, loveseat, and lampshades. When the sun illuminated the room, it often felt like I lived inside a Creamsicle.

There was a pocket kitchenette with a fold-down table-for-one, mini fridge (and I mean mini), sink, stovetop, and two sets of dishware. It had everything one needed and not a morsel more. With no guests to entertain, I washed the same bowl, plate, glass, fork, spoon, and knife while the other set of dishes remained untouched in the cupboard, a domestic reminder of my newfound state of solitude. There was an impossibly thin balcony with French doors that overlooked Rue Cornavin. Living on the same street as the train station Gare Cornavin made me feel like a true nomad. Traveling by train in Switzerland was akin to gliding through a cinematic fairytale with no villains; pure, enchanted magic. At a moment's notice, I could board a train and find myself strolling along the Seine in Paris.

One weekend, I indulged this fantasy. I took an early morning train from Geneva to Paris with just a backpack and three hours later I was re-tracing Elizabeth's steps, visiting all of her old haunts: the Ritz Hotel, Café de Paris, Angelina's, 255 Rue Saint-Honoré—the first Parisian Red Door Spa was then a by-appointment-only couture lingerie shop called Cadolle (Herminie Cadolle was credited with inventing the bra in 1889, thus liberating women from the corset) and 2 Rue de la Paix—the second Parisian Red Door Spa in Place Vendôme was occupied by Maison Massaro, a bespoke shoemaker, and La Colombe, a café bistro. I saved the best stop for last: Shakespeare & Co., one of Elizabeth's favorite places to peruse, the historic bookstore owned by her friend, Sylvia Beach. A bell gently chimed as I opened the door and I envisioned myself as Elizabeth, crossing the threshold into the shop and seeing Sylvia behind the counter. I felt the ghost of their presence in every cozy corner of the book nook. The experience was "hauntingly calming," as I wrote in my red journal on the train ride back to Switzerland. It was as though Elizabeth had been trying to tell me, *"You're in the right place."* I was exhilarated by my first, real solo travel expedition ("Two countries in one day!" I wrote) and in awe of exploring Europe as Elizabeth had a century earlier.

***

One of the most challenging parts about getting ready while living alone was that I had no one to do up the zipper on my work dresses. My solution was to cover the back of my undone dresses with a blazer—it was the worst on sticky summer days when I had to keep the blazer on, lest someone discover my shoddy zipper solution, but I was proud of my resourcefulness. There was also one small, cracked mirror (that I was too short to see) above the sink in the bathroom of my apartment, so to get a glimpse of myself, I had to stand on the toilet, lean sideways, and duck down awkwardly. Because of this, I applied my makeup in the morning before work with a tiny Arden compact, but I left the house mostly sight unseen. But disassociating with my self-image in the mirror became a refreshing way to live. Prior to Arden, I associated makeup with vanity; applying it was only to *look different on the outside,* but the more I learned about the history of cosmetics, I came to appreciate the idea of holistic beauty from a mind, body, and soul perspective. Over the course of my three internships, I had gradually honed my skincare and makeup skills, but it was the application process itself, rather than the end result, that I enjoyed more than anything. Putting on makeup became less about how it altered my appearance, and more about the internal boost I got from allocating a moment to myself at the beginning and end of my day. My "beauty routine" went beyond the surface and included spending time meditating, journaling, stretching, reading, and preparing nourishing foods. The ritualism of carving out time for myself was gradually enhancing my external *and* internal confidence. And I had Elizabeth to thank for championing that concept.

Living in Switzerland, there was an absence of eyes on me for the first time in my young life; no one to supervise, bear witness, or even care what I did or didn't do. My days were unencumbered in a way I hadn't experienced before. The freedom was both exhilarating and terrifying—I wasn't used to operating without a set schedule and regular check-ins from my parents, professors, and peers. Other than work, my first few months in Geneva were spent alone. Switzerland had a relatively large expat community, but the majority of people were older, in a different life stage, with spouses and kids. Determined to stave off the creeping loneliness (and the excess of cheese, croissants, chocolate, and wine), I took up running and began surveying the breathtaking beauty of my new environment on foot. "Going to the gym" was a laughable concept in Europe when the great outdoors beckoned at every turn. Before I knew it, running turned into a daily ritual. I looked forward to tying my laces, putting on my headphones, and setting off to explore, destination unknown. Often, I would get so lost in a monotonous trance that I'd arrive back at my apartment a couple of hours later, unaware of how much time had passed, on a tingling high from my blissful blackout state.

On weekends, I also started hiking, a popular pastime in Switzerland. Hiking along the top of the Téléphérique du Salève, a high alpine ridge in neighboring Veyrier-du-Lac, became a favorite Sunday activity. I took the bus from Gare Cornavin, and it dropped me off across the border in France. After a short gondola ride to the top, there were different trailheads with spectacular views of Lake Geneva, the French Alps, and Mont Blanc. On my first hike, the sky was a vast, fearless blue, and the summit air was crisp. I looked out over my new home, straddling two borders. I inhaled slowly; the fresh mountain air swirled around my ribs like a ribbon enveloping my lungs. I exhaled in a long, deliberate breath. I wanted my mind to be as present as my body, to commit this feeling of complete freedom to muscle memory. Although I was alone, in moments like that, I never felt lonely.

Gruyères was a quintessential Swiss town, about an hour by train from Geneva, known for its delicious homemade cheese of the same name. Cows with bells around their necks and plump chickens roamed around the grassy knolls surrounding the medieval fortress of Chateau St. Germain. I visited this magical place on a whim, but felt so calm, so at home there, that I returned too many times to count. I devoured charcuterie boards and nursed glasses of wine at the castle's H.R. Giger Bar where I spent hours reading and writing in my journal at a table for one in the corner. The bar was truly otherworldly, like something out of *Lord of the Rings*, with a cavernous ceiling made up of fossilized vertebrae and oversized skeletal chairs. While that may sound like the antithesis of cozy, when the rain fell on the green hillsides outside of the oversized oval windows, any anxiety or self-doubt bubbling beneath the surface subsided; for I felt safe inside the belly of the beast.

While my coworkers were kind, we rarely socialized outside of work. They endearingly referred to my attempts to speak French as "mignon" (cute), but with my vocabulary whittled down to a few choice phrases, I was unable to elaborate on stories and articulate my thoughts. My subpar French skills made my personality come across like unsweetened oatmeal: boring and bland. To be honest, I wouldn't have wanted to hang out with me either. The language barrier was especially noticeable in loud restaurants and bars. After my colleagues had a few drinks, their French seemed to come out in inaudible rapid fire, and I struggled to keep up with the fast-paced flow of conversation, so I sat silently or snuck home unnoticed. I was frustrated being unable to express myself as I was used to, but it made me even more determined to improve my speaking skills before I returned to Manhattan. It also made me realize how much I had relied on witty nuances to connect with people, and as such, my coworkers never got to know the "real" me. *In hindsight, I didn't know who the "real" me was either.* It was an eye-opening experience that made me reflect on the identity I had carefully crafted over the years. *Who was I without words?*

Looking back, it was a big reason why I dove so fiercely into blogging and journaling about my lived experiences during this chapter of life. Writing became my only true outlet for self-expression and how I preserved some semblance of my sanity. On the page, I could express freely, whereas in person, my thoughts were suppressed.

Just when I thought I would be spending every weekend alone, a girl from my hometown (who I had attended backyard birthday parties with as a kid) reached out to me after learning through my blog, *Matterhorn Maven*, that I had recently moved to Geneva. Although we hadn't seen each other since we were tater tots, I was excited at the prospect of reuniting with a familiar face. Tasha Tacchi was completing her master's degree in hospitality management at Les Roches in Crans Montana, Switzerland. We agreed to meet for lunch in Montreux, which was roughly halfway between Crans Montana and Geneva (an hour and a half by train each way). After fifteen years of no contact, Tasha and I jumped instantly back into a friendship. Although we were both determined to improve our French, it was refreshing to speak English freely again, and to commiserate with someone else experiencing the novelty of European life. We were both slated to be in Switzerland for a year before returning to North America, so we planned an aggressive bucket list of places to explore over the coming months, keen to maximize our time.

Logan and I had continued to keep in touch through near daily emails. We were in that post-breakup stage of trying to be friends. There are so few people in life who really know you that it seemed a shame to completely throw it all away. We shared so much personal history that "being friends" was our way of preserving the past within the present, but deep down, I knew our friendship was fraudulent; I just didn't want to be the first to surrender my façade. How did people distill intense romantic feelings down into platonic ones? My love for Logan lingered like a leaky faucet; even when I tried to turn it off, it kept trickling out.

One day, Logan asked if I wanted to try talking through Google Voice. I had never heard of it before, but it was, as Logan explained, a way to make international calls without a cell phone (which I still didn't have). I found a secluded corner in the Starbucks down the street (my apartment Wi-Fi was unreliable) and soon my laptop was ringing like a giant telephone. I put my headphones in and "picked up" the call and heard the familiar cadence of Logan's voice: "Hey, Lou." Two little words and tears streamed down my face. I hadn't realized how close my homesickness was to boiling over. Logan and I talked for hours about everything and nothing at all, until the Starbucks manager told me they were closing. In a strange land full of strangers, speaking with someone who really knew me was a boost to my spirits, but made me ache for what I had left behind.

At the end of my first summer in Switzerland, I was running along the lake when I came across a waterfront hill filled to the brim with young, twenty-something couples and groups of friends. Some sat in retro lawn chairs while others huddled on picnic blankets, passing around bottles of wine and snacking on seasonal fruit and fresh baguettes. If you added a few bowler hats and lace-fringed parasols, it looked like Georges Seurat's *A Sunday Afternoon on La Grande Jatte*. Projected on a giant white screen was the Audrey Hepburn movie *Roman Holiday*, with French and German subtitles. I stopped mid-stride to fully absorb the dreamy scene. It reminded me of the outdoor movie nights with my friends in New York's Bryant Park. We cheered when a red balloon was released at sunset to signal the start of the movie and watched as it disappeared into the golden hour light. The city smog and bright office towers in New York had hindered the visibility of stars, but I knew they were there, out of sight in the universe. At the bottom of the slope, there was a white tent with twinkle lights that served popcorn and cotton candy, and an old-fashioned crêpe stand, operated by an elderly man who looked like he belonged in a barbershop quartet, humming French lullabies as he whipped up his crêpe creations. The moon glistened above the picturesque scene, illuminating the mountains and Lake Geneva below. The warm breeze was subtle, causing the occasional ripple across the water. As darkness fell, I continued running, feeling both euphoric and melancholic. I took the scenic route home along the lake with a clear sky full of stars guiding me home.

Chapter 11

The World of Tomorrow

New York

1937–1940

New York's World Fair debuted to record crowds of over six hundred thousand in Flushing Meadows, Queens in 1939. The World's Fair was meant to lift global spirits following the Great Depression and was an "expression of international faith, courage, and peace for the future despite the present threatening world situation," said President Roosevelt in the opening ceremonies, telecasted worldwide, in an era when the whole world was troubled by the threats of war.

The front page of the *New York Times* on Monday, May 1, 1939, captured the awe and wonder of the biggest exposition in history—and even mentioned Elizabeth Arden's contribution to the World Fair.

WORLD FAIR OPENS AS A SYMBOL OF PEACE;
VAST SPECTACLE OF COLOR AND WORLD PROGRESS THRILLS
ENTHUSIASTIC CROWDS

Silk-hatted dignitaries, sailors on shore leave, men and women of all ages dressed for fair weather and a great holiday as they came in hordes down the railroad and subway ramps, forty and fifty abreast, to gaze upon the medley of sound and color.

Wealthier fairgoers climbed into motor-driven and man-powered chairs for their first tour of the grounds, while hundreds of thousands preferred to make it on foot and puzzled over maps to find various exhibits among 1,216-acres of fair grounds.

Green trees, lawns, playing fountains, pavilions and restful benches make a garden scene of this artificial city within a city. The dominating scene was the Trylon, the world's largest escalator, connected to the 200-foot Perisphere where visitors peer into the huge crystal ball to see what "the World of Tomorrow" will be like.

Bugle notes, brassy and thin, sounded and echoed from all corners of the field while drums rolled and fifes piped sharp marching tunes as a parade representing nearly all countries of Europe, Asia, and the Americas gathered with spectators at the Court of Peace for the opening ceremonies.

The Army band played "Stars and Stripes Forever" and navy officers cried "Present arms!" as troops saluted President Roosevelt, whose son helped him to the lectern. Scores of reporters and moving-picture photographers waved microphones below the stage to capture his speech. He welcomed the global crowd and stated how he hoped the greatest contribution from the fair would be showing people of every nationality and racial strain they could eliminate hatred and live together in harmony and friendship.

Mrs. Roosevelt, the President's wife, wore a brown silk dress covered in tiny Trylons and Perispheres, with matching hat and purse, to announce the fair's opening of the World of Fashion building: dusty pink and powder blue stripes with glistening doors that look like giant sequins keys the mind to the beauty that awaits within. [The World of Fashion building] is Fifth Avenue in miniature. The ground floor is serpentine, so its drama is not revealed all at once. Live models continuously step out of gargantuan bird cages. Prominently placed at each end of the "Hall of Labels" are the exhibits of

Helena Rubinstein and Elizabeth Arden. Both are temples of beauty in which women will learn much about the art of cosmetics.

As visitors journeyed homeward at the end of the night, they were bewildered by the surprising beauty and magnificence of modern lighting effects; fireworks combined with flame, water and color glowed above the Lagoon of Nations, bathing the fair grounds and heavens above.

Elizabeth was delighted to have a prominent exhibit at New York's World Fair and wasted no time maximizing the opportunity. She asked Eleanor Roosevelt, a friend and frequent spa guest at Maine Chance, to award the winning model from the opening ceremony fashion show with an Elizabeth Arden beauty kit and she hosted twice-daily beauty demonstrations on the fair's main stage. The World's Fair brought an influx of foreign travelers and tourists to New York City for the first time, so the coveted brand exposure for Arden attracted a plethora of new clients to the Fifth Avenue Red Door Spa. As a result, Elizabeth launched "Doorway to Beauty," in what would become one of her most successful campaigns, with ads depicting her signature, oversized red door.

THE DOORWAY TO BEAUTY

Elizabeth Arden extends a cordial invitation to come to her New York Red Door Spa during the World's Fair season. Fair days will be tiring, nerve wearying and "Fair Faces" will show the signs of fatigue. The Red Door Spa will be open early each morning and late each night for a special series of all-day staying makeup and quick, refreshing skincare treatments, including body molding massage, Miss Arden's superb hair coiffure, and of course, you can bring home her incomparable face treatments and cosmetic products—the perfect souvenir.

For visitors from the World's Fair who wanted to continue the "Red Door way of life" once they returned home, Elizabeth created the "Arden At-Home Five-Point Plan: for beauty, youth, slenderness, grace, and health," that detailed how to do face treatments, apply makeup, exercise routines, and implement healthy eating habits at home. Holistic beauty was still a revolutionary concept and Elizabeth was ahead of the trend in empowering women to find time to reconnect with themselves on a daily basis. Elizabeth personally followed up with women who received the Arden At-Home Plan with the purchase of her "beauty kits."

My Dear Miss Humphrey
October, 1939

After trying my new Arden At-Home Plan, I feel I must write to you as I want to be quite sure you are getting the wonderful benefits which this proper daily care can bring.

Do be sure to cleanse…cleanse…cleanse. I feel as though I could not say that enough, for so few women realize that a clean, softly receptive skin is the canvas of cosmetics. If the dust-laden air is your enemy, combat it with generous quantities of my Cleansing Cream and cool pattings of my Ardena Skin Tonic applied with firm upward movements.

There will be moments when you will have special questions, so please turn to me freely with any and all of them. It is always a pleasure to answer letters from women who are seeking more direct ways to loveliness. It is that which makes my work worthwhile.

Faithfully yours,
Elizabeth Arden

The World's Fair skyrocketed Arden's international acclaim so much that she outgrew her manufacturing facility in Manhattan and bought, in $190,000 cash, an eighty-thousand square foot, four-story factory building in Long Island City to accommodate her expanding business. The same year, she was asked by the president of the National Federation of Business to serve as key-note speaker at New York's Women in Business event, held at the Hotel Brevoort, to discuss women's place in business. In the late 1930s, Elizabeth was dubbed "the Tiffany of her trade" by *Fortune* magazine, as "she has earned more money than any other woman in U.S. history…none have been able to achieve the size or the prestige of Elizabeth Arden's own particular business."

On the brink of WWII, Elizabeth had achieved her goal of becoming one of the wealthiest self-made millionaires in the world, but when she looked around, there was no one to share in her accomplishments. It was lonely at the top. Despite her external riches, Elizabeth felt socially impoverished. Chronic loneliness had crept up on her, and she began projecting her sadness as anger. At the office, Elizabeth became merciless and mercurial with her staff, firing treatment girls for minor infractions, like a wrinkled uniform or misplaced ribbon. She tried to fill the personal void in her life with material possessions. Elizabeth's extensive wealth now allowed her to maintain a robust entourage of help at her home in Manhattan and Maine Chance, including housekeepers, gardeners, maids, chefs, butlers, and chauffeurs who drove her around in either her Rolls Royce or Bentley.

Elizabeth still hadn't spoken to her brother William since he took Tommy's side in the divorce, but she showered her three nieces, Beattie, Ginnie, and Pattie with gifts and now that they were older, she hired them to work as her personal assistants—handling social invitations, organizing her closet, packaging product for royals and celebrities, or typing out her daily diary notes. Elizabeth trusted few and kept her circle tight. She made sure to be surrounded by people at all hours of the day, as she had developed severe anxiety, and hated being left alone in a room too long. Her insomnia returned with a vengeance, and she called Lanie, Teddy Haslam, and Gladys late into the night from bed in her silk nightgown.

More and more, Elizabeth turned to her greatest form of stress relief: her horses. Everyone, from household staff to her nieces, noticed how Elizabeth's demeanor softened at the stables—horses were her longest running source of joy and provided a familiar sense of comfort. By channeling her pent-up energy into the art of horse racing, Elizabeth's passion progressed from a hobby into a full-time vocation.

Elizabeth's first foray into the elite sport began with horse shows. Old Gold and Cherry Red, Elizabeth's prized ponies, were housed at Belmont Park in Elmont, New York and won blue ribbons at shows across the country. Elizabeth caught the racing bug after witnessing the exhilaration of racing season at Saratoga Springs, one of the oldest racetracks in the US, opening in 1863. She immediately joined the Belmont and Saratoga Racing Associations and rented barns at both tracks year-round. For her racing persona, Elizabeth created a new identity: Mrs. Elizabeth N. Graham, a composite using her original surname and a married prefix (despite being single), and further called her principal stables "Mr. Nightingale's," combining a masculine prefix with her original middle name. Forever ahead of her time, Elizabeth was never one to conform to gender norms. She spared no expense when it came to buying and housing her horses, going by the adage: "to make money, one must spend money." In the span of a week she bought seven yearlings for $54,000, to be trained for the next racing season. None of those yearlings turned out to be winners, but that didn't stop Elizabeth from hiring the best trainers, jockeys, stable boys, and groomers. She coordinated the colors of her racing silks to match her beauty business: cerise (a vivid reddish-pink), white, and blue. She had Mr. Nightingale's (her stable) painted in matching hues. Everything had to be "on brand."

Elizabeth's spending habits on horses soon bordered on manic—Lanie, her closest friend in Manhattan who was recently promoted to Arden treasury director, warned Elizabeth that she was starting to siphon money faster than she was earning it. Without a return on investment for her hobby, she was endangering the mass fortune she had worked so hard to achieve—but horse racing was beginning to consume Elizabeth. It made her feel fulfilled, something she hadn't felt in a long time. With the amount of excitement and energy she put into her passion, maybe it was time for a new direction—but was it worth giving up her beauty empire?

- LOU -

La Fête Nationale Suisse (Swiss National Day; Switzerland's Canada Day/Fourth of July holiday) was celebrated on the first of August with great fanfare; shops closed, Swiss flags hung from balconies, and there were yodelers, bonfires, and fireworks. Tasha trained from Crans Montana to stay with me for the weekend, my first visitor, to experience the Swiss spectacle. Throughout the day, we strolled along the cobble-stoned streets watching parades of people in traditional alpine attire, women in delicately embroidered dirndls, their hair in milkmaid-style braids, some in straw hats with ribbons dangling from the brim, and men in lederhosen wearing Bavarian Tyrolean felt hats with feathers tucked in the brim. I felt transported in time, as though I was Heidi, from the book by Johanna Spyri, venturing down from the high Alps into the village for the first time. Cows were artfully decorated with wildflowers, and you could hear the chime of their cowbells ("More cowbell!" I cheered, but no one got the SNL reference).

We listened to alphorn music and a melodic choir sing the Swiss National Anthem. At sunset, Tasha and I sat on rocks overlooking Lake Geneva, sipping wine directly from the bottle and waving tiny Swiss flags in salute to passersby waiting for the les feux d'artifice. We watched the alpine afterglow as the salmon sky faded to an inky-indigo above the mountains. And then, the night sky erupted into the most dazzling display of pyrotechnics. Bursts of light, color, and sound went off in synchronized succession, choreographed to a classical orchestra. A round, full moon and a speckling of stars appeared after the fireworks show, like they had been hiding in the wings, awaiting their turn on the main stage.

Arm in arm, Tasha and I walked back to my apartment amidst a crowd of happy drunks, forgotten confetti, and streamers on the street. The Swiss are reputed for keeping to themselves, but that night, it was as if everyone came alive for the first time—under the glow of the cherub moon, we were werewolves shedding our sheep's clothing.

Early the next morning, I walked Tasha to the train, and there was not a soul nor a leftover piece of confetti in sight. It was as though Geneva had thrown a wild party but somehow managed to clean up before its parents arose. Everything was back in its proper place, just as it had always been.

Switzerland was making me more introspective. I hadn't noticed how much stimuli I had been bombarded with on a daily basis, until I escaped the white noise. Solitude gave the space and time to foster self-awareness. In a sense, my exile from society was an entry into my own mind—and an awakening to new possibilities of what made me feel truly, not artificially, fulfilled.

Six months into my new Swiss life, I had my first progress report at work with Giovanni. We met in a conference room where, to my relief, he told me essentially to "keep doing what you've been doing," but at the end of the review, he mentioned there were going to be some changes made to our team moving forward.

The next day, Noémie was fired.

Although Noémie had never warmed toward me, I instinctively felt terrible. Gossip around the office was that her output was too slow and consistently full of mistakes, which was creating a bottleneck with the global marketing team in New York. Apparently, she blamed her mistakes on others in the chain of command, but despite forewarnings, Noémie was blindsided by the news. After Giovanni told the team,

Noémie came to my desk (she never came to my desk) and asked if we could talk outside. Her tone made me uneasy, but I agreed.

"Everyone in the office think it's your fault I was fired," she began.

"What are you talking about?" I asked, stunned by her bluntness.

"Before you arrived in Geneva, no one even knew you were joining the team, including Vivienne and Giovanni. We only found out when Dominique in HR asked where we should set up the new girl's desk. I already *was* the marketing coordinator, there's never been *two*," she said.

Looking back, I should have realized it was weird to have two marketing coordinators in a small office doing different tasks, but essentially the same job.

"Everyone thinks you fucked the CEO to get here," she said, hitting me with the real venom.

Too dumbfounded to speak, I turned to walk back to the office, but Noémie followed. The accusation was so outlandish, so wildly untrue, it didn't deserve the dignity of a response. When we got back inside the building, Noémie's tone changed to one of concern, in a bizarre Jekyll and Hyde circus act.

"If they fired me, your job isn't safe either. Except maybe they won't be as hard on you because of your *reputation*," she said, miming giving a blowjob.

I bolted for my desk before she could continue harassing me. My mind tried to process the onslaught of information Noémie had just unleashed. None of what she had said was remotely true, but I couldn't help but wonder if everyone in the Geneva office believed her? I went to the office bathroom, leaned against the cold concrete of the stall, and cried. All of the loneliness, homesickness, and self-doubt bubbling beneath the surface poured out of my eyes like the Jet d'Eau in a steady stream of emotions.

When I got home later that night, I pulled out my red journal. It had been a while since I last dedicated an entry to "Dear Liz." Part of me wished Elizabeth would beam down and unleash her mercurial side onto Noémie, but hurt people, *hurt people*. As I wrote, I realized Noémie was projecting her own anger and frustrations, imposing her feelings onto me. Elizabeth had been betrayed far worse by people in her life and I wrote down a saying she used often: "Some people feel the rain. Others just get wet." It was the exact lesson I needed to learn in the moment; a reminder that anytime it "rained" (or conflict arose), I had the power to control how I reacted and could choose to wallow in self-pity or hold my head high and see the best in any given situation.

After the confrontation with Noémie, I had to work alongside her for another month, and then she was gone. I never saw nor spoke to her again, and despite my fears that everyone in the office secretly believed what she had said to me was true, nothing ever came of her slander. Shortly after she left, a new girl joined the company (on the finance team) and sat next to me in the Arden cafeteria and she became my first office lunch buddy. "Salut, je m'appelle Elin, et tu?" she said, introducing herself with a warm grin. Elin's English was on par with my French, so there was a bit of a language barrier, but it allowed us to practice and we became proficient at reading body language to understand what the other meant without speaking.

In early fall, Elin invited me to her family's farm for the weekend. Elin had grown up as a champion equestrian and still rode for fun in her spare time. Her family lived north of Neuchâtel in the scenic Franches-Montagnes region of Switzerland. They bred Freiberg horses on their farm, the only Swiss breed of horses that had originated in the Jura mountains. I instantly felt myself relax in Franches-Montagnes. The area was a natural wonderland of open pastures and pine forests at the base of the alps. I had only ridden a horse once as a kid around a small stable enclosure, but Elin was an expert guide. After grooming the Freibergs' lustrous manes in the stables, we loaded saddlebags with snacks and water and trotted leisurely along a trail passed verdant meadows with ancient castles bursting through the forested hillsides. I inhaled the earthiness of the grass and subtle perfume of wildflowers. Every so often in the distance, we would hear the melodic chimes of cowbells. Afterward, we filled our bellies with a fondue dinner, lots of red wine, and a bonfire with her family before falling into a deep, restful sleep. In a foreign place, I was finally starting to feel more at home.

Chapter 12

Cracks in the War Paint

Kentucky, New York, Paris
1940–1945

Elizabeth's horse-racing hobby showed no signs of slowing as the war in Europe picked up speed. Her newfound obsession was bleeding money, but her beauty business was still holding steady, so she purchased land in Lexington, Kentucky, to house and train more thoroughbreds. In addition to Mr. Nightingale's, she called her second stables "Maine Chance Farm," not to be confused with her destination spa of the same name. Elizabeth tried to convince an up-and-coming architect named Frank Lloyd Wright to design her new stable complex, but after what he described as "several heated meetings" with the "bullheaded" Ms. Arden, Frank declined the commission.

After Seabiscuit, the unlikely champion, beat Triple Crown winner, War Admiral, Tom Smith became the most sought-after horse trainer in the world. Known as "Silent Tom" because of his quiet nature, Elizabeth somehow convinced the man who had been responsible for Seabiscuit's success to train her thoroughbreds. Money was no object when it came to "her darlings," as she called her horses—and she even started carrying photos of them in her wallet, like a proud parent.

Silent Tom helped put the Maine Chance Farm racing stables on the map. Elizabeth won her first major race in Saratoga with a three-year-old horse named Great Union. She had grown accustomed to being one of the only women in business, but after winning her first major race at Saratoga, she could also add one of the first female owners in horse-racing history to her list of accolades. Silent Tom and Elizabeth became a tour de force and her thoroughbreds began receiving recognition as major players on the American horse-racing circuit. Elizabeth was on her way to conquering (what was considered to be) yet another "man's world," but not without jumping over a few hurdles first.

A devastating fire broke out at Belmont Park in New York, killing three of Elizabeth's top thoroughbreds and badly burning the others. Elizabeth rushed to the stables and stayed up all night applying over a gallon of her Eight Hour Cream to the injured Belmont horses in an attempt to soothe their burns. A couple of years later, tragedy struck again when a fire at a racetrack in Chicago destroyed twenty-two horses owned by Maine Chance Farm. The stables' new star colt, Jet Pilot, narrowly survived the blaze as he had been shipped to another racetrack mere hours before. Elizabeth was beside herself, as the "horses were like her children," stated Mrs. Marylou Whitney, the wife of another racehorse owner in an article about the fire.

Elizabeth had developed a pattern of easing grief by buying real estate. After Bessie died, she purchased the adjacent property in Maine and after the devastating fires killed and injured many of "her babies," she once again turned to real estate therapy. In 1938, she bought a large Victorian-style home in Summerville, South Carolina at 208 Sumter Avenue. The breathtaking property was originally built in 1891 with over fifteen rooms, a pool house, double wraparound verandas, a gazebo, fountain feature, and of course, an oversized red door. *Years later, my friend Tasha and I would visit the Red Door Estate, also known as the Elizabeth Arden House, as it still exists today, outside of Charleston.*

Elizabeth stayed at the Red Door Estate in South Carolina while her trusty interior designers, Nicolai Remisoff and Rue Carpenter, renovated her new apartment back in New York where Elizabeth had also bought a sprawling penthouse at 834 Fifth Avenue, a short walk from her Red Door Spa at 691 Fifth Avenue.

When she returned to Manhattan to see what Nicolai and Rue had done with the penthouse, she was floored by the beauty. From the pastel color palette to the opulent chandelier in the dining room (imported from a Russian palace) to the prancing pink horses in the drawing room to the flower-filled private terrace, Elizabeth absolutely adored her "forever home," as she called it. The penthouse had a panoramic view overlooking Central Park, which gave her the sense as though she was living in a bird's nest, high above the chaos of the city. True to her word, Elizabeth would live at 834 Fifth Avenue for the rest of her life, never once updating the décor, that suited her tastes, but was described by some visitors as "being inside a box of macarons."

***

Winter had covered Manhattan with a quilt of snow as the holidays drew near. Elizabeth was used to being alone for Christmas, given Gladys was in Paris and she was estranged from most of her family. But gift-giving season following the Macy's Thanksgiving Day Parade was always Arden's busiest time, so Elizabeth was glad for the excuse to focus on work.

On Christmas Eve, Elizabeth invited Lanie over to her apartment under the guise that there was a lot of work to do, but mostly because she wanted to stave off the loneliness. Lanie, who had never married, fell asleep in an overstuffed armchair as Elizabeth chatted away to her into the wee hours. Between Christmas Day and New Year's, Elizabeth hosted an annual holiday open house at her apartment for staff and industry acquaintances, like Edna Woolman Chase—who substituted as family. She indulged the spirit of the season by giving employees generous bonus checks and extending the invitation to their partners and families—however, once Elizabeth was assured everyone was enjoying themselves at her holiday party, she would slip unnoticed to her bedroom and was not seen again for the rest of the night.

For New Year's Eve, Elizabeth was always invited by someone in her society circles to a glamorous countdown celebration at either the Plaza, the Waldorf, or the Met. She never told anyone that December 31st was also her birthday. As the clock counted down to a new year, Elizabeth— dressed in blush rose chiffon and draped in diamonds—would watch from the wings as everyone waltzed around the ballroom, until they kissed and cheered at the countdown, while every New Year's Eve at midnight, Elizabeth would raise a glass of champagne and whisper "Happy Birthday," toasting to herself. On New Year's Eve in 1940, no one knew she turned sixty-two.

***

As winter stormed into spring, so too did the troops across the Atlantic. Due to wartime shortages, people found economic and creative solutions to stretch the purse strings—and makeup turned out to be one of them. During the war, metallic lipstick cases were made from the same molds as bullet casings; hence when a woman gave a soldier a kiss "that made his heart stop," it was known as hitting him with a "lipstick bullet." Also, in an effort to reuse the metal tubes (instead of throwing them away), rouge refills became popularized. Just as in WWI, Elizabeth amped up her contributions to the war effort and made her cosmetic campaigns overtly patriotic:

`TIL VICTORY!`

`Elizabeth Arden has four exquisite shades: Stop Red, Victory Red, Magenta, and Redwood, available in her famous lipsticks and NEW refills to match your makeup to your costume. Remember, it's patriotic to make your metal lipstick cases last so save metal AND money by buying Arden refills for 80 cents.`

Many people believed women should have never been allowed to serve in the military or don "masculine uniforms," so in a show of public support for female fighters, Elizabeth cheekily launched an exclusive lipstick called "Montezuma Red" with proceeds in support of the U.S. Marine Corps Women's Reserve. The ad featured a black-and-white portrait of a strong female Marine with pops of red showing on both her uniform *and* lips. "Montezuma Red was inspired by the brave, true red of the hat cord, scarf, and chevrons of the Marine uniforms and is a tribute to some of the bravest women in the world," declared Elizabeth. From WWI to WWII, red lipstick played a patriotic role. Adolf Hitler famously hated red lipstick on women, so wearing Montezuma Red became not only a sign of patriotism but also a statement against sexism and facism.

Elizabeth also made wartime headlines for sharing her exercise program called, "Seven Rules for Fitness," with over eighty-thousand service women at a national training institution, although the news story focused less on fitness and more on what the women would be wearing.

ELIZABETH ARDEN OFFERS SEVEN RULES FOR FITNESS FOR SERVICE WOMEN

The American Women's Voluntary Service (AWVS) held a style preview yesterday at the *New York Herald Tribune* auditorium for the smart new powder-gray, brass-buttoned uniform prescribed for its 80,000 members. The basic uniform, consisting of a tunic, skirt, and service cap in twill cuts smart military lines and is terribly cute.

Elizabeth Arden demonstrated a physical fitness course to be given on a nationwide basis to AWVS members. The women heard the following "Seven Rules for Fitness":

1. A burning desire to win
2. Courage to carry through
3. Desire to exercise
4. Determination to diet
5. Breathe deeply
6. Maintain perfect posture
7. Willingness to sacrifice comfort

While Elizabeth contributed to the war effort from New York, she was terrified by the reports she was hearing from overseas as Britain and France declared war on Germany. Her friend, Edna Woolman Chase, had traveled abroad on assignment for *Vogue,* and while she was lunching at Claridge's in London with Teddy Haslam, she received an urgent message from the concierge that her daughter, Ilka, had called the hotel to implore her mother to cut the trip short—threats of a German bombing campaign in England were imminent. Edna Woolman Chase managed to get on the next ship, the SS *Manhattan,* right before the Blitz. Teddy Haslam stayed in London and somehow managed to survive the targeted attacks.

Elizabeth checked in often with Gladys in Paris, who insisted she was all right, except in a tight financial situation, as supplying, staffing, and sales had dramatically stalled across Europe with the war. In a letter Elizabeth wrote to Teddy Haslam, she confessed: "I spoke with Gladys today and sent her $10,000, she seemed broke in a dual sense!"

Despite the economic downturn, Elizabeth was surprised that lipstick sales soared. She intuitively tapped into the "lipstick effect," whereby people afford themselves little luxuries when times were tough. Even Britain's prime minister, Winston Churchill, declared that lipstick was a morale booster through hardships. A dab of color on the lips was a small reminder that there was beauty in the midst of sorrow. However, lipstick sales weren't enough to offset the mounting debts, as most Red Door Spas were forced to temporarily close while the war intensified. Never one to admit defeat, Elizabeth quietly sold $350,000 worth of shares to pay bank loans. And then, with Elizabeth unable to catch a break, someone broke into her Manhattan office and stole $2,000 in cash (over $30,000 today). The burglary made the *New York Times* on May 18, 1944.

BEAUTY SALON IS ROBBED

ELIZABETH ARDEN SAFE LOOTED OF $2,000 BY BURGLARS

Burglars ripped open a five-foot safe at Elizabeth Arden's beauty salon at 691 Fifth Avenue last night and escaped with $2,000 in cash.

The burglary was discovered about 9 a.m. by employees and within a few minutes squads of detectives were searching the building on Fifth Avenue for clues and fingerprints.

The Arden company occupies seven floors of the twelve-story building and the safe was in the office on the sixth floor. The police believe the burglars hid in the building, which is normally closed to the public at 7 p.m. The thieves then used an electric drill to make large holes in the safe and ripped it open.

Despite her financial difficulties, spring soon transitioned into summer racing season, and Elizabeth was glad for the distraction. She was more desperate than ever for her stables to start making a substantial profit. By 1945, Silent Tom helped put Elizabeth's pocketbook back in the black after her thoroughbreds won over $500,000 (approx. $7,115,000 today). In the midst of WWII, Maine Chance Farm was the top money-winning stable in the United States—and then, like clockwork, scandal struck.

"TRAINER TOM SMITH BARRED IN DOPING: JOCKEY CLUB SUSPENDS MAINE CHANCE HORSEMAN FOR DRUGGING," read the headlines across the sports section of every newspaper.

Silent Tom was banned for a year after a saliva test showed evidence that ephedrine had been administered to Elizabeth's horse, Magnific Duel, a one-to-two favorite for the Triple Crown (composed of three races: the Kentucky Derby, the Preakness Stakes, and the Belmont Stakes). Both Silent Tom and Elizabeth declined to comment on the story, but behind closed doors, Elizabeth fumed about the suspension of "poor Tom." Elizabeth had to forfeit all purse winnings of Magnific Duel, but all other horses from Maine Chance Farm were luckily still eligible to start the racing season—under the stipulation that they were placed under the care of a licensed trainer approved by the Jockey Club.

Elizabeth hired a trainer named Roy Waldron, but he resigned after one week as he couldn't handle Elizabeth's overbearingness. She then went to the press in a public appeal to get the Jockey Club to allow her to appoint Jimmy Smith, Silent Tom's son, as her trainer, until his father was able to resume the position. "I'd like to have Jimmy Smith train my string, but I'm apprehensive that my motives might be misinterpreted," she said. The Jockey Club worried Elizabeth had somehow found a loophole to keep working with Silent Tom during his year-long suspension, but ultimately agreed to let his son act as trainer, so long as his father wasn't present.

While Elizabeth fretted over the future of her racing career without Silent Tom, she received a telegram from the Count that chilled her to the core: Gladys had been arrested by the Nazis in Paris on account of "espionage and communicating with the enemy."

To aid in the war effort, Gladys had started volunteering with the French Red Cross and had been discovered concealing and caring for a young Allied aviator whose plane was shot down by the Germans and crashed over France. Gladys took a great risk hiding him from her own husband, who had ties to the opposition, but she thought of the boy's family and how she hoped another mother somewhere would have done the same for her son. Gladys hadn't seen or heard from John Jr. since he left Paris as a teenager to live with his estranged father, but she had discovered through the International Red Cross that he was a lieutenant in the United States Air Force, previously stationed in California.

Gladys was caught off guard when the Gestapo stormed her Parisian home in Place Vendôme to arrest her. She was sent with six hundred other prisoners from Paris to Ravensbrück, a women's only concentration camp in Germany, just north of Berlin.

Elizabeth was frantic and hysterical when she heard the news from New York, but all she could do was plead with Gladys' husband, the Count de Maublanc, to use his royal connections to get her sister released. She had never felt so helpless.

After three months of unlivable, torturous conditions at Ravensbrück, Gladys was transferred to another prison camp in Vittel, France, where she struggled to survive for nearly a year. Gladys was freed, no thanks to her husband, but after the camp was captured by the Allies at the end of the war in 1945. She was one of the lucky few to walk out alive.

Elizabeth was sixty-seven the year Gladys was released from the concentration camp in France and WWII ended. After weathering the Great Depression and two World Wars, Elizabeth realized that for all of her wealth and success, she hadn't been able to buy her sister's freedom—a reminder that family was the greatest fortune of all.

- LOU -

Elizabeth's life lessons began pulling at me in more profound ways than just wanting to follow in her footsteps in the beauty industry. My draw to Elizabeth was never about direct comparison, but looking behind her surface story to find the deeper meaning. Nothing in my life would ever compare to the atrocities Elizabeth and Gladys endured, but their resilience reinforced while I was consumed with chasing career goals to not lose sight of the importance of family.

As my first winter in Europe approached, my problems were insignificant compared to the devastations of war, but I was beginning to battle a severe case of homesickness. There were no overt warnings signs, no fever or cold sweats to alert me of its arrival, just the slow creep of its presence until wistfulness weighed heavy on me. Homesickness is a silent predator and soon I fell into a cycle of chiding myself for having the audacity to miss home, a childish yearning, while there were far worse issues in the world, but on my first Thanksgiving alone, I longed for my family and the comforts of home. I imagined them sitting down to a festive feast: mountains of mashed potatoes, turkey, gravy, stuffing, and pumpkin pie—and my empty seat at the table.

***

Geneva brightened slowly as the sun switched places with the moon above the mountain peaks. Early morning sailors floated gently along the shores of Lac Léman; the swans nuzzled their necks into their chests for warmth. My feet crunched as I stepped on fallen leaves, and the alpine air awakened my lungs on a sunrise run. Jogging through the Swiss countryside allowed me to escape my fortress of self-pity, and the hit of endorphins provided an emotional cleansing. Aloneness heightened my ability to self-reflect, as I had more time to process my thoughts, but it was a double-edged sword: too much overanalyzing made me spiral into self-doubt, but contemplation also let me delve deeper into my psyche and get reacquainted with the real me—void of outside influences.

Running became a form of escapism from my internal conflictions—an implementation of Elizabeth's notions on holistic self-care and the internal benefits that resulted from taking time to nurture oneself: mind, body, and soul. I ran by a field of wild horses and thought of Elizabeth, who was in her sixties when she discovered her passion for horse racing; I hoped it wouldn't take me as long to discover outlets outside of the beauty industry that made me feel fulfilled, but Elizabeth had shown it was never too late to pivot from a preprogrammed path.

On a whim, I signed up to run the Geneva Marathon that year. I had never competed in any sort of organized race before, but I felt compelled to challenge myself. It also offered a welcome distraction from that pesky, reoccurring bout of homesickness. My self-imposed training schedule allowed me to see most of Geneva on foot and cross over into France many times. I liked the idea of being in two places at once, often slowing my stride to straddle the invisible borders. After a few months of running, I noticed the transformation the training was having on my body; I felt lean and strong. The internal changes taking place weren't as evident yet to the naked eye.

***

Halfway through my sojourn in Switzerland, I awoke to frost spidered against the window. My eyes slowly adjusted to the kaleido-scope of snowy light streaming through the crystalline flakes. From beneath my cozy cocoon of covers, I could see winter had officially arrived. Peeking through the curtains, I got a glimpse of Geneva's first snow, and marveled at how beautiful the city looked blanketed in an ivory cloak. Snow had an enchanting effect on the ordinary, covering up the earth's blemishes, if only for a season.

Training for the marathon and devoting every other waking hour to work became my new norm and helped suppress the ache of what I thought I was missing back home. My former life, including the people in it, was getting smaller and smaller in my mind, like a bunch of balloons let loose disappearing into the sky—no longer visible, but subconsciously still out there floating in the abyss. I started traveling a lot throughout Europe for work, mostly to the London office, which was one of our most profitable markets. I felt like Elizabeth riding business class on the train, as though I were on my way to visit Teddy Haslam at the London Red Door Spa, and pulling up in a black cab to my Mayfair hotel, just as Elizabeth had a century before me. I came to adore everything about the British branch and English sensibilities. The UK team was the perfect mix of professional and proper, but could easily throw back a couple pints at the pub. I felt at home on those work trips and could picture myself living there someday.

I was starting to adjust to my new solo Swiss life when my family surprised me by announcing they were coming to celebrate Christmas, or "Swissmas," as we called it. I was so excited that I wouldn't have to spend the holidays alone that I could barely sleep leading up to their arrival. My dad and sister, Grace, had never been to Switzerland before, and it was the first time my mom and Meredith, who had helped me first get settled, would get to see the gorgeous country in all of its snowy glory. The five of us stayed in my studio apartment as I played Geneva tour guide: we visited the Marché de Noël (Christmas market) on Rue du Mont-Blanc, sipped vin chaud (hot mulled wine), and perused the holiday huts selling artisanal trinkets, like hand-painted ornaments and knitted wool sweaters. We ate dinner at my favorite fondue and raclette restaurant, Edelweiss, which looked like a vintage Swiss ski chalet and had a live band playing traditional folk music every night, yodeling and alphorns included.

After a few days of showing my family around Geneva, we traveled by train to Interlaken. From there, we hopped on the Bernese Oberland Railway to Jungfraujoch to see the spectacular views and breathe in the icy air of the Aletsch glacier, coined "the top of Europe." The part of the trip I was most eager to experience was Zermatt, home of the infamous Matterhorn (and my blog's namesake), where we skied and celebrated Christmas Eve/Day. Zermatt's chilled alpine air was so invigorating, like living inside a big breath mint; when I inhaled, I could feel it beneath my bones into the fibers of my being. Witnessing the majesty of the Matterhorn in person exceeded every expectation; seeing the skyscrapers of Manhattan for the first time would forever be one of my fondest memories, but it was incomparable to nature's towering beauty. The Matterhorn's striking pyramidal peak straddled the Switzerland-Italy border, so we had to bring our passports to the top of the mountain to ski from one side to the other. The ability to cross an alpine border on skis never ceased to amaze. Elizabeth's late-in-life realization that family was the greatest fortune of all, hit me with force during that trip. I embraced the quality time spent untethered from technology with my family, whether it was gazing up at the magnificent Matterhorn from the chair lift or watching the world whizz by as we played cards on the train. I was grateful for moments where my body and brain synced, and allowed me to appreciate people and places in real time. Usually, we are only able to ruminate on good times by looking back on the past, so it was a rare treat to feel an overwhelming sense of gratitude for what was happening in the present.

After Christmas in Zermatt, we stopped at as many Swiss villages as we could fit in, such as Grindelwald, Spiez, Gstaad, Vevey, and Luzern, on the train ride to Zurich for New Year's Eve, our last stop before my family flew home to Toronto. Ringing in 2012 with my family, I couldn't help but think of all the years Elizabeth had spent celebrating December 31st alone, so I raised a glass of champagne to toast Elizabeth on what would have been her one hundred and thirty-fourth birthday.

Spending time with my family in Switzerland reinforced that there was a transformative power in seeing the familiar from a new perspective. Our rapport fell back into its old rhythms, as though nothing had changed, but I felt like a different person—less hurried, more introspective—at the same time. After tearful, Hallmark-special hugs at the airport, I took the tram back to my pied-à-terre. My sisters and I had shared beds for the past two weeks together, so it was strange to get under the covers alone again. I couldn't help but still curl my body to one side of the bed, leaving space for someone else to crawl in beside me.

My family's visit had temporarily cured my homesickness, but there was a constant push and pull between solitude and loneliness. I feared loneliness yet flirted with solitude. I enjoyed the glamour of living alone, recognizing it as a fleeting privilege. Solitude fostered independence and the bandwidth to reimagine my identity, whereas loneliness was an intense ache that made me question what kind of life was worth living without someone to share in the sorrows and successes.

It was a contradictory revelation: I both despaired yet desired aloneness. I was doing what Elizabeth had done in her early years: leaning hard into independence and isolation to build a career in beauty, but later in life Elizabeth found herself desperately lonely, craving connection and companionship. Was I destined for the same end? What did that say about a life well lived?

Chapter 13

A Runaway Success

New York, Kentucky

1945–1948

The morning was overcast in Louisville, Kentucky, on Saturday, May 3, 1947. Over one hundred and fifteen thousand people cascaded into Churchill Downs, the largest attendance ever recorded in its history. The threat of thunderstorms couldn't dampen the crowd's excitement for what was about to transpire that day. It was the seventy-third annual Kentucky Derby, and Cornelius Vanderbilt's horse, Phalanx, was the overwhelming favorite, with two-to-one odds. Female-owned horses were rare in the racing circuit, let alone Triple Crown contenders, but Elizabeth N. Graham's thoroughbred, Jet Pilot, of Maine Chance Farm, was favored second to win, followed by Faultless, from Calumet Farm.

As the melody of "My Old Kentucky Home" floated over the racetrack, Elizabeth stood on the sidelines, draped in fur, pearls, and a stylish fascinator, with a mint julep in hand to calm the nerves. Her one-thousand-four-hundred-and-fifty-pound "darling baby" appeared from behind the corral with Silent Tom, who had returned to Maine Chance Farm to take over from his son Jimmy after serving his one-year suspension from the sport. Jet Pilot, a handsome, chestnut brown race-horse, and his twenty-two-year-old jockey, Eric Guerin, "known for his cool head and steady hands," said Elizabeth, wore Arden's signature racing silks with a cerise and white sash, blue cuffs on the sleeves, and a matching cap.

The crowd roared at the sight of the twelve racing beauties competing in the Derby. The stadium fell silent, tensed with anticipation; the gun sounded. *They were off!*

Jet Pilot, number eleven, fired out of the gate. He managed to maintain his position, just slightly ahead of Cornelius Vanderbilt's horse, Phalanx, but Faultless was slightly ahead. Out of nowhere, Phalanx shot ahead, and the three racehorses charged ahead neck-and-neck. The sprint to the line was so close the judges had to debate who was the winner over a grainy, black-and-white photo finish. Elizabeth nearly pinched her skin raw with her nails until the final results were in: Elizabeth N. Graham, Jet Pilot's proud owner, had won the seventy-third Kentucky Derby by a nose.

In the winner's enclosure, Elizabeth beamed with pride, hugging her trainer, Silent Tom, and her jockey, Eric Guerin, as a blanket of roses was placed onto Jet Pilot. The victory was remarkably sweet for Elizabeth, as she was not only the wealthiest businesswoman in the world for nearly two decades, but now the winning owner of America's most prestigious equestrian event. After the press and crowds dispersed, Elizabeth stayed in the stables and rolled up her pristine sleeves to massage Eight Hour Cream into Jet Pilot's legs and hooves. She sang him a lullaby as she covered him with a cashmere blanket while he rested after winning the biggest horse race in history.

Elizabeth's luxurious grooming routines had become notorious on the horse circuit and elicited eye rolls from traditional horsemen who thought her cajoling was over-the-top. Elizabeth decorated her stables as tastefully as her salons. She walked around spritzing her Blue Grass fragrance, "Just because it's a barn, doesn't mean it has to smell like one," she said. She played music with a portable phonograph, and hung plants in the stalls to circulate a better oxygen supply. Elizabeth was emphatic about feeding her horses special clover for nutrients ("It's their spinach," she said), and organic fruits and vegetables picked fresh from her farm. She banned blinders for aesthetic reasons ("They're too ugly for my beauties," she said), and implemented a strict no-whipping policy—blaming the jockeys and farmhands for any mistakes or mishaps. Humans were flawed; horses were flawless.

In one instance at Maine Chance Farm, Elizabeth was feeding an orange to one of her horses (supposedly his favorite snack) when he bit off the tip of her finger. A stable boy later remarked that Elizabeth didn't lash out or panic; she calmly picked up her fingertip, as if it were a fallen feather, and asked him to put it on ice while her chauffeur pulled up the car to take her to the closest hospital. The tip of her finger was sewn back on later that night. If it were a *person* who had harmed her, their bags would have been packed at once, but as always, Elizabeth's beloved horses could do no wrong. "The poor baby just got excited," she later told a reporter, as the biting incident turned into an international news story. The Queen of England sent a letter to Elizabeth through her lady-in-waiting, writing: "Her Majesty was so glad to have seen you last week and does so hope your finger is growing!"

After her historic win at the Kentucky Derby, *Time* magazine featured Elizabeth in a multi-page spread and the first businesswoman on the cover, calling her, "The Queen who rules the sport of Kings." Maine Chance Farm continued to rake in over $590,000 per year (over $8 million today), making it the most profitable stable in North America. Elizabeth, who had grown up tending horses on a farm in Canada, had accomplished more than most people dreamed of in a lifetime, and forty years after running away from home, had somehow come full circle to find fulfillment in a once forgotten pastime.

Approaching her seventieth birthday, an age when most people considered retirement, Elizabeth's ambitions strengthened, rather than withered—mostly to distract from her crushing loneliness. "I'm not interested in age," Elizabeth always said; but although she felt younger than her years, her old age was getting harder to hide on the outside. That's the thing with façades; they can only protect you from the harsh realities of the world for so long, until they inevitably wear off.

- LOU -

I decided to run away from home when I was nine because I wanted an adventure worth writing about in a book before I turned double digits (an age I considered very old). For a few hours, I hid behind big trees on various neighborhood lawns, but once my snack rations were gone and the temperature dipped as the sun dropped, I was cold, tired, and hungry so I made the executive decision to postpone my escape until another day. When I got home, the door was unlocked. I smelled dinner cooking in the kitchen and heard the blare of the TV in the living room, so I snuck unnoticed upstairs to my bedroom and unpacked my runaway supplies. "Girrrrrrls, dinner's ready!" my mom called. It was my favorite, cacio e pepe (but back then I called it "cheese and pepper pasta"). I skidded into my seat at the supper table, searching my family's faces for relief that I was back, but no one so much as blinked. My family hadn't even noticed I'd run away.

Fourteen years later, morning light flooded my small Swiss studio on September 12, 2012 and I remembered it was my twenty-third birthday. The revelation left me unfazed. I rotated onto my side and fell back asleep. Tangled in a web of fabric, I felt around the sheets for my glasses when I re-awoke a few hours later. I had fallen asleep with them on while reading, and the lenses were cloudy with fingerprints when I finally found them. Church bells kept me honest, so when the local "église" chimed, I reluctantly rolled out of bed. The sky had turned dark by late morning, and the rain that persisted throughout the day gave me permission to do nothing.

It was a Wednesday, but I had taken the day off from work. In Geneva, I was allotted four weeks of holiday, and Vivienne had reminded me a couple of times I needed to use them up. Wrapping myself in a silk robe (it made me feel fancy), I boiled water on the stove for my French coffee press and made pancakes, the foolproof kind where you just add water. I poured a splash of milk into my coffee, drizzled maple syrup onto the pancakes, and sprinkled the stack with fresh raspberries and blueberries. The breakfast presentation was just for me, but when can you treat yourself if not on your birthday? I put Edith

Piaf on the record player to fill the silence and lit a tea-light candle, placing it on top of the pancakes. Sitting on the couch, I whispered "Happy Birthday" to myself, and blew the candle out.

After a slow morning, I opened my laptop and worked on a PowerPoint presentation for an upcoming work trip to Italy. When I was an intern in New York, I felt as though I lagged far behind Elizabeth, like I was reaching my hand out, flailing to catch up on the career ladder. In Geneva, I finally felt as though I had reached a pivotal rung on the corporate climb. Becoming CEO of Arden, which I considered to be "reaching the top," was still far off in the distance, but when I looked back at my interning days, I could see how far I'd come. But as the rain pelted outside my window and I celebrated my twenty-third birthday alone, I wasn't so sure what it meant to be "successful." What did it feel like to be "full of success"? Other than pancakes, I didn't feel full of anything at the moment.

I made myself another cup of coffee and cracked open my red journal to muse about this idea further. The term "FOMO" didn't exist yet, but the "Fear Of Missing Out" on milestone events was real. Halfway across the world, I may have existed in the virtual sphere, as *Matterhorn Maven*, but I was nonexistent in the physical sense to family and friends. The computer acted as a portal to my past, where I watched other people's lives progress while I lived in a semi self-imposed limbo. For my entire life, I had always been on the same path as my peers, yet now that I was on track to reach professional success at Arden, I suddenly felt light-years behind on the parallel path of personal development. *Had I mismanaged adulthood?* My move to Geneva was supposed to be temporary, but the longer I stayed, the more I felt like I no longer fit in back home. I still trusted Elizabeth's life map to guide me on where I needed to go in the beauty industry—it had gotten me this far in my professional life—but I was starting to question what the possibility of a detour might look like, as I was beginning to dissociate from the picture-perfect *Matterhorn Maven* identity, I had created for myself.

After journaling, I packed my laptop and notebook into my backpack, grabbed my umbrella, strapped on my rain boots, and went for a stroll along Lake Geneva. I watched my favorite furry ballerinas, the swans, as they pirouetted across the glacial water that was stippled with raindrops. On my way back to the apartment, I stopped at Café Boréal to siphon their Wi-Fi before it closed. I had been avoiding civilization all day, but I was curious to see if anyone had emailed to wish me a happy birthday. Along with sweet messages from my family, there was one from Logan, "Lou! Happy Birthday! You're likely celebrating on a yacht in St. Tropez or something!" From comments people left on my blog or said in emails, I had become aware the perception back home was that I was living a ritzy European life, jet setting on weekends and working at a glamorous job in a chic Swiss city. I perpetuated the myth by posting photos of my travels and only writing about the highlights on *Matterhorn Maven*. I didn't blame anyone for assuming my life in Geneva was all glitz and glamour, because that's exactly what I portrayed. I kept my public updates upbeat, and privately internalized the struggles. Logan had always been the one person who knew me the best, but his birthday message made me pause: what did it mean now that *he* could no longer differentiate between the real me and the façade?

Several months had passed since my last Google Voice call with Logan, and while we still emailed here and there, I could feel him pulling further away from me. I knew with an ocean between us dating was an impossibility, but I had been holding onto hope that once I returned to New York (a less than two-hour flight from Toronto), we would have a better chance to rekindle our romance. However, as Logan's responses grew fewer and sparser, I recognized my lingering love was unrequited. It was a weird feeling, being acutely aware you were in the midst of being forgotten. I couldn't necessarily feel the pain yet, but I knew it was coming, like an epidural for heartbreak.

After thanking Logan for his birthday message, I closed my laptop and walked home in the rain. I left my wet boots to dry on the doormat and took a long, hot shower before changing into my coziest pajamas. I put Edith Piaf on the record player again and *La Vie en Rose* played in the background as I poured myself a glass of cabernet sauvignon and prepared dinner: cacio e pepe. By my twenty-third birthday, I had finally succeeded in running away.

Chapter 14

Life's a Marathon, Not a Sprint

New York

1945-1953

Elizabeth was in her New York office when Lanie burst in and broke some troubling news: Tommy Lewis, Elizabeth's ex-husband, was now working for Helena Rubinstein, her biggest competitor. The divorce clause, which had banned Tommy from working in the beauty industry, had expired, and he jumped at the chance to betray his former wife one last time. The charismatic, affable Tommy that Elizabeth had first fallen in love with no longer existed. The beauty business was Elizabeth's firstborn baby, and Tommy had no qualms about feeding it to the wolves. For over fifteen years, he had been privy to the inner workings of Arden's proprietary formulas and marketing strategies—and was no sheep in sharing the secrets of her success with the competition. As the former director of Arden's wholesale division, Tommy poached many key industry contacts and brought them over to Helena Rubinstein's. To Elizabeth, going to work for her corporate competitor was more duplicitous than the cheating that led to their divorce.

Tommy was eventually promoted to president and general manager of Helena Rubinstein's Prince Gourielli division and worked there until his retirement in 1968. He remarried a woman named Margaret W. Pease, a socialite from Preston, Connecticut, and according to his obituary, they lived at 21 East 90th Street in Manhattan's Upper East Side until his death at the age of ninety-five in 1971. Elizabeth did not attend the funeral.

Dating had been the furthest thing from Elizabeth's mind for over a decade following her divorce, but spry as ever, she finally decided to dip her toe back into the dating pool as she approached her seventies.

Elizabeth was introduced to the Russian prince Michael Evlanoff at a charity gala in Manhattan by Princess Mikeladze (whom Elizabeth had met through her interior designer, Nicolai Remisoff).

Prince Evlanoff was enamored by the cosmetic tycoon and immediately asked her to accompany him to the dance floor where he told her about his royal background: he was the son of the late prince Basil Evlanoff and late princess Helen Koudacheff, whose family history dated back to the Tartar war lords of the twelfth century. He had graduated from the Russian Artillery School in St. Petersburg in 1914 and served in World War I. After the Russian Revolution he settled in Paris, but a few months prior had moved to New York and was living at the Sherry-Netherland, a luxury hotel with long-term accommodations, on the corner of Fifth and 59th.

Elizabeth adored all things royal and had always been slightly envious her sister Gladys held the title of countess, so she allowed herself to be swept away by Prince Evanloff's advancements. The Russian prince was persistent in winning Elizabeth's affections and showered her with bouquets of American Beauty deep pink roses, her favorite flower. The bundles consisted of thirteen, instead of a dozen roses, as he remembered Elizabeth was superstitious about the number twelve (the reasoning remains unknown). The thoughtful attention to detail charmed the often-elusive Elizabeth, and although Prince Evlanoff was eighteen years younger, he filled the deep void of loneliness in her life.

Their courtship progressed quickly, and soon the twosome was seen dining all over town together. Elizabeth was giddy with delight when head waiters at 21 Club bowed and said, "This way, Your Highness," when she arrived arm in arm with Prince Evanloff. Everything seemed almost too good to be true.

The Russian prince told Elizabeth that he had a large trust fund established in his name, but after moving to Manhattan, he was still awaiting dispensation from the king of Sweden. Elizabeth was used to footing the bill, and happily covered expenses for her new beau, as he awaited the transfer of funds to his US bank account. Prince Evlanoff was a smooth talker and prone to exaggerating stories into fibs, but Elizabeth ignored any red flags. A couple months into their whirlwind romance, the Russian prince proposed and Elizabeth accepted, without hesitation.

Elizabeth asked Teddy Haslam to walk her down the aisle, and although he was skeptical of this flash in the pan romance, the ever-loyal Teddy flew in from London to be by her side for the nuptials. The wedding had a short mention in the *New York Times:*

ELIZABETH ARDEN BECOMES A BRIDE WEDS PRINCE MICHAEL EVLANOFF

Elizabeth Arden was married yesterday afternoon at All Souls Unitarian Church to Prince Michael Evlanoff, member of a prominent family of the former Russian nobility. The bride, escorted by Edward M. Haslam, European manager of her firm, dispensed with attendants. She wore a dark blue duvetyn and satin traveling costume with hat to match and a corsage of red roses. A small reception was given at the bride's home afterward.

A couple weeks after the wedding, the newlyweds traveled to Tucson, Arizona, to look at an estate for a secondary Maine Chance destination spa, on their way to Nassau, Bahamas, for their honeymoon. Elizabeth arranged for her new husband's belongings to be unpacked in her Fifth Avenue penthouse while they were away. She converted her library into a bedroom for him (she believed everyone should have a room of one's own) and sent her linens to be monogrammed with their new royal crest. Elizabeth also left instructions for household staff to start referring to her as *Princess,* yet another alias to add to her growing repertoire. But while in the Bahamas, the marriage ended as quickly as it began.

"Get everyone to stop work on my apartment immediately," wrote Elizabeth in a panicked cable to Lanie. Her time as a princess was short-lived.

The prince's demeanor toward Elizabeth changed after they were married. He issued orders to his new bride to transfer her fortune over to his bank account. Elizabeth had written a worrisome letter to Teddy Haslam after the wedding night but still went on the honeymoon: "The prince waited until you had gone to show his true colors. Just as soon as you left, he did his best to break my spirit. He told me a frantic story about owing over $27,000, saying his debtors were pressing him and wanted me to give him a blank check."

"The shock didn't stop there," as Elizabeth told Lanie when she got home. Prince Evlanoff had invited someone else to join them on their honeymoon—his boyfriend. Elizabeth was flummoxed. She had always prided herself on her ability to read people; how had she missed all of the warning signs that the prince preferred men for pleasure but women for money (and later, as she discovered, for American citizenship)?

Elizabeth requested an emergency divorce. Mysteriously, a "friend" of Prince Evlanoff's tried to blackmail Elizabeth into giving him a "settlement sum" of $100,000 as hush money. Instead, she hired a private detective to investigate Russian prince Michael Evlanoff. What she learned was astounding. Elizabeth was a smart lady, but she had been royally duped.

The detective discovered Prince Michael Evlanoff's title was fake, as was his imaginary trust fund. Elizabeth felt she should have known there was something fishy about an aristocrat being unable to pay for their lavish dinner dates due to "administration" problems with the king of Sweden (whom he had never met). Michael Evlanoff was drowning in debt, and throughout his courtship with Elizabeth, had racked up even more bills by using her famous name to pay for everything on credit. The "royal riches" and engagement ring he gave her had all been purchased on commission under the name "Elizabeth Arden."

Unbeknownst to Elizabeth, she had paid for every bouquet of red roses, Tiffany & Co. jewels, and her very own wedding ring. The *New York Daily News* reported on the divorce, but Elizabeth was so embarrassed that many details were purposely kept from the press.

LIZ ARDEN SHEDS SECOND HUSBAND

Liz Arden, who has made millions out of making women beautiful, shed her second husband today after it seems they couldn't make a beautiful life together. The famed beautician was granted a divorce after she testified that the Russian refugee "abused her mentally." Liz Arden was also permitted by the court to legally return to her maiden name, Florence Nightingale Graham.

With enough alter egos to fill a rolodex, Elizabeth decided to return to her roots before her seventieth birthday and legally changed her name back to Florence Nightingale Graham during the court proceedings. She lost touch with Michael Evlanoff after the divorce. According to an obituary in the *New York Times*, he died in 1972 at the age of seventy-six—ironically, at the Florence Nightingale Nursing Home, an assisted-living facility in East Harlem, Manhattan.

Soon after, in 1949, Lanie passed away in her sleep. Elizabeth was devasted by the loss of her longtime friend and first employee. Elizabeth never took sick days, but she sequestered herself in her bedroom for over a week, curtains drawn, in mourning. "Miss Florence G. Delaney, finance director and treasurer of Elizabeth Arden, died today at her home. Miss Delaney joined the Arden firm in its infancy over thirty years ago as a bookkeeper and rose through the ranks," read her obituary.

While the 1940s ended on a heavy note, the 1950s began jubilantly with Elizabeth attending the coronation of Queen Elizabeth II on June 2, 1953. The heir to the throne arrived at Westminster Abbey in a gold state coach led by a team of eight horses wearing a white satin, embroidered coronation gown, designed by Sir Norman Hartnell. After the ceremony concluded, newly anointed Queen Elizabeth II set off on a marathon procession back to Buckingham Palace. The route had been designed to allow crowds to get the best chance of viewing their new queen, proudly holding her orb and scepter, wearing the bejeweled imperial state crown. The queen won the hearts of thousands along the processional by refusing to raise the roof of her carriage for protection from the rain, waving gleefully as she made her way under the magnificent arches and scarlet banners bearing the royal monogram. Queen Elizabeth II's coronation was the first to be televised and was watched by over three hundred and fifty million people worldwide. Queen Elizabeth II (along with her six maids of honor) were ready for their closeups as their faces were artfully made-up with Arden cosmetics.

Elizabeth made acquaintance with an American journalist named Jacqueline Bouvier, who was covering the historic event for the *Washington Times-Herald*. She would go on to become First Lady Jackie Kennedy and later met the queen on multiple occasions as policy intersected. As formidable women in power, Queen Elizabeth II, Elizabeth Arden, and Jackie Kennedy formed a mutual respect for one another, and socialized often in London and New York.

After the coronation, Elizabeth returned to Manhattan where the city and the beauty industry were entering into a golden age. Although Elizabeth had been in the beauty business for over forty years, hungry newcomers were starting to infiltrate her territory. Elizabeth was starting to question how much longer she could maintain her status as queen of the cosmetics kingdom?

- LOU -

I was nearing my one-year anniversary in Switzerland when Giovanni abruptly called me into a conference room where Elisabetta Ricci, the head of Arden's European division, was waiting for me. Giovanni closed the door, and I braced myself for the phrase: "YOU'RE FIRED!" I distinctly remember wondering if it would sound less harsh in his lilting French: "VOUS ÊTES VIRÉ!" had the same meaning, but less visceral impact.

"Vivienne is enceinte, or how you say, pregnant," Giovanni blurted out. That was *not* what I'd been expecting. "She departs for her congé maternité, errr maternity leave, in a couple months," he said. How had I not noticed that the petite Vivienne had started wearing looser clothing to hide a growing baby bump?

"Elisabetta and I would like to promote you to *directrice* (manager) and cover Vivienne's position while she's *en congé*," Giovanni said, looking at me expectedly.

Elisabetta chimed in, "I know you were expecting to return to the New York office, but accepting this promotion would require you to stay in Geneva." I've spoken to Dominique in HR, and we can continue covering your rent for another year, and file the paperwork to extend your visa. What do you think?"

The news caught me completely by surprise. I had never considered an alternate universe where I would stay in Switzerland longer than a year. But I recognized it was rare to be promoted to manager so early in my career, and understood the significance of the offer.

"Can I take a few days to think it over?" I asked. What I was really thinking: *I need to call my mom and dad to ask them what I should do, because I'm actually still a child, not a real adult, who can't make a decision by herself.*

"Bien," said Giovanni. I shook their hands and returned to my desk. Vivienne caught my eye above our computer monitors and gave me a wink. She had known what the meeting was about.

"Félicitations!" I mouthed.

"Merçi," she said, "Félicitations to *you*," she said, with a smile.

That night, I opened a bottle of red wine and poured a generous glass. I chose Ella Fitzgerald to put on the record player and sank into the couch to collect my thoughts. I had immediately emailed my parents asking what they thought I should do. Their response was a unanimous "TAKE THE OFFER!" I knew that they were right. How could I pass up paid accommodations, a salary in Swiss francs, and managerial experience at twenty-three? I should have been jumping for joy, but I couldn't shake the overwhelming feeling of being a fraud. People's expectations of me, versus the real me, felt misguided. Couldn't everyone see that behind the confident front I put up, I was struggling to figure it out as I went along? I grabbed the wine bottle and gave myself another healthy pour. I had been busting my butt and the promotion was proof, a milestone marker, that I was on my way to the elusive goal of achieving "success," so why did I feel undeserving, even unfulfilled?

When Side B of the Ella Fitzgerald record finished, I switched over to Billie Holiday. I topped off my wineglass and put the empty bottle by the door. The effects of the alcohol softened my internal restlessness and allowed me to stop wrestling with the insecurities of my ego. Limbs loose, I turned up the volume to Billie Holiday's "Body and Soul" as I got ready for bed. Billie's raspy voice crooned amidst the crinkling of the record as I drifted into a deep sleep.

> *My days have grown so lonely…*
> *What lies before me*
> *A future that's stormy*
> *A winter that's gray and cold*
> *Unless there's magic, the end will be tragic*
> *And echo a tale that's been told so often…*
> *I'm all for you, body and soul…*

That Monday, I accepted the promotion—and with that, my stint in Switzerland extended from twelve months to two years. I no longer tried to shrink time down into manageable components; months had turned to years.

Every season looked good on Switzerland. It was impossible to pick a favorite. Just when I thought I loved the crunchy leaves and crisp atmosphere of autumn, the snow-covered Alps dazzled me with their sparkling purity in winter. Then, the wildflower fields bloomed in spring, and lake life peaked in summer, unveiling layer after layer of Switzerland's natural beauty.

In Geneva, the first sign of the changing seasons was "L'Horloge Fleurie in La Jardin Anglais"—the outdoor flower clock in the English Garden located along the waterfront. The flower clock, which holds the record for the longest second hand in the world at 2.5 meters, was created in 1955 as a symbol of the country's renowned reputation for luxury watchmaking and dedication to nature. Groundskeepers refreshed the clock's design by planting over sixty-five hundred variations of flowers, shrubbery, and plants, depending on the season. Throughout the winter, a white coat of snow hid the clock's numbers, but the ticking hands remained visible on the surface, like a pop-out card concealed by silvery glitter.

Spring had arrived when I walked by the flower clock on route to Café Boréal for my weekend croissant and caffeine fix. Flowers bloomed in a smorgasbord of shades from blush pinks and pallid lilacs to fruity oranges and canary yellows. The temperature had warmed, and the clouds parted to reveal a fearless blue sky mantling the mountains. Spring in Geneva looked like a green-screen backdrop, too cinematic to be real. Swiss alpine flowers blossomed in the surrounding meadows with names that sounded like a merry band of forest fairies: primrose, daisy, bellflower, and buttercup. I half expected a yodeler to announce from a nearby hilltop, like a modern town crier, that spring had officially sprung in Switzerland.

Despite the beauty of the changing seasons, time ticked on, the same as always. The flower clock was tangible proof of time's never-ending journey. Springtime also signaled the reality of the upcoming Geneva marathon, which consumed me and induced perpetual panic right up until race day.

A few days before the marathon, my mom arrived from Toronto as she had decided to run the half-marathon, which would allow her to watch me cross the finish line at the end of the full. My mom was the true marathon maven (having multiple races under her belt), and she was the inspiration behind my belief that running 42.195 kilometers was remotely in the realm of possibility. I was glad there was someone to cheer me on and bear witness to the completion of my first marathon because, at the end of the day, all any kid wants is to make their parents proud. I thought of how Elizabeth had lost her mother early in life, and wondered if the strong inner drive that made her strive for greatness was to make her mom proud—an invisible force cheering her on.

The morning of the marathon I awoke early. Truthfully, I hadn't really slept. Instead, I tossed and turned until sunrise in spurts of sparse slumber. I was so nervous; I had no appetite. My mom forced me to eat a piece of toast with peanut butter and banana. We helped each other attach our bib numbers to the front of our shirts with safety pins. (I only pricked myself twice.)

The race started in the village of Chêne-Bourg. The route wound through the picturesque countryside up into the Alps and finished in the heart of the city, along the boardwalk in front of the Jet d'Eau. The half marathon began at 8:30 a.m., and the full one started at 9:45 a.m. I double-knotted my shoelaces, and my mom showed me how to tuck them in tightly so they wouldn't come undone. We hugged and wished each other "good legs" (seemed more practical than "good luck"). "Can't wait to see you cross that finish line, Lou!" she yelled as she set off on the half.

I stood behind a banner that said DÉPART in a thick human clump that spoke only French and German, waiting for the marathon to start. Finally, the gun sounded. *I was off!* With my heart pounding, I moved with the stampede like it was the running of the bulls. Bodies jostled in unison until there was enough room to break free; we were a herd of caged cattle flooding through the ranch gates. I kept with the natural flow of traffic until I had enough personal space to pick up speed.

My blue iPod shuffle was clipped to my waistband and my headphones were fed underneath my shirt so the cord wouldn't hit me in the face while running. My biggest fear was the iPod would die mid-marathon, and I would be forced to trudge along listening to nothing but the sound of my pounding heart. My mom never ran with music, but I needed the upbeat rhythms to drown out the internal feedback loop of fear.

Adrenaline coursed through my veins and I fell into a comfortable cadence. Wary of exerting too much energy too quickly, I zoned out from the other runners and focused on steadying my stride. It didn't matter how fast I ran; the goal was to keep running the entire way. I knew if I let myself walk, it would be that much harder to pick up the pace again, as my legs would turn to lead.

Every five kilometers I rewarded myself with a pink lemonade energy chew from my fanny pack, like a dog getting a treat. It was a mental way for me to break down the mammoth route in front of me. An hour into the marathon, I felt strong, even taking the time to soak in the scenery around me. *Switzerland is breathtaking*, I thought as I passed a lavender field and a charming chalet that looked like a life-sized cuckoo clock. The sky was bright blue and dotted with fluffy marshmallow clouds. The Alps seemed to smile down upon me, cheering me on.

While the majority of the marathon was in the rural backcountry, I was surprised to look around at one point and discover I was completely alone. Every now and then I passed a rogue runner, or one passed me. Whenever the latter happened, it became a competition to overtake them again. This mental game distracted me from the increasing physical exhaustion.

From what I had seen of marathons on TV, there were people lined up with signs, clapping and cheering like a coronation processional.

Along the first leg, there were no crowds on the sidelines, only the serenity of nature, which lulled me into a hypnotic runner's trance.

While the path wasn't visibly steep, I knew I was gaining altitude by the shortness of my breath. My body still had a lot of steam left in it, but the thinness of the alpine air, coupled with the beating sun, made me lightheaded. Despite my previous apprehension of using a fanny pack, I'd gotten used to the weight of it resting on my lower back, like a hand gently nudging me forward.

I slowed to a jog, reached around to grab water, and guzzled as much as I could while continuing to run. Before I knew it, the bottle was empty so I squeezed the last drops onto the top of my head and let the lukewarm liquid trickle down my face.

My playlist was streaming steadily along to "Keep the Car Running" by Arcade Fire. I was too scared to press any buttons and risk breaking it somehow, so I refused to skip songs and listened in full to whatever was playing on shuffle.

I felt solid until I hit the half-marathon marker. The idea that I had to do that *ALL OVER AGAIN* was mentally tough to swallow. I could no longer ignore the cramps in my side, like dull daggers, and the dead weight of my calves.

"Mind over matter, mind over matter, mind over matter," I muttered to myself. That was the only way I knew to get through the rest of the race; it was more mental than physical. Just after the halfway point, the blue sky suddenly turned dark gray. The towering Alps now looked more menacing than encouraging. Rain pelted heavily, causing the dirt path we were on to turn to mud. An ominous feeling washed over me. Tears streamed as I trudged uphill, single file, getting splashed in the face with sludge. What was I trying to prove and to whom? Why did I always feel the need to achieve? Was it for myself or for other people? My mind was starting to lose the battle with my body. At that moment, I would have given anything to curl up and have someone carry me home to my warm bed. The only silver lining was that the rain disguised my tears.

Eventually, the terrain plateaued, the clouds reined in their water-works (I reined in mine), and for the last fifteen kilometers, we came down from the mountains to finish the rest of the race through the paved streets of the city.

Crowds now lined the route, and their cheers gave me a much-needed boost. By then, I was running on pure autopilot. My body no longer belonged to me. I felt like a robot programmed to keep moving until I combusted.

For the last five kilometers, it felt like I was hallucinating. The entire time I had been so worried my iPod would stop working, but for the final stretch, I allowed myself to play DJ roulette. When "Dog Days Are Over" by Florence and The Machine came on, a surge of adrenaline hidden in my reserves kicked in, and I started sprinting. I thought my body was depleted, but my muscles expended the last energy stores they had been hoarding for the grand finale.

I crossed the finish line, and the expulsion of emotions that hit me caught me by surprise. It was as though I had chugged the most potent cocktail of endorphins and enervation; the highest highs mixed with the lowest lows. It was a feeling I haven't felt since, and one I'll never forget.

As soon as I stopped running, someone placed a completion medal around my neck and pointed to a table filled with bananas, granola bars, and water bottles. I looked around for my mom but couldn't find her. I walked away from the crowd toward the water's edge and watched the swans glide gently along Lake Geneva as I burst into tears.

The word *marathon* comes from Pheidippides, a Greek messenger who was sent from the battlefield of Marathon to Athens to announce that the Persians had been defeated in the Battle of Marathon (in which he had just fought) in 490 BC. He ran the entire distance without stopping before rushing into the assembly and exclaiming, "We have won!" Then he collapsed and died. COLLAPSED AND DIED. Why would anyone willingly run a marathon after that tragic history? And yet, I had just done it. I had completed a real-life marathon. M-A-R-A-T-H-O-N. 42.195 kilometers. The word lost all meaning, but unlike poor Pheidippides, I lived to tell the tale.

My mom eventually found me down by the water. She ran over and embraced me in a hug. "I'm so sorry I didn't see you, Lou! I was stuck in line getting our bags," she said. She had flown halfway across the world to watch me finish my first marathon, and she had missed it. At first, I was disappointed. I so badly wanted to make her proud, but I quickly realized it didn't matter. I had trained alone so it almost felt fitting I finished alone. I didn't need my mom as a witness to know it had happened. The hardware around my neck and the lactic acid in my legs proved it was *real*. It was a lesson Elizabeth had experienced a century before me: the biggest rewards in life were the goals you accomplished while no one was watching.

Although no one I knew had seen me cross the finish line, thousands of smiling strangers had supported me in that final stretch. The more I thought about it, the more I realized my family *had* paid witness to it as well. They had cheered me on from the sidelines my entire life. Some things didn't need to be seen to know they were true, like my cosmic connection with Elizabeth. For all the times I had felt homesick or lonely, it was a reminder I was never truly alone.

In an Epsom salt bath later that night, I examined my nakedness. New muscles had formed. My stomach was concave with defined indents that ran vertically beneath my chest to my hips. Bathwater dripped off the end of my nipples and trickled along my abdominal lines, the way water ebbs and flows through rivers. I gazed down at the legs that had carried me for over forty-two kilometers, the mass of muscle a means of transportation. What used to be soft had sharpened. Bones jutted angularly. I was the same, yet different. Like a block of butter left in the fridge, somewhere along the way, I had hardened.

Self-doubt was beginning to transform into a newfound self-resilience. Before I fell into a deep sleep, I crossed "Run a Marathon" off of *Lou's Life List*. No matter what obstacles I encountered from thereon, I related the experience to running a marathon. If I could put in the hard work, dedication, and persevere through that mental and physical challenge, I could accomplish anything. It was a marked shift where I began asking less WWED and more WWID: what would *I* do?

Nearly a year later, I found myself back in Elisabetta Ricci's office. Our relationship had organically evolved into one of mentor-mentee and pseudo-mother-daughter. I was up for another promotion. There wasn't a role currently available at my level in New York, but there was a job in London. I wasn't supposed to have "favorite children" when it came to the European markets, but the Arden London office was hard not to fawn over. Located between Oxford Circus and Tottenham Court Road, the team was lovely, and the office was located in a lively part of the city. Whenever I visited for work, they put me up at the Marylebone, a boutique hotel in the posh Mayfair area. It reminded me of being back in the hustle and bustle of Manhattan, except with better accents and an undeniable British charm.

Without hesitation this time, I accepted the London offer. I was starting to trust myself more when a door of opportunity opened, to always walk through. There was a rapid sequence of action as Dominique in HR helped me procure visa paperwork and find a flat in Mayfair (the domain name for my third blog iteration was almost too easy: *Manhattan, Matterhorn, and Mayfair Maven*; the alliteration could live on).

A few months later, after I had mentally and physically prepared to move to London, Elisabetta dangled a shiny new carrot in front of me. Breaking news: a position had become available on the Celebrity and Designer Global Fragrance team…in Manhattan. On one hand, this was my ticket home; on the other, what was home anymore? I wished then that I could hover above myself, like a ghost, and float forward into my future to see which fork in the road was the best choice in the grand scheme of my life—London or New York?

After careful deliberation, many pro/con lists, I accepted the Manhattan offer. It wasn't an easy conclusion, but there was no time to second-guess my decision, only a rapid series of action—an abundance of fresh paperwork arose, and I had to find a place to live in New York, STAT.

As luck would have it, my first roommate in the city, Laura, had since moved back to New York from London to work in digital marketing at Chanel and was on the hunt for a roomie. She found us a three-hundred-fifty square-foot apartment at 529 Broome Street in SoHo. There was a makeshift cardboard wall separating our rooms, and it was on the fifth floor of a walk-up (no elevator), but we didn't care; the location was perfect, and rent was reasonable for New York standards.

Within a matter of days, I had gone from *Mayfair Maven* back to *Manhattan Maven*, and from solo living to shacked up. While London would have been a grand adventure, there was something in my bones that told me it was time to return to New York City, the place where it all started.

My last day at the Geneva office, the wine and waterworks flowed at my farewell lunch. Those people had become my family, and that place had become my second home. Even my French had vastly improved, reminding me how much I had learned along the way. Like Mary Poppins, who only stayed in one place until the winds changed, I felt as though I had accomplished all I had set out to do in Geneva. Throughout history, especially during WWII, Switzerland was a safe haven, and living up to its reputation, behind the red flag, I, too, found refuge.

My final weekend in Geneva, I walked along, trying to commit every last morsel of the mountainside city to memory. I savored my tiny espresso, waved forlornly to the swans, and absorbed each cobblestone of the quaint city that had once felt so foreign but was now so familiar.

Cities have such a profound effect on those that come to them, yet in return, they show only apathy. Once I left, I would be forgotten. Someone new would move into my pied-à-terre and take my place in the metropolitan melting pot. I would miss Geneva, even though I knew it wouldn't miss me back. But I guess that's *amour*.

For the last time, I walked by the flower clock. The begonias had begun to wilt, and Lake Geneva looked like glass in the background. The way the powerful Jet d'Eau hit the water made it appear as though the fountain was rebounding off of cement when in reality, the stream continued plunging far below eye level. There was a rainbow mist in its wake, another trick of the light. It reminded me of the iceberg analogy: how people were mesmerized by the external beauty of the Jet d'Eau, yet the true extent of its power was hidden beneath the surface.

I examined the flower clock in motion, mesmerized by its steady rhythm. *Tick. Tock. Tick. Tock.* I watched as the metal blades made their circuitous journey, never stopping, never-ending as the hands marked a new revolution. Clocks make time visually appetizing; humans created them so time could be worn on the wrist, hung on a wall, checked on a phone, or admired from a garden in Geneva. Time has become a touchable, traceable, transferrable accessory, but in truth, the perpetual passage of time is invisible to the naked eye. The benefits cannot be seen, only felt—as I was discovering to be true with things that mattered most in life.

Adulthood in Geneva began full of possibility and with the assumption that I would continue to up-level by blindly following Elizabeth's lead, as I had done in my internships. But by the end, my views tapered to something increasingly introspective—and the realization that I, alone, was responsible for my life.

Part III
LEGACY
New York, New York

"The desire for beauty is not all vanity. In fact, I believe vanity is the least part of it. The most important gift that beauty brings to a woman is not beauty itself, but a **cloak of courage**."

—Elizabeth Arden

Chapter 15

The Nifty Fifties

New York and Los Angeles
1950–1955

The 1950s in New York was a golden time in the city's history and for the beauty industry. There was a future-focused mindset of prosperity post-war; the economy was booming and progress went vertical. Slick glass-and-steel office towers began to replace the ziggurat, "wedding cake" style buildings in midtown. Times Square was not a tourist mecca but a ritzy date-night spot for New Yorkers to enjoy a steak dinner at Tad's Steakhouse (where a T-bone, baked potato, garlic bread, and tossed salad cost $1.09) and a movie at the Mayfair Theater, whose marquee sign showcased the names of Hollywood's biggest stars from Joan Crawford to James Dean.

From the outside, Manhattan appeared to be the mecca of the world, but beyond the shiny exterior, there was an undercurrent of unrest. The rich were getting richer, but there was an influx of poverty, racial segregation, and the dawn of the Civil Rights Movement and the Cold War. Suburbanization incentivized couples to move to the city's outskirts to raise families, resulting in the "baby boom." However, the cultural push for procreation and domesticity had an isolating effect on women, confining them to the perimeters while their husbands continued to work in the city. Media messaging like "Femininity begins at home," "Remind her it's a man's world," "At least you didn't burn the beer, dear!," and "The harder a wife cooks and cleans, the cuter she looks!" urged women to leave the workforce and embrace their role as housewives and mothers. The idea was hardly a new one, but there was a growing dissatisfaction for women who wanted a more fulfilling life. Ambitious, career-driven women who *also* wanted a family were discouraged and disadvantaged by the institutions employing them without maternity leave or advancement opportunities. In Betty Friedman's *The Feminine Mystique*, she argued that the 1950s suburban boom was "burying women alive," which contributed, in part, to the rebirth of the feminist movement in the 1960s.

The beauty industry was in full bloom, but the migration of women to the suburbs meant a dip in regular, in-person visits at the Fifth Avenue Red Door Spa. More than ever, Elizabeth understood the need for women to carve out time for themselves, so she created a "Day of Beauty" itinerary for women to recreate an Arden Red Door Spa day at home. In a *New York Times* feature, Elizabeth wrote: "I'm revealing my recipe for those unable to receive pampering at my pink-and-blue Fifth Avenue salon so you can treat yourself at home. Start with a simple breakfast: boiled egg, orange juice, toast, and coffee, while reading the morning paper. Next on the serve-yourself-salon agenda is a facial with a bowl of ice cubes, my cleansing cream and skin lotion, followed by my makeup routine. Allow adequate time to recharge before facing the demands of your family," said Elizabeth.

With more disposable income and wartime rationing over, the luxury makeup market took off—and Elizabeth Arden was at the helm. Hollywood's silver screen starlets, like Elizabeth Taylor, Marilyn Monroe, Audrey Hepburn, Grace Kelly, Natalie Wood, Doris Day, and more heavily influenced the cosmetic trends. Cream and liquid foundations were set with a powder and then a rose-colored blush was added to the cheeks for what was known as the "mask effect," a heavily made-up, yet flawless looking complexion. Thick, full brows with a strong arch were popularized by Audrey Hepburn and Elizabeth Taylor, and bold, defined lips in reddish-pink hues were in style. The doe-eyed look of the 1940s gave way to the cat eye in the 1950s, with black eyeliner, eye shadow, and mascara. Arden launched the best-selling Eye Stopper eye pencil with its own sharpener (one of the first), and sets of false lashes, made of natural hair woven on fine silk, flew off the shelves. Elizabeth's marketing prowess kicked in with her

"Two is Better than One" campaign that promoted the practice of blending two lipstick colors for the launch of Arden's Duet Lipsticks: a double-headed tube in coordinated shades that came in a bejeweled case. Arden's Looking-Glass Lipstick, with a built-in, rolling mirror, was also a popular product for easy touch-ups on-the-go.

"Hormones" became a trendy buzzword in skincare marketing, so Elizabeth created the Ardena Special Hormone Cream and Joie de Vivre Cream. "A new combination of natural estrogenic substances adds vitalizing hormones to help replenish aging tissues and restore your complexion to radiant loveliness," read one ad. At her Red Door Spa, clinicians used organic ingredients, and Arden's "Egg and Oil" facial (exactly as it sounds) became a sought-after treatment.

Teenagers emerged as a new consumer market in the 1950s, the first generation to grow up with TVs in their household (subsequently influenced by commercials and product placements), with spending power from allowance and odd jobs. Elizabeth's clientele was mostly wealthy, middle-aged to elderly women who had grown up with her, but in an attempt to appeal to the changing styles of the decade, she added "perms," and hair highlighting services to the hairdressing arm of her salons and launched a new cleanser called "Ardena Complexion Clear for Young Moderns" for acne-prone skin targeted at teens. Elizabeth also shot a campaign with college-aged women at her Maine Chance Health Spa and offered a reduced rate, from $500 to $200 a week, to promote the idea of a fun "girls' getaway" for the debutante set. The idea never took off like Elizabeth hoped, as many high-school and college-aged women married young, moved to the 'burbs, and were morally shamed for leaving the care of the children with their husbands (more often it was a babysitter) to indulge in a spa weekend with their friends.

Before leaping headfirst into television advertising, Elizabeth tried her hand at radio. Elizabeth's friend and *Vogue* editor Edna Woolman Chase hosted a popular radio show, "Luncheon at the Waldorf," where she interviewed people over lunch at Manhattan's Waldorf Astoria hotel and Elizabeth was featured as a guest. On the show, Edna introduced her to the listeners: "She's the richest self-made woman in America, building an industry independent of masculine aid, holding onto it against the encroachment of banks and other syndicates, yet hides her brains and poor past behind a baby face and practiced voice." Elizabeth was stunned that Edna had so astutely seen through her façade—when had the veneer slipped? Elizabeth worried her unmasking on air might make the press dig further into her past, but there were no public repercussions.

Elizabeth loved radio as a format, but preferred to be the interviewer, rather than the guest in the hot seat. She snagged a thirteen-week contract with NBC to host The Elizabeth Arden Radio Show. On the weekly segment, Elizabeth covered a new cultural topic and answered callers' questions related to beauty and lifestyle, much like a modern-day podcast. Eddy Duchin's orchestra performed the opening and closing musical sequence, and Elizabeth shamelessly plugged her products throughout. Ever the perfectionist, Elizabeth wrote and rewrote her scripts several times before she was satisfied, much to the frustration of the production crew. Despite her best efforts and enthusiasm, The Elizabeth Arden Radio Show failed to catch on, as radio was a medium for the mass market and not a good fit with Elizabeth's prestige brand. Her thirteen-week contract was not renewed.

After dabbling in radio, Elizabeth became captivated by the newfangled invention of television. "There will be nothing but television after the war, I feel sure, and it's good to get in on the beginning," she famously predicted before WWII. In 1948, 90 percent of people in the US had never seen a television program, but after a massive advertising push that marketed TV sets to suburban families, more than 7.3 million were sold by 1950. Elizabeth was eager to leverage new technologies to reach new audiences, but the challenge for marketing makeup on TV was that the transmissions were all in black and white (until the 1960s), so Elizabeth's gorgeous pigments, hues, and colors were wasted. However, the film industry had progressed from silent monochromatic movies to higher-quality, widescreen Technicolor pictures by the 1950s. The cinema was a weekly escape for people wanting to be transported on a glitzy adventure for a few hours, like *An American in Paris*, which won seven Academy Awards in 1951. Attractive, starry-eyed dreamers flocked to Tinsel Town to make it on the big screen.

Elizabeth recognized the power of color cinema and desperately wanted to break into Hollywood, so she created "Screen and Stage Makeup," a line of cosmetics for professional use on movie sets and in theatre productions:

LIGHTS! CAMERA! ACTION! BEAUTY!
Elizabeth Arden sets the stage with beauty.

The great stars of Hollywood have found the answer to the relentless cameras and hot lights with my Screen and Stage makeup, a complete departure from ordinary heavy greasepaint. It is perspiration proof without clogging pores, photographically superb before footlights, and clings to the skin for hours without renewal.

Arden's Screen and Stage line couldn't compete with Max Factor's Pan-Cake makeup, a matte foundation with a lightweight finish that resolved the reflection issues on Technicolor film sets. Elizabeth tried to extend Screen and Stage makeup for general use at "that extra-special party, masquerade gala, or professional photography session," but retailers were (rightly) convinced people wouldn't convert to this formula, and her clients' preferred the original Arden cosmetics.

In 1953, Elizabeth was in Los Angeles, California, to visit her Red Door Spa at 3933 Wilshire Boulevard and attend the premiere of *How to Marry a Millionaire* on behalf of her client and friend, Marilyn Monroe, who had won Hollywood's Fastest Rising Star in 1952. Elizabeth and Marilyn shared the same beauty philosophy, that makeup was meant to be an accessory to one's natural state and provide a moment of self-care before braving the world. "I want to grow old having the courage to be loyal to the face I have. Lipstick and mascara are like clothes; they improve my looks as much as a nice gown," said Marilyn. On the day of the premiere, Elizabeth sent one of her Red Door stylists ahead to Marilyn's third-floor suite at the Beverly Hills Hotel to do waxing and bring eight sets of false lashes (a signed pink receipt says Marilyn paid $20.60). Marilyn's personal makeup artist, Whitey Snyder, prepped her skin with Arden's Eight Hour Cream to keep it soft, hydrated, and glowing; lined her eyes with the Eye Stopper eyeliner in black; used the Ardena stick shadow in White Luster up to her brow bone as a base, followed by the Ardena cream shadows in Autumn Smoke and Pearly Blue; false lashes; and a swipe of Arden's berry-orange red lipstick. Marilyn spritzed on Chanel No. 5 (Elizabeth hadn't been able to convert her to Blue Grass) and added dangling diamond earrings before being sewn into an ivory crepe-de-chine dress, with long white evening gloves and matching fox stole and muff. Marilyn described the premiere "as the most beautiful night of my life." *How to Marry a Millionaire* went on to gross over $2.5 million, and Marilyn, who had received third billing in the movie behind Lauren Bacall and Betty Grable, was a breakout star and became the top-billed actress of the decade.

In 1955, Marilyn moved to New York from Los Angeles to study at the Actor's Studio, temporarily staying at the Waldorf Astoria, while Elizabeth helped her find an apartment at 444 East 57th Street in Sutton Place (where Bessie had lived) and a ten-minute cab ride from both the Fifth Avenue Red Door Spa and Elizabeth's apartment. After a short-lived marriage to Joe DiMaggio (her second husband), Marilyn was the mistress of playwright Arthur Miller until the press discovered the affair, and Arthur left his wife to marry Marilyn at a courthouse in White Plains, New York. By the mid-fifties, Marilyn was a media darling and hounded relentlessly by paparazzi who staked outside the Arden Red Door Spa and Elizabeth's penthouse to capture a shot of the movie star.

The invention of the flashbulb and portable 35mm Leica camera made candid ("unflattering") photography of public figures all the rage during the golden age of photojournalism. Photographers captured Marilyn in a series of photographs outside of the Red Door Spa on Fifth Avenue, gazing up admiringly at the oversized red door, and even a sneaky shot of her inside the plant-filled pink lobby. Paparazzi was a new phenomenon for Elizabeth who was used to having more autonomy over when and how she presented herself to the press. Although she wasn't hounded as aggressively as Marilyn, she wasn't used to her unauthorized image being splashed across magazines and newspapers— but more troublesome to Elizabeth was how the tabloid images held up a mirror to the visible signs of aging she could no longer hide. Elizabeth was seventy-seven in 1955, and despite her religious beauty routines, the candid reflections of her appearance in photographs demoralized her. *Years later, the same could be said of social media—no matter how good someone feels about themselves in "real life," scrutiny over images on the internet, especially in comparison to others, negatively affects self-esteem.*

Paparazzi and tabloids were a part of the new cultural zeitgeist, and Elizabeth realized she had no choice but to adapt or risk getting left behind. Instead of shying away, she took matters into her own hands. Long before the invention of Photoshop, Elizabeth began trying to take control of her public image by sending lists of extensive retouches to photographers at every major media outlet. Retouching in those days could be done directly on the negatives using a piece of cotton or leather to carefully scrape away dark shadows and facial lines with powdered chalk, but it was cumbersome work and rarely used. Elizabeth's request for retouching was denied, so she sent over a small selection of "approved headshots" she had curated in lieu of paparazzi "candids."

At home, where she had more sovereignty over her visual representation, Elizabeth commissioned artists to paint large-scale portraits of her, with strict stipulations that they take liberties in smoothing her skin and adding rouge to her cheeks for an overall youthful appearance. In

1955, Elizabeth hired Simon Elwes, recommended by Queen Elizabeth II, as he had painted portraits of many prominent figures in history and was favored by the British royal family. Elizabeth wore a red and white Nina Ricci dress for the several sittings it took to complete the portrait. In the end, Elizabeth absolutely hated how she looked. Simon Elwes framed it for her anyway, but she refused to show the portrait publicly.

Marilyn continued to be a loyal Arden lover, but her friendship with Elizabeth faded by the latter half of the decade. Marilyn began partying with a younger crowd and started relying heavily on drugs and alcohol. Publicly, she was maintaining a picture-perfect façade, but behind closed doors, Marilyn was having issues in her marriage, suffering from depression, anxiety, chronic insomnia, and mercurial mood swings. One of the most beautiful women in the world struggled with low self-esteem and severe self-doubt, which serves as a stark reminder that true beauty begins within—and when women are free to be their whole selves, respected for the magnificence of their multitudes.

- LOU -

Back in New York, I felt a familiar jolt of electricity, the same one I had experienced as an eighteen-year-old intern arriving for the first time. The streets steeped in historical significance; my footprints stamped the same ground as generations of dreamers and achievers who came before me. It was eerily comforting to know we were all just moving particles through time. The faded signs, alleyway graffiti, limestone buildings, and water towers dotting the skyline were relics of our shared past.

My previous internships had lasted the length of the smoggiest months, from May to September, in the sweltering heat of the beast, so Manhattan and summer were intrinsically linked for me, but after moving from Geneva, I got to experience the city in all its shapes and seasons. I had always been dazzled by New York's shiny shell, but like a snail in spring, there would be times when the ugliness of its under-belly was exposed.

Returning to the Arden office in Union Square made me feel like an alumnus at homecoming. The hallways were familiar, but it took a minute to get back into the swing of things. The Global Celebrity and Designer Fragrance Marketing team (a mouthful to say and an even more cumbersome email signature) was exciting new territory for me. I attended "Scent School" at International Flavors and Fragrances (IFF), an olfactorium where my team and I learned about fragrance notes and experimented with scent designs in the lab. Fragrances have top, middle, and bottom notes—the top is what you smell when you first spray it, but over time, the notes evolve and combine with your natural pheromones. I learned that all fragrances are unisex; the difference between a woman's perfume and a man's cologne is a marketing myth used to sell bottles. The chemistry of mixing musks and florals, blending masculine and feminine notes was fascinating and made me feel like Elizabeth in her early years, creating formulas in the back-office laboratory on Fifth Avenue. We studied Arden's Mémoire Chérie, which had been Elizabeth's personal favorite scent and won the Grand Coupe D'or in 1960, as one of France's finest fragrance, but it was discontinued in 1980. Mémoire Chérie was a cool floral with green undertones, notes of bergamot, neroli, fresh apricot, chamomile, soft honey rose, violet, amber, musk, and vetiver. I loved how scents evoked moods and piqued memories; Mémorie Chérie transported me back in time and gave me a sense of what Elizabeth had smelled like, a tangible trace of her essence.

Celebrity fragrance lines weren't popular in Elizabeth's era, but over time, as celebrities starting morphing into "lifestyle brands," one of the first steps was creating a signature scent. Elizabeth Taylor led the way for the celebrity fragrance category and was the first to make it a viable, sustainable business. Elizabeth Taylor, a loyal friend and fan of Elizabeth Arden, partnered with the company to create and distribute her signature fragrance line. When she launched Passion in 1987, it was an instant success and she became the first celebrity to win a Fifi award (the Oscars of fragrances). White Diamonds was her next runaway hit in 1991 and is still considered one of the best-selling fragrances of all time. Other fragrances in her collection include: Violet Eyes, Forever Elizabeth, Gardenia, and Diamonds & Sapphires. Elizabeth Taylor's fragrances did $1.5 billion in sales over thirty years as an Arden-owned celebrity line.

By the early 2000s, nearly every pop star and actor had a signature scent and the profitability for companies like Arden, who celebrities tapped to create, produce, and distribute the fragrances, was huge. In 2013, when I was working at Arden, celebrity and designer fragrances composed nearly 75 percent of the company's sales, while the Arden branded makeup and skincare products were roughly 25 percent.

The celebrity and designer fragrance portfolio that I worked on included Britney Spears, Hilary Duff, Taylor Swift, Justin Bieber, Mariah Carey, Ed Hardy, John Varvatos, Juicy Couture, BCBG, and Elizabeth Taylor (my grandmothers fangirled over the White Diamonds gift sets I sent them). For each celebrity, their management team sent over "briefs" (descriptions of what the celebrities liked and disliked), and my team would create a library of scent compositions, conceptualize bottle designs, and ad campaigns to fit each celebrity's brand identity. Some clients were more involved than others in the making of their namesake perfume, but they always had final approval. I knew the ins and outs of the marketing process, but dealing with celebrities (and their team of handlers and managers) required an added layer of diligence in working with big personalities while still churning out quality products. I learned in "Scent School" that while individual tastes are varied, the masses are predictable. Vanilla, light florals, and musk were usually guaranteed to be commercial successes in the celebrity fragrance arena, as they were "sweet, but not too sweet."

The heyday of celebrity and designer fragrances peaked around 2011, but would fall out of fashion by the end of the decade, with indie brands like Le Labo becoming popularized. The dip in celebrity perfumes began once they trickled down from aspirational items to kitschy objects sold in Walmart and Kohls. People were initially interested in the commodification of their favorite singer or actor's likeness, but if the stars didn't wear the scents themselves, the appeal was fleeting.

Britney Spears was a notable exception to the rule, and little-known fact—she built a billion-dollar empire with her fragrance line at Elizabeth Arden. Britney's first perfume, Curious, launched in 2004, and became the top-selling fragrance across all categories, selling over five hundred million bottles and making $100 million in sales in its first year. Over Britney's twenty-plus year career, she sold one hundred million records—her perfume sold five times more units in twelve months. In 2013, when I was on the team, Britney's fragrances had grossed over $1.5 billion worldwide, and she released a song called "Perfume" about leaving her signature scent on an ex-boyfriend—the music video was a product placement paradise. Today, Britney has twenty-eight perfumes and counting.

Juicy Couture and Ed Hardy were also interesting brands to work on in 2013, as their fashion houses were suffering post Paris Hilton and Kim Kardashian hype, but like bellbottoms and record players, trends repeated themselves, and the fragrances were in a cycle of being "cool," "retro," and "nostalgic" again. Everything, including people, can experience a renaissance.

When celebrities came into the office for the final stages of the process, I was initially starstruck, in the wide-eyed sense of seeing someone you *think* you know, but the celebrity mystique was soon lost. By getting a peek behind the curtain of their double-lives, I felt empathetic; the exhaustion of constantly "being on," adhering to expectations, of maintaining a faultless exterior—their humanity stifled behind curated personas.

I learned how delicate and fragile identities are. People deserved to be handled with care, unwrapped gently and examined from all angles, without judgment—but put anyone under society's harsh microscope, and they suffer like ants beneath a magnifying glass on a sunny day. Working on celebrity fragrances was a lesson in how others can never truly know us as intimately as we know ourselves.

Outside of work, Laura and I settled into our apartment at the corner of Broome and Thompson in SoHo (an acronym for **So**uth of **Ho**uston) above a lesbian bar called The Dalloway, after the Virginia Woolf character. We transformed it into a bohemian chic abode on a budget ("Boho in SoHo"), wallpapering the fridge in funky designs to match the living room décor, stringing twinkle lights, and hanging hand-painted wooden signs that said "LAURA" and "LOUISE" above our side-by-side bedroom doors. We had a shelving unit called the Diva Station, as by the nature of our jobs at Chanel and Arden, we accumulated a lot of samples. Our fairly low-maintenance morning ritual consisted of a pit stop at the Diva Station on the way to work, spritzing and spraying each other with various lotions and scents. Laura's boyfriend dubbed our apartment "The Dollhouse," based on its small square footage and in reference to us being floppy rag dolls feigning adulthood and playing house (he wasn't wrong).

SoHo had elements of Geneva's Vieille Ville with its cobblestone alleyways, cast-iron architecture, tucked-away boutiques, cozy cafés, and celebrity residents who hobbled outside in the early hours like bridge trolls with good bone structure, to get their caffeine fix before the weekend tourists descended and demanded selfies (the age of the autograph had dwindled, but paparazzi were ever-present).

I purchased my first iPhone (with a built-in camera!) after being cell-free for nearly two years, but never took to the increased cultural reliance on texting. I hated the daily pressure of being reactive to a device; I preferred being left to my own devices. How did anyone accomplish anything with that hunk of metal beeping and buzzing nonstop? While in Switzerland, I had craved connection, but now that I had contacts at my fingertips, I almost missed the anonymity.

However, I was thrilled at the prospect of taking photos on-the-go. It was the golden days of a relatively new app called Instagram, without ad-riddled feeds or "influencers," as people posted unfiltered photos in the moment. The philosophy of social media—to capture memories and connect with friends and family—was similar to why I started blogging, so I joined the 'gram using the same handle as my reincarnated blog: @ManhattanMaven. The instant gratification of having a portal to people's lives was stimulating, but like my blogs, it was easy to forget social media was still a curated version of reality; a highlight reel, not the full story.

Blogs had continued to increase in popularity since I first began in 2008, but "blogger" as a profession was still far from mainstream; it was a place where the personal essay, as an art form, found room to flourish. Hitting "publish" on my words catapulted my private writing practice into the public sphere. With an audience, I was more inclined to organize my anecdotes and opinions into structured paragraphs with opening and closing statements and articulated points of reference, whereas in my red journals, my stream of consciousness flowed freely, unencumbered from social constructs.

I clung to my red notebooks (by now I had amassed a neat stack) as a sacred place to house my truest thoughts. I lived somewhere in between the extremes of two realms: the confident, career-climbing businesswoman I presented on my blog/Instagram, and the guileless girl trying to figure life out in her journals. Years later, I recognized another thread that connected my presentation of self to Elizabeth's a century prior—we both tried to control the narrative of our public-facing personas, but along the way, our real selves had become endangered species.

For the finishing touches in my Broome Street bedroom, I tracked down on eBay the 1946 *Time* magazine featuring Elizabeth as the first businesswoman on the cover, with a multi-paged article detailing as much about her supremacy in the beauty industry as her success in horse racing; monumental achievements that seemed to have faded from mainstream consciousness. I framed the historic cover and hung it on my wall alongside gorgeous black-and-white prints I found of Marilyn Monroe in cat-eyed sunglasses and a fur coat in front of the Arden Red Door Spa on Fifth Avenue. Whenever I felt myself being seduced by the city, as one cannot escape its around-the-clock temptations, the framed *Time* cover reminded me to stay focused on my end-goal of becoming a corporate success at Arden. Otherwise, who was I?

I flew to Toronto for my first Canadian Christmas in years to see family and friends, where, unbeknownst to anyone, Logan and I kissed at a New Year's Eve party (on Elizabeth's birthday). Seeing Logan in person made all of my old feelings for him come flooding back. We exchanged numbers (now that I had a cell phone again) and discussed the possibility of visiting since we were only a one-hour flight a part, but after I returned to New York, time got away from us as the seasons shifted from winter to spring to summer. Logan quoted Ferris Bueller in one of his texts and I wrote the saying in my red journal, as it described how I felt in that particular phase: "Life was moving pretty fast, and if I didn't stop to look around, I just might miss it."

Chapter 16

Think Pink

New York

1955–1960

In a visionary move, Elizabeth capitalized on the growing men's toiletry market (estimated to be a $150 million market in the 1950s, according to the *Wall Street Journal*), and she became the first major manufacturer of women's cosmetics to put out a men's line. In 1956, Elizabeth introduced Arden's first men's range, ARDEN FOR MEN, packaged in gold and charcoal containers with the logo of a horseman and scented with sandalwood. The line consisted of talc, foam shaving cream, aftershave lotion, cologne and hand and bath soap, and later included other products like stick deodorant and lip balm. While many of Arden's male sales staff scoffed at the idea of beauty products for men, Elizabeth forged ahead as planned. Unfortunately, she was *too* ahead of her time on marketing makeup to men, which still remains a relatively untapped market. ARDEN FOR MEN was a valiant effort, but a sign Elizabeth was starting to lose her Midas touch.

In 1957, Elizabeth experienced more loss with the death of Edna Woolman Chase. Her *New York Times* obituary made mention of Elizabeth's attendance at her funeral: "Leaders in the publishing, fashion, and society fields were among the four hundred people who attended the funeral for Edna Woolman Chase, editor emeritus of *Vogue* magazine, one of America's most formative figures in the world of fashion, and mother of Ilka Chase, writer and actress. Mrs. Chase, whose home was at 333 East Fifty-seventh Street, died of a heart attack in Sarasota, Florida at the age of 80. Among those close to Mrs. Chase notably in attendance at the service were Mrs. Natica Nast Warburg, Mrs. Sally Kirkland, Miss Nancy White, and Miss Elizabeth Arden."

A bright spot that year was the release of Arden's "Think Pink!" campaign, which inspired the famous scene of the same name in the 1957 blockbuster, *Funny Face*, starring Fred Astaire and Audrey Hepburn. The romantic musical comedy was about a fashion magazine editor (an homage to Edna Woolman Chase) who discovered a shy bookseller (played by Audrey Hepburn) at a bookshop in Greenwich Village as the next big face in fashion, for women were rarely depicted as "both beautiful and intellectual." While filming in New York, Audrey Hepburn was pampered at the Red Door Spa, and Arden's "Think Pink!" ads were everywhere: "Elizabeth Arden thinks pink! Hot pinks, cool pinks, blush pinks, dusty pinks, pinks the color of flamingos, and bougainvilleas lend a becoming glow to every complexion."

Nearing the end of the 1950s, Elizabeth was in her late seventies and had lost Bessie, Lanie, and now Edna. She still had her beloved Teddy Haslam and sister Gladys, but they lived in Europe, and she was achingly lonely. Elizabeth hired her youngest niece, Pattie, to move in with her. Pattie adored her aunt Liz and agreed to be her live-in companion, moving into the guestroom at 834 Fifth Avenue penthouse.

To ring in 1958, Elizabeth attended a New Year's Eve party in Lexington, Kentucky, hosted by her wealthy neighbors and equestrian friends Leslie Combs and his wife, Dorothy, heir to the Colombia Gas and Electric Company fortune. The Combs were renowned on the racing circuit and owned Spendthrift Farm, a sprawling one hundred and twenty-seven acres in Lexington, where their annual New Year's Eve party was held. Leslie was the man responsible for advising Elizabeth about which thoroughbreds to purchase, including her beloved Kentucky Derby winner, Jet Pilot.

For the Combs' extravagant New Year's Eve party, Elizabeth chose a pink chiffon evening gown with delicate crystal beading and her signature string of pearls. Couples waltzed to a live band and sipped champagne cocktails. At 11 p.m., Elizabeth told her hosts she was feeling under the weather and got her chauffeur to bring the car around early.

As the clock struck midnight, Elizabeth lay awake in her pastel nightgown under her white satin duvet, with no illness except for a bout of insomnia. At the eleventh hour, she couldn't bear to spend her eightieth birthday in another room full of people, yet all alone.

At this time, Elizabeth turned down an offer from Scottish publisher Sir William Darling to write an autobiography about her, as she believed, despite being eighty years old, she was too young for a memoir. "They're for the elderly or the deceased," she said.

To commemorate fifty years since her arrival in Manhattan, she did an in-depth, sit-down interview with *The Daily Record*:

I sat with Miss Arden in her office, where one wall was covered with photographs of racehorses and the opposite was lined with sedate flower prints, while her desk was littered with lipstick tubes, new cosmetic samples, and stacks of business documents.

"I'm not here very much, so I've just never bothered to fix up my office," Miss Arden explained.

She is not in the office, her employees explain admiringly, because she insists on personally looking in on all departments of her vast beauty empire, which she built in the past 50 years from a few jars of cream, an idea, and a loan. She also likes to supervise the training of her racehorses. She is likely to visit her stables at Belmont race track before breakfast in the morning and whip up a new lipstick shade in her laboratory before noon.

Under the name Mrs. Elizabeth N. Graham, the beauty expert owns the Maine Chance racing stables. She is an exacting employer in her Fifth Avenue business office and a sentimental stable owner who calls her horses "my darlings."

"It is much better to look natural, whatever you do," Miss Arden said, discussing the progress women have made in recent years in retaining youthful faces and figures. "But you must spend some time on yourself each day," she continued.

At an age generally estimated to be around seventy (she'll neither confirm nor deny), Miss Arden fortunately is an excellent example of her teachings, for she looks at least twenty years younger. Her formula, she says, is "10 minutes of exercise and stretching each morning, 10 minutes devoted to the face and at night it's important to remove makeup and apply proper creams. I average only a few hours of sleep each night, I'm still trying to learn how to relax," she added. When it comes to her future, she hints at no succession plans. "I laugh at the threatening finger of Old Age," she said.

- LOU -

Sheryl Sandberg's book, *Lean In*, was published in March 2013 and widely touted as an inspirational guide for women on how to lean into your career. I eagerly read it cover to cover, hoping for motivation on my climb to the top of the corporate food chain, but for some reason, it quietly shook the shaky foundation of my house of cards.

I began an internal audit regarding my ideal future and started thinking about what life would look like as a Manhattan CEO with a family. Elizabeth had abandoned the "family" part of the success equation altogether (whether by choice or circumstantial), so I couldn't look to her story for advice on this important life scale.

In Elizabeth's generation, women were only expected to fulfill the role of mother and wife, whereas Sheryl Sandberg pointed out, we had come so far as to recognize motherhood as a small part, but not all of a woman's worth. I was thankful to have more choices than Elizabeth when it came to how I wanted to identify, but as I observed the reality of what it meant to dominate both realms, I struggled with the practicality of how in the hell I could possibly "do it all," and "do it all *well*."

My interpretation of *Lean In* was that if I wanted to become a CEO, there would have to be major sacrifices in my personal life. Subconsciously, I had always *known* that from witnessing Elizabeth's rise to the top, but as I grew older and took better note of my surroundings, I recognized the toll these dueling pressures took on women in my direct environment.

Rachel Wilson was the new vice president of Global Skincare Marketing. She was sharp-witted, savvy, stunning, and the company's Home Shopping Network (HSN) darling. Her Julia Roberts megawatt smile could have sold out used toothbrushes in minutes. Rachel commuted into the city from Connecticut, where she lived with her handsome husband, two toddlers, and a new baby—the framed photo of them on her desk looked straight out of a J. Crew ad. Polished and powerful, Rachel made marriage, motherhood, and executive management look like a breeze. I was in awe of her, but I was reminded later that when anything *looked* easy on the outside; there was a lot of hard work going on behind the scenes.

Midmorning at work one day, I exited the stall of the ladies' washroom and washed my hands beside Rachel, who stood at the sink reapplying her lipstick.

"OH FUCK," she said out of nowhere.

I never pictured such a composed, perfectly-put-together woman like Rachel swearing, so it caught me off guard. I looked in the communal mirror at her reflection and saw a giant wet patch on her silk blouse.

"Oh my God, I am so sorry! Did I splash you?" I asked, mortified. Had I zoned out washing my hands and sprayed *the* Rachel Wilson with water?

"No, no, my breast milk is leaking," she said, while attempting to dab the spot dry with paper towel. "I have a meeting right now, but I need to go pump," she said.

"Can I do anything?" I asked, feeling helpless.

"Actually, would you mind going to conference room 7B and telling them I'm caught up on a call and will try to make the tail end of the meeting when I can?"

"Absolutely, no problem," I responded, happy to be of service.

"Thanks, you're an angel," she said as I dashed out the door.

After delivering the message, I grabbed a cup of coffee in the office kitchen and headed back to my desk, when I passed by the janitorial supply closet. The door was slightly ajar, and inside, sitting on top of an overturned mop bucket, was Rachel with a contraption strapped to her chest that looked like something out of Frankenstein's laboratory. The machine sounded like a wheezing donkey (*"hee-haw, hee-haw"*). Rachel gave me a subtle shrug, her expression forlorn as she pulled the door shut.

Over the next couple of years, I would witness my fair share of leaky breasts, mad dashes to the nearest fire-escape stairwell or janitor's closet, and women cutting their (already short) six-week maternity leave in half to return to the office early.

"I just couldn't stay away from work a minute longer," they would say, which I learned was code for "There's no way I'm letting my short-term substitute become my long-term replacement."

Freezing eggs was a painful, invasive, and expensive procedure that became a buzzed-about "solution" so high-achieving women could excel in their ambitious careers, which coincided with their prime childbearing years. While it was an advancement that offered another choice for women contemplating both careerhood and motherhood, to me, it also prolonged the pressures many women faced. Even with hired help, women, for the most part, bore the brunt of child raising and household duties, while maintaining a demanding, full-time jobs in the city. How on earth did women manage to nurture a career and a family at the same time? I internalized the message that it was important to *lean into* my career in my twenties and early thirties to be successful—but then what? Would I look up from my desk at thirty-five (forty?) and pick my private life up off the back burner and pluck my carton of embryos out of the freezer? I had worked in marketing for too long to unknow that what it felt like we were being fed, as a young generation of women with more opportunity than Elizabeth's era, that without systemic change, the shiny sales tactic of "having it all," seemed not just unsustainable, but on a track toward a breaking point.

In my red journal at this time, my musings reflected frustration with the systems that placed a dual burden on women and ways corporations could be restructured to include lactation rooms, on-site childcare, and "period days" in addition to "sick days." Witnessing how women had to adapt their needs to fit institutions created by men for men—even at a company like Arden with a predominantly female workforce—was formative in shaping my early thoughts about marriage, motherhood, and managing an empire. Those who did it all, like Rachel Wilson, were heroes to me, but also struck me with a mix of awe and dread. I was years away from starting my own family, but I was confused: to *lean in*, or not to *lean in*?

Outside of the office, I found myself avoiding large crowds and post-work drinks, preferring to retreat to the solitude of my bedroom, where I escaped into the confines of a book, blogged, or watched old movies on my laptop. I had a nostalgic obsession with 1950s films starring Marilyn Monroe and Audrey Hepburn: *Some Like it Hot, The Seven Year Itch, Roman Holiday, Funny Face, Sabrina,* and *Breakfast at Tiffany's.* In the aftermath of my life in Switzerland, I found I had come to appreciate aloneness, but I knew my inwardness couldn't last, for only the aggressive survived, and the passive perished in a city like New York. I had to relearn how to belong.

Chapter 17

Changing of the Guard

New York and London

1960–1963

When the swinging sixties entered the world's stage, Elizabeth had a hard time relating to the vibrant, sexually uninhibited culture of the 1960s. This new generation bought transistor radios, records (the new seven-inch EPs), and portable record players to listen to bands like The Beatles and the Rolling Stones. Lava lamps, banana-seated bicycles, beaded curtains, miniskirts, and pot were also popular. The youth of the 1960s dared to go bold with their cosmetic hues and painted their faces in avant-garde geometric strokes.

Elizabeth tried to attract a younger demographic by releasing "Sounds of Beauty," a vinyl record that came with the purchase of her products tailored for "Young Moderns," as she called the new cohort. The album had a voiceover of Elizabeth describing how to use her products, but unsurprisingly, it was not successful in attracting the groovy group.

Competition in the beauty industry intensified, and the beauty category became saturated with niche brands entering the space fighting for a scrap of the market share. Elizabeth's major rival had only been Helena Rubinstein, but there were new kids on the block. Charles Revson and his company, Revlon, catapulted into the cosmetic sphere with an enormous ad spend after WWII, launching Fire and Ice, the first ad campaign that overtly linked makeup with the concept "sex sells." In 1955, Charles had taken his company public and became a multimillionaire overnight. By the 1960s, every person in America knew the name Revlon after a successful promotional stint on the CBS game show *The $64,000 Question.* The neon "REVLON" sign above the contestants became one of the earliest and most successful product-placement campaigns.

Charles was known for his many mistresses and wild yacht orgies, but it was his professional prowess that worried Elizabeth, as Charles made no secret he was vying to overtake Arden's prestige territory. He went so far as to hire an ex-FBI agent to wiretap the lines of Arden's Fifth Avenue office to eavesdrop on her product innovation plans.

When the two moguls crossed paths at Le Pavillon restaurant in Manhattan, the maître d' knew to seat them on opposite ends. Elizabeth never warmed to Charles and referred to him only as "that man," when absolutely necessary. Revlon soon dominated the mass market, but Arden continued to reign supreme in the prestige space at high-end department stores and Red Door Spas worldwide.

Helena Rubinstein was having a harder time than Elizabeth keeping up with modern trends. Helena was eighty-eight years old in 1960, and the wear-and-tear on her brand was starting to show. "If you live long enough, you find you've either worn out your competitors or outlived them," said Elizabeth in relation to the battle of the brands.

Josephine Esther Mentzer, a feisty little firecracker from Queens, New York, quietly snuck onto the cosmetic scene, while Elizabeth was busy expanding her empire, operating two Maine Chance spas, and nurturing winning racehorses. Josephine had grown up idolizing Elizabeth, and took a page out of her idol's playbook by creating an alter ego and adopting the same name as her new company: Josephine Esther Mentzer became Estée Lauder. (She thought the French version of her middle name sounded fancy and tweaked her husband's original surname, Lauter).

For a few years, Estée slid under the radar, building her business from the ground up, the same way Elizabeth had done fifty years prior. She was a savvy saleswoman with a hands-on approach who easily charmed the cosmetic buyers at department stores. Her products filled a modern gap in the prestige market, as her formulas and packaging were new and innovative. Estée was described in media publications as "particularly attractive—small, blonde, busty, and bubbly." It wasn't until Estée's wildly successful Youth Dew took off at Bonwit Teller that Elizabeth took notice of the woman, whom the press referred to as "her younger doppelgänger." Age and time had caught up to Elizabeth, and her grip on her sovereign empire was slipping.

In 1961, Elizabeth mingled with Audrey Hepburn at the Red Door Spa while she played Holly Golightly in the film adaptation of *Breakfast at Tiffany's*. Elizabeth was enraptured with the storyline: country girl turned New York café socialite, as it mimicked her real-life narrative. While most books, movies, and television shows featured women as ornaments with supporting roles, *Breakfast at Tiffany's* was different, as the protagonist was not only female; she was complex, outspoken, and opinionated—someone who Elizabeth could see parts of herself in.

Marilyn Monroe, who divorced Arthur Miller the same year, had been Truman Capote's preferred choice for the part of Holly Golightly, but Paramount Pictures refused to cast her due to fears she was unreliable in showing up to set and remembering her lines. Marilyn's mental health had worsened, and she developed a dependency on amphetamines, barbiturates, and alcohol. After six years in Manhattan, Marilyn moved back to Los Angeles. She returned to New York on May 19, 1962, at John F. Kennedy's (JFK) request, to sing "Happy Birthday, Mr. President" at a Democratic fundraiser, also his early forty-fifth birthday celebration. JFK had met Marilyn at a dinner party at Bing Crosby's Palm Springs estate. Marilyn spent the day getting ready at Arden's Fifth Avenue Red Door Spa before shimmying onto the stage at Madison Square Garden. She shrugged off her fur coat to reveal a sheer, skintight dress with glittering rhinestones, and sang a breathy, sultry rendition. Tabloid gossip intensified that JFK and Marilyn Monroe were secret lovers, as the president's extramarital affairs were widely known, and his wife, Jackie Kennedy, was conveniently at the Loudon Hunt Horse Show in Virginia with the children. Elizabeth was in attendance at the after party that night at executive Arthur Krim's townhouse at 33

East 69th Street, where Marilyn and JFK were photographed speaking intimately, and it was largely speculated she stayed the night at JFK's thirty-fourth-floor suite at the Carlyle Hotel, where he used the warren of underground tunnels to sneak mistresses in and out to avoid detection. Three months after the purported affair, Marilyn Monroe died of a barbiturate overdose at her home in Los Angeles on August 4, 1962, at the age of thirty-six. A year later, on November 22, 1963, John F. Kennedy was assassinated in Texas at the age of forty-six. Elizabeth, who had been friendly with Marilyn and Jackie Kennedy, attended both funerals.

Elizabeth was deeply distraught in 1962 when Teddy Haslam, her oldest and dearest friend, died. Teddy had been an integral part of her European expansion with the flagship Red Door Spa on Bond Street, but above all else, he was her cherished friend, who walked her down the aisle at her wedding to Prince Evlanoff, and answered her calls at all hours of the night. Teddy was one of the few people who ever truly understood the real her. At age eighty-four, Elizabeth flew to London and personally oversaw and paid for all of Teddy's funeral proceedings. It was a changing of the guard, of sorts, resulting in a lingering melancholy that would stay with Elizabeth for the rest of her years.

- LOU -

Not drunk, but not yet sober, Laura and I clinked our plastic Gatorade bottles together, *"Cheers!"* We hadn't slept, and the cab speeding up Sixth Avenue was our last-ditch effort to get to work on time. I used to be the first one in and the last one out.

I had been in New York for nearly a year when my self-esteem started evaporating, like a pinprick in a bicycle tire. The deterioration was invisible from the outside (for the time being), but was wreaking havoc on me internally. The previous me, the responsible perfectionist who lived diligently by her day planner, took vitamins, went running, read books, and wrote stories, was emerging less and less. Instead, a new version of myself was appearing more and more: one who passed out in the previous night's makeup, was perpetually hungover, whose diet consisted mostly of coffee (in the morning) and wine (at night), and began avoiding everyone she cared about.

Between my blog self, my work self, my after-hours self and, my true self (wherever she was), it felt like I was a one-woman show, scarily out of sync. Dark circles rolled in under my eyes like a pack of Hell's Angels at a roadside diner. I was working hard and drinking harder. My face was dry and puffy from daily alcohol consumption, poor nutrition, and limited sleep. One morning, while brushing my teeth, I caught a glimpse of myself in the mirror. There were crevices, lines, and shadows I had never seen before.

Throughout our tenure as roommates, Laura coined many new terms and phrases. The most frequently used at the top of our vocabulary list were "peaks and troughs" and "PAB," which stood for post-alcohol blues. We were in a continuous cycle of chasing only "peaks"—adrenaline-pumping, serotonin-inducing events. But then, almost exclusively on Sundays, "PAB" would kick in, and we'd hit a "trough," the emotional crash and burn that followed. Our true feelings, ones of disillusionment that we tried to suppress with alcohol and jam-packed schedules, oozed out of our pores like molten lava.

Sitting cross-legged on the couch on Sundays, we would have real, honest conversations about what we missed back home in Canada. "I think I would be content to live in a cabin in the woods," I would trail off dazedly, "surrounded by colorful bookshelves, with one of those sliding ladders, like in *Beauty and the Beast*, where I could drink coffee and write books all day." When I daydreamed about my future, the scenes never included where I currently lived, what I currently did, or the people I was currently surrounded by—but I didn't connect those dots back then. A timeline was also, always, exclusively missing from our conversations—everything would happen "eventually," "someday," in the lofty, "distant future," as though by happenstance. Time was a luxury commodity in our twenties.

I received an email from Logan that he had a new girlfriend. His phrases were concise and cold, a speech pattern I didn't recognize from him. It made me want to melt into a puddle of my own bones. He signed off the last line with a reference to a Drive-By Truckers song: "Maybe, for us, the secret to a happy ending is knowing when to roll the credits." The line stuck with me because, at the time, I disagreed: I felt like we hadn't reached the cinematic climax when everything was about to work out. In my own naiveté, I had convinced myself our relationship sabbatical was more or less mutual, a way for us to have space and time to discover who we were as individuals; a means to an end, and in the end, we would end up together.

Logan deleted me from his phone, social media, and all other traces from his life. A strange phenomenon of modern dating, one Elizabeth never had to contend with, was being systematically erased online, deleted with the click of a mouse. To have felt so known by someone, and then to feel so unknown, was gut-wrenching. For a love that had once felt so infinite, so, too, did the pain of feeling forgotten, like none of it had existed at all. I kept replaying the narrative like I could rewrite the ending, but romantic rejection was a chemical crash, out of my control.

No one knew Logan and I had stayed so interconnected throughout the years, so I couldn't confide in anyone about the immense sadness his complete exit from my life brought to the forefront, as from the outside, family and friends thought we had broken up a couple years prior. Heartache hit me gently, then profoundly—memories were so deeply encoded, it took a long time to detach from them. Heart-healing happened the same way, and in time, I learned that it was healthy to leave a whisper of a hole in the heart; it left room for someone new to fill it back up again.

Eventually, I came to believe that closure was a benign concept and change was the only constant—and maybe, just maybe, *the secret to a happy ending was knowing when to roll the credits.*

Months later, I dipped my toe into the murky waters of Manhattan's dating pool. I was with Laura at a bar in the East Village when I met Ben. He was five years older than me, but in New York, everyone was basically the same age. Ben's brother was married to a New York City Rockette (a fact I found interesting despite it having nothing whatsoever to do with him). He had deep dimples and worked at an organic baby food company in Brooklyn, which made him an exciting divergence from the peacocking Wall Street suits.

I thought things were going well, when after several dates over the course of a few months, Ben ghosted me (a new millennial term that described a rather callous dating ritual where someone abruptly ceases all communication without explanation).

"It's the paradox of choice," I said to Laura. "With all these apps, the options are endless, or it's a glaring case of *He's Just Not That Into Me*," I reasoned. Had dating always been this hard?

"Don't torture yourself; on to the next," Laura said.

An hour and a bottle of wine later, Laura suggested we call Ben. She dialed his number through an app that blocked caller IDs. After a few rings, she left a voice mail:

"Hi, Benjamin. My name is Cleo, and I'd like to place an order for twelve hundred kegs of your finest organic breast milk. If you or someone from your team at Little Fuck Organics could respond at your earliest convenience, that'd be great," she said, and hung up.

Years later, Ben found me on the internet and sent a private message that said:

```
Hey! Hope all is well with you. Sorry for being such
a dick back in the day. I was going through a weird
time. Tell Laura, I mean Cleo, I'm still working on
fulfilling that order for twelve hundred kegs of our
finest organic breast milk.
```

Several months after the ghosting incident, Laura and I were leaving Houston Hall when a guy stopped us on our way out.

"Louise Johnson, is that you?" he asked.

"It's me," I responded, failing to recognize him.

"It's Jack Thomas. Not sure if you remember me, but we interned together at Arden a few years ago," the guy said.

"Oh my God, Jack, hi! Yes, of course I remember you," I said, although truthfully I hadn't recognized him. His hair had turned a dark auburn, and his scrawny boy build had transformed into a man's muscular physique. He was also dressed casually, in jeans and a T-shirt, not the flashy, expensive suit he wore when we were interns.

"I wasn't sure if it was you, but then I saw that beautiful smile," he said, laying it on thick. "Let me grab your number. I need to take you out for dinner to prove to you I'm not the douchebag I used to be," he said.

It had been a while since anyone had flirted with me, so although it was cheesy, I blushed and agreed to go out with him. Jack's conceitedness had seemingly turned into a confidence and persistence I found attractive. One dinner date turned into a handful, but quicker than it started, the brazen charm wore off, and Jack's patriarchal beliefs about women's place in society ("I'd hate if you made more money than me," "Ew, shave your legs,") grew intolerable. Our compatibility was scant, but I had welcomed the companionship. After a couple months I ended things. Like Ben before him, Jack faded from my life as easily as he had entered it. How strange it was that people came into our lives in blips, for a short while, until they were merely a part of our past, characters in a story we told about a particular phase in our lives. I wondered if Elizabeth ruminated on the fluidity of relationships as much as I did, or if she preferred it that way?

Chapter 18

Dr. Feelgood

New York and Ireland
1963–1966

The early sixties were off to a sad start for Elizabeth after Teddy Haslam's death, as more of those around her began to dwindle. By then, she had outlived all of her original employees and barely recognized the staff that roamed the halls of her 691 Fifth Avenue building. The press no longer courted her as much as they had at the height of her fame, but Elizabeth's travel schedule was just as grueling in the 1960s as it was throughout the 1930s. Elizabeth fell in love with air travel and couldn't believe how quickly she could be transported from one place to the next. Flying Pan Am, she donned her signature pink and pearls on a trip to Paris to visit Gladys, who continued to run the European operation like a well-oiled machine, and whose husband, Count Henri de Maublanc, had recently died of a heart attack.

Elizabeth hopped over to London, her second-favorite city after New York, to check on the Bond Street Red Door Spa, where Eight Hour Cream continued to fly off the shelves, but the place felt strange without Teddy Haslam there to greet her.

Seeking a change of scenery, Elizabeth journeyed to Ireland. She was becoming more impulsive in her old age and continued her pattern of coping with grief by indulging in real-estate therapy. After Bessie's funeral, she bought Maine Chance Farm, and after Teddy's funeral, she upped the ante by buying a castle in Ireland for $200,000— sight unseen.

The Barretstown Castle, outside of Dublin, came with over five hundred acres of rolling green hills and was fit for a queen. Elizabeth hired local designers to "pinken up" the castle's "drab décor." She purchased horses for the stables, even though she had stopped riding, and only visited the Irish castle once a year.

Back in Manhattan, Elizabeth continued to splurge and bought a dog, as she couldn't very well bring her beloved horses home from the stables to cuddle. She named her furry pal Pee-Wee, as it took the pup a while to become house-trained. Pee-Wee became (wo)man's best friend, with Elizabeth feeding him caviar and wrapping him in fur minks when he slept beside her in bed.

Terrified by the depths of her own loneliness, Elizabeth became a compulsive hostess, with sometimes as many as one hundred people squeezed into her penthouse. She had always eaten cleanly, never smoked, and exercised daily, but she began drinking more frequently during her nightly dinner parties. Only alcohol helped temporarily dull her inner demons.

To ward off sickness, Elizabeth began taking regular vitamin injections, amphetamine-based shots by Dr. Max Jacobson, dubbed "Dr. Feelgood," after being introduced to him by Jackie Kennedy, another one of his clients.

Despite Elizabeth's best efforts, her own health was weakening after multiple trips to the hospital for pneumonia and kidney infections. Her hair was severely thinning, and her left leg and hands swelled often enough that she had to take heavy doses of Novocain for the pain. By 1963, Elizabeth had suffered two minor strokes yet continued on with work and travel plans as though nothing had happened after her recovery. A noticeable sign to her staff was that she began to forget people's names, which she said was "not a sign of her strokes or her age, but a sign of her busy mind."

In 1964, at age eighty-six, Elizabeth was excited to fly from Los Angeles to New England to meet her friend Mamie Eisenhower at Maine Chance Spa but before the flight, Elizabeth fell so ill that she was confined to bed rest and around-the-clock nurse's care at the Beverly

Hills Hotel. Mamie Eisenhower who had already arrived at Maine Chance, told her friend not to worry and that she "enjoyed every minute of her stay in the Garden of Arden," as she detailed in a telegram delivered to Elizabeth's hotel bedside.

On April 1, 1965, Helena Rubinstein died in New York at the age of ninety-three. Despite her own increasingly poor health, Elizabeth rebuked the possibility of her demise. Neiman Marcus was the only brave soul to ask Elizabeth what would happen to her company after she was gone. Years later, he described the experience in a letter to a friend: "Death was a subject Miss Arden refused to contemplate, and any reference to it was met with icy silence. I'm confident that she was convinced she would never die but would merely pass on into a Blue Grass-scented heaven, anointed by Eight Hour Cream."

Dying was something that happened to *other* people, not to her. Much to the dismay of the company's stakeholders, Elizabeth refused to discuss a contingency plan for the future of Arden, as though she would live on forever.

- LOU -

Meanwhile, I was still burning the candle at both ends, but if Elizabeth could handle Manhattan's rat race into her eighties, I needed to toughen up. Plagued by a bad bout of insomnia, I had taken to going on long walks at night to tire myself out. The never-ending soundtrack of the city drowned out the stress swarming my synapses until I got lost in the rhythm of my own breath.

My sisters, Grace and Meredith, came to visit for a weekend— apparently the family was worried about me, so my mom sent them as foot soldiers. Seeing Grace and Meredith, bright-eyed and in awe of the city's splendors, reminded me of my former self, a version I once liked. I could tell my sisters weren't impressed with what they saw in me: a burnt-out, unmotivated shell of their formerly goal-oriented, ambitious sister. I justified my "unhealthy habits" in that I had spent my whole life planning ahead + working hard to *achieve, achieve, achieve*, that I deserved to indulge in a few vices.

Grace, Meredith, and I went to the Plaza Hotel for high tea at the Palm Court. The imported palm trees, ornate glass skylight, and oval vintage mirrors dripped of opulence and old-world charm. During our tea service, I noticed an elderly woman sitting alone a few tables away from us. Her elongated neck was adorned with so many strings of pearls, like a pageant giraffe, it was a mystery to me how she maintained any semblance of elegance under the weight of the beads. She wore a vintage Chanel suit in pink tweed, and her bottle-blonde hair, with silver streaks, was pulled loosely into a chignon. Soft makeup was delicately applied, save for the bright pink lipstick that rimmed the edges of her mouth and teacup. For being so dolled up, I assumed she was waiting for someone—her husband, children, or a socialite companion—to join her for afternoon tea.

The way she sat there, dipped in pink and pearls, the picture of independence, reminded me of Elizabeth Arden. I was drawn to her, for so often youth is associated with beauty, but the woman was so striking and poised in her own skin. I could only imagine how many heads she had turned in her younger years, but even now, the wrinkles that framed her features were attractive in their own right; horizontal exclamation points that highlighted her long lashes and sparkling baby blues. But beneath her beauty lurked a shadow of loneliness. I sensed it from the way she kept adjusting her rings and glancing at the hotel doors. Or perhaps I was projecting my own increasing unease in my skin.

I looked away from the woman and got lost in conversation with my sisters as we sipped overpriced tea and ate tiny crust-less sandwiches that disappeared in one bite. I was mesmerized by how full of life my sisters were, how lighthearted they seemed as they threw their heads back with genuine laughter. My mind felt foggy, somewhere on the periphery of their merriment, but I hoped it didn't show.

On our way out of the Plaza, I noticed that the elderly lady was still sitting at her table. A fresh pot of tea replaced the old, and she was now deeply immersed in a book. The pink tassel on the end of her bookmark dangled over the white tablecloth, ticking back and forth as if it would never stop. A pang of admiration rose up inside of me. I realized my assumption had been wrong: the woman waited for no one.

Chapter 19

End of an Era

New York

1966

On Tuesday, October 18, 1966, Elizabeth Arden died of a heart attack at Lenox Hill Hospital in New York City. No one was certain of Elizabeth's real age when she died, just as she liked it. Her obituary wrongly stated she was eighty-one, but she was actually eighty-eight (88) years old. In some cultures, the number eight signifies new beginnings and is a sign of infinity, which would have been a lucky omen to Elizabeth, who believed in her own immortality.

ELIZABETH ARDEN IS DEAD AT 81; MADE BEAUTY A GLOBAL BUSINESS
October 19, 1966—The *New York Times*

Ms. Elizabeth N. Graham (Elizabeth Arden and Florence Nightingale Graham), who built the billion-dollar beauty industry and was one of the country's leading race-horse owners, died of a heart attack yesterday morning at Lenox Hill Hospital.

She was stricken Monday evening at her ten-room apartment at 834 Fifth Avenue. Her niece called her physician, Dr. George W. Slaughter, who admitted her to the hospital at 7 p.m. Over the years, she managed her company's affairs down to the last detail, and she had worked Monday, as she customarily worked every day, at her office at 691 Fifth Avenue.

A sociological and historical phenomenon, and a woman of uncommon business talents, she made her fame and fortune in the last fifty years from rich women and fast horses. Both gave every appearance of loving her pampering. Her thoroughbred, Jet Pilot, won the Kentucky Derby in 1947.

Elizabeth Arden manufactured more than 300 cosmetic products sold in department stores and salons around the globe. The bulk of her trade was done at her major temples of glamour, over fifty Red Doors in principal cities across the United States, Canada, Mexico, Peru, Europe and Australia, and two beauty-restorative resorts in Maine and Arizona. The New York salon occupies eleven of twelve floors at 691 Fifth Avenue and like every other major Arden salon, it is entered through a bright red door.

In Paris, the Arden Red Door Spa is in Place Vendôme, a few steps from the Ritz. It is managed by Miss Arden's sister, Countess Gladys de Maublanc. In London, the Arden Red Door Spa is on Bond Street and members of these European salons have included the Queen of England, the Duchess of Windsor, Princess Charles d'Arenberg, Olivia de Havilland, the Begum Aga Khan, and other distinguished guests.

Through her clients in the beauty business and her friendships in the horse world, Ms. Graham became prominent in society. She gave many parties at her duplex apartment on Fifth Avenue. She was a patroness of annual luncheons, fashion shows, the Philharmonic orchestra and sponsored the annual Blue Grass Ball (named for one of her perfumes). She was a pioneer in advertising beauty products in fashion magazines and newspapers.

In whichever of her worlds Ms. Graham was present, she could appear fragile and fluttery. Although she stood only a little over 5 feet tall and was slender, anyone who mistook her wispiness for indecision quickly discovered she had a will of steel and the power to execute it.

She was undeniably ageless, a circumstance she accentuated by concealing her birth date. Whatever it may have been, Ms. Graham, in her sixties and seventies, looked twenty years younger, even on close inspection of her face. Moreover, her hair never grayed publicly, but remained a beige-blond.

Ms. Graham lived suffused in pink. Early in her business career she came to the conclusion it was the most flattering color in the spectrum and never changed her mind about its power to make drab subjects glow in its reflected warmth. Pink was the signature color of her jars and products. She once halted production because the shade was slightly off, costing $100,000. Even Elizabeth Arden press releases were mimeographed on pink paper.

Pink also dominated the décor of Ms. Graham's Manhattan residence, her cottages at Belmont and Saratoga race tracks, her Maine Chance Farm in Lexington, Kentucky and winter residence near Charleston, South Carolina. Pink was in evidence, too, in her 12th-century gothic castle in Ballymore Eustace, 20 miles outside of Dublin, part of a 500-acre estate for horses and cattle.

Miss Arden herself was always well dressed, either in a trim suit or a gently flowing gown. She dressed mostly in pink or its variations (once in a great while she wore blue or beige) and she once doused her hair in a pink rinse. She invariably wore diamonds, a pearl necklace, and earrings. The scent of Mémoire Chérie, an Arden perfume, was rarely absent nor was a handbag, a small alligator one, which she carried even in her own living room.

The chief ingredients of beauty, in Miss Arden's view, were a healthy lifestyle, clean skin, natural makeup, and a simple hairdo.

She married Thomas Jenkins Lewis in 1915, as she believed a wed woman inspired more confidence in her customers. He managed the Arden wholesale division, but after they divorced, he went to work for Helena Rubinstein, Elizabeth's arch-rival in the beauty field. There was a second marriage to Prince Michael Evlanoff, but it ended quickly in divorce.

Miss Arden was a hard taskmaster. She demanded perfection from her employees and herself. Her passion for detail was legendary, extending to every phase of her business—the color of her packaging, the wording or mood of an advertisement and the naming of a perfume.

Ms. Graham lived with her niece, Patricia Graham, and is the aunt of Beatrice and Virginia Graham. She is survived by her sister, Countess Gladys de Maublanc. A funeral service will be held on Friday at 11 a.m. Elizabeth Arden salons throughout the world will be closed Friday in memory of their founder.

Elizabeth was buried at Sleepy Hollow Cemetery in a pink ruffled chiffon dress, custom made for her by Oscar de la Renta, a string of pearls, and her signature pink lips. The adjoining plot remained empty, as though she waited for a companion who never came.

In 1966, Elizabeth Arden Inc. was a billion-dollar global company with Red Door Spas in major cities around the world. A *billion* dollars was an unfathomable sum, and an unimaginable possibility for Florence from the farm. She had exceeded every expectation she set for herself.

In Elizabeth's will, she left the majority of her multimillion-dollar fortune to her sister Gladys, and nieces, Pattie, Beattie, and Ginnie. The company was grossing approximately $60 million per year, but the US government billed Arden for $37 million in estate and corporate taxes when she died. The board sold off her assets to raise funds: Arden-owned manufacturing factories, Maine Chance Farm, private estates, the Arden Castle in Ireland, her New York apartment, and the license to the Red Door Spas.

Elizabeth died before the first man walked on the moon in July 1969. Instead of being impressed, she would have questioned where the female astronauts were, as for all of the strides women had made in her lifetime, there was still a long way to go.

After her death, and after her homes, horses, and business were swept up by strangers, only the legacy of the name Elizabeth Arden remained—and that, too, had been a mere figment of her wildest dreams.

-LOU-

I took a taxi to Sleepy Hollow Cemetery, clutching a bouquet of thirteen red roses on the fifty-minute cab ride from my apartment in Manhattan to Sleepy Hollow, New York. The final resting place of Elizabeth Arden was tucked under a row of trees. Her tombstone was a plain, cement block engraved with "ELIZABETH N. GRAHAM 1966." I don't know what I was expecting, but I lay the flowers on the grass, and smiled at how even on her grave she had left out her birth year, and how even in death, her name remained a compilation of identities. "Thank you," I whispered, "May you rest in peace."

I had since moved into my own apartment in the East Village after Laura moved in with her boyfriend. It was across the street from the 1831 Marble Cemetery, where prominent New Yorkers were buried—my neighbors were many of Elizabeth's wealthy friends. "Great bones," I said to the landlord when he had showed me the place.

Elsewhere, living across from a graveyard might be eerie, but in Manhattan, green space was a welcome reprive, and it meant unobstructed rooftop views when watching the skyline turn taffy pink and tangerine. Elizabeth and I were both specks along New York's timeline, lucky enough to have lived amidst the skeletal framework of the city and its historic past.

***

My sickness came on without warning. That isn't entirely true; there were signs: headache, stomach pain, nausea, brain fog, insomnia, and vomiting, but I chose to ignore them until my body sent a signal loud and clear.

It took a gamut of tests, but the doctor diagnosed me with something that sounded like the final stump word in a national spelling bee: helicobacter pylori, a bacterial infection that had entered my body and taken up residence and caused an ulcer in my digestive tract.

"It's possible you acquired the bacterial infection on the subway from touching a pole and rubbing your eyes or lips," said the doctor.

"I could have gotten this just from riding the subway?" I asked, amazed.

"It could have been the final straw, especially if your immune system was already suppressed. Stress, anxiety, lack of sleep, binge drinking, are all contributing factors," he said. Hearing from a medical professional that my own vices had destroyed my immune system was a moment of reckoning. *What was I doing with my life?*

I spent half a month off work in my sick cell of solitary confinement. The illness got worse before it got better. Sleep, sweat, shiver, vomit, hydrate and repeat. The only silver lining of my body hitting rock bottom was the rare opportunity for reflection and profound transformational breakthrough.

Sickness had stripped my immune system, but also the borders of my identity. It demotes people to the rawest version of themselves, breaking down our external armor. In a strange way, getting sick brought me closer to the core of myself that I had suppressed for so long. In this in-between moment, a pause from real life, I finally admitted to myself that what I wanted for my life was starting to look different than it once did at eighteen. Why did it always take darkness to truly see the light? I harbored introverted tendencies in an extroverted city, and when I let my mind go into long-range view, the future I envisioned for myself was no longer becoming CEO Elizabeth Arden 2.0. I had unwittingly tied my self-worth to what I did rather than who I was. Transformation didn't happen overnight, but I needed to reconsider not what success *looked* like but what it *felt* like—for me.

There was a thunderstorm the night before I returned to work after being sick. Drizzle from the day had turned into a torrential downpour. I took a warm shower before bed. Scrubbing myself anew, I listened to the competing sounds of rainwater outside the window versus the rushing showerhead. There were sharp bolts of lightning and loud booms of thunder. I thought about the humdrum of human connectivity I would return to the next morning. Despite the chaos outside, I felt calm, untouchable by the elements.

After what seemed like hours, I stepped from the shower, slipped on a bathrobe, and wrapped my hair up into a towel. The room was humid, the mirror fogged, and the candles flickered. Barefoot on the cool tile, I rubbed a clean circle on the mirror. I took great care moisturizing my face in slow, deliberate strokes. The cream absorbed immediately into my thirsty skin. I layered the lotion everywhere until my whole body softened in renewal.

The next morning, I walked to work, rejuvenated. I absorbed the mosaic of faces hurrying along the busy sidewalks. Manhattan was a mirror, and in its crowded reflection, I had finally found myself.

Chapter 20

Beyond the Red Door

New York

1967–Present

With no named successor, Gladys took over control of the company from Paris after Elizabeth's death in 1966. She already owned and operated the European subsidiary, so it was a natural progression. However, by 1969, Gladys was no longer able to run the business on her own, as she was old and quite ill. Gladys sold the company back to the American board and lived sickly, yet simply for two more years in her beloved Paris.

"Countess Gladys de Maublanc, sister of the late Elizabeth Arden, the cosmetics maven, died at the American Hospital in Paris. She was 87 years old. The former Gladys Graham managed the French branch of Elizabeth Arden and the well-known Paris salon since it was opened in the early 1920s. During World War II she was interned at Ravensbrück by the Germans. Her spirit and encouragement kept the strength and morale of other prisoners high. She received the French Legion of Honor for her military services. The City of Paris gave her the Silver Medal for her contributions to the cosmetic industry. She leaves a son, John Graham," read her obituary in the *New York Times*.

Maine Chance Farm closed permanently in 1970 after a fire destroyed the spa treatment center—the heat under the wax for an Ardena paraffin bath had been left on.

Elizabeth's Barretstown Castle in Ireland was bequeathed to the Irish government before Canadian businessman Garfield Weston took up residence. The interior remains relatively untouched from when Elizabeth redecorated and refurbished it. Horses graze at the stables she built, and best of all, the main door to the castle is still painted bright red.

In 1970, Eli Lilly, a global pharmaceuticals company, acquired Elizabeth Arden for $38.5 million and turned her independent enterprise into a multinational conglomerate. With more chefs in the kitchen, the decade marked a focus for large corporations to drive profit and increase the bottom line, rather than investing time and money into innovation and creativity.

In 1988, as the cosmetics market slumped, Eli Lilly sold Elizabeth Arden Inc. to Fabergé for a reported $700 million. The following year, in 1989 (when I was born), Unilever acquired both Fabergé and Elizabeth Arden for $1.5 billion.

The great era of the Red Door Spas was over in 1990, as Unilever set to task cleaning up what they perceived as "deadwood," which meant closing nearly all of the Red Door Spas worldwide.

At the end of 2000, Unilever sold Elizabeth Arden to a Florida-based company, FFI Fragrances. The share-and-cash deal cost close to $240 million. Scott Beattie, the CEO of FFI at the time, changed the company name back to Elizabeth Arden and remained chairman, president, and CEO of the company until 2016.

"Elizabeth Arden is one of the most classic beauty franchises in the United States and internationally, and we're going to capitalize on that and grow it," Scott Beattie said in an interview with *Women's Wear Daily*. By the millennium, almost four decades after her death, Elizabeth Arden's company was finally about to be revived.

Under the helm of Scott Beattie, Elizabeth Arden reopened the Red Door Spas around the world as part of the global expansion program. Eight Hour Cream rejoined the best-seller ranks, and Catherine Zeta-Jones was tapped as the celebrity face of the brand.

In 2016, Revlon acquired Elizabeth Arden Inc. in a reported deal worth over $870 million. The acquisition undoubtedly made Elizabeth roll over in her grave, for she had prided herself on having beat out "that man" (Charles Revson) in the prestige market. Now, his company owned her life's work.

In 2017, Reese Witherspoon became the face of Elizabeth Arden Inc. as the company's Storyteller-in-Chief. "As one of the first female entrepreneurs, Elizabeth Arden paved the way for women like me. It's an honor to carry on her legacy and be part of such an iconic company that is committed to serving women," Reese Witherspoon said in a statement to the *Hollywood Reporter*.

By 2023, the global beauty industry is proejcted to be worth over $805 billion, according to *Reuters*.

As for me, I couldn't shake the lasting impact Elizabeth Arden had on the direction of my life. I worked at Arden from 2008 to 2014, starting as an intern to senior global marketing manager and working at both the North American and European headquarters. It truly was a dream job in a dream city, but I discovered another calling that couldn't be ignored. I had arrived in New York to *become somebody*, and I left to return to myself.

With the passage of time and the company changing hands, Elizabeth's inspiring legacy was at risk of getting lost in history, so I felt pulled to preserve her story as it intertwined with mine. In this fast-paced world, it was important for me to slow down and allow for thoughtful introspection in the writing of this book, which helped to examine my own coming of age within the beauty industry.

Elizabeth was that person for me, so let me be that person for all of you who are on the journey to becoming your best self. Allow me to leave you with a beauty analogy on finding lasting fulfillment in life: go ahead and try on as many shades of lipstick as your heart desires until you finally land on the one that feels truest to YOU.

Epilogue
The Final Red Door
2014–2016

Moving out of Manhattan happened in vignettes: the packed boxes in my empty apartment, my last day of work, the taxi ride to the airport, the view from the plane as Legoland below got further and further away.

The decision to leave Elizabeth Arden came the same way it had arrived: through snail mail in a big white envelope with a red logo. I had decided to leave the red door of Arden in New York for the crimson halls of Harvard University in Boston to pursue my master's degree in journalism. Cambridge, Massachusetts, was bursting with curiosity in an environment engineered to harvest new ideas, and it seemed to offer an opportunity for reflection and growth. To many people, this left turn in my life was puzzling. I already had a successful marketing career in the beauty industry. Who gave all of that up for the unknown, especially to become a *writer*, which had an invisible prefix of "struggling" attached to it?

My friend Steve later said it best: "Marketing is storytelling at its core, so you didn't actually change direction; you've been doing both your whole life." For me, I couldn't articulate it any other way other than it wasn't so much of a choice as a calling that couldn't be ignored.

Most people who move to Manhattan make the trip once and stay forever. You rarely read stories about those who left, only the tales of those who came and conquered. They say, "If you can make it in New York, you can make it anywhere," but I never hear any accounts of what happened to the strange souls that left. *Did they really make it somewhere else?*

Manhattan elicited an optimism that everything was within your grasp, yet just out of reach. That was the beauty and the beast of the city: the infinite power struggle between *having* everything you dreamed of yet always *wanting* for more.

While I would forever love New York, I wanted to re-evaluate my place in the cosmic void and see what else the universe had in store for me. There's the clichéd saying if you love something, let it go, and if it's meant to be, you will find your way back. With that mantra, I left Manhattan with a peaceful state of mind.

***

The timing was right to lay my "Maven Blogs" to rest. Eventually, I created a new website, this time under my own name, no pseudonym. It made me feel legitimate, like I had a flag in the ground, a proud plot owner staking her territory among the infinite landscape of the World Wide Web.

Louise Claire Johnson
Welcome To My New Home

Welcome to my new place in cyberspace. As my location has been in flux for the past few years, I figured it was time to find a more permanent place to hang my hat.

I started "The Maven Diaries" when I was eighteen as a way to keep in touch with family and friends while documenting my escapades in new cities. Those blogs feel like cozy blankets and indelible reminders of moments in time, but they also weren't representative of the full spectrum of my identity.

I showed my life as I wanted it to be, not always the complete story of what I was really feeling at the time.

260

I'll be honest; writing under **Louise Claire Johnson** makes me feel vulnerable. Before, I could hide behind my "Maven" alter egos. Now, there's no more hiding.

I've finally let myself acknowledge that throughout all of the years, my dream of dreams has been to be a writer.

I equated my worthiness with success and internalized the idea I wouldn't find it through creative writing, but little by little the voice in my head became so overpowering I knew I had to make a change.

It's been a humbling journey with an infinite horizon.

Thanks for reading,

— Lou

I spent the summer after I left New York at my parents' cottage in Norway Bay, my version of Maine Chance. I stacked up all of my red journals from over the years, their spines full of secrets, and read cover-to-cover every word, including my earliest *Dear Liz* entries. Beneath the shiny exteriors, the pages of the notebooks were a wealth of imperfections: inkblots, coffee stains, food smudges, teardrops, ripped corners, scratched-out words, incoherent ideas, and scribbly handwriting. They were a mess of thoughts, and yet, the truest, tangible version of me lived behind their gilded exteriors.

Red would forever remind me of Elizabeth Arden and the red door that had unlocked so many opportunities for me. I opened a brand-new red journal and set to task filling it from beginning to end at a little writing desk overlooking the water, surrounded by shelves of books, determined to find a way to share Liz's stories with the world.

***

Walking through Harvard Yard in early September was a surreal dream. I felt like Hermione, seeing the magical wizarding world of Hogwarts for the first time. Looking up at the majestic Widener Library, whose stacks run deep underground, I realized I was standing on top of rows of books older than both Elizabeth and myself. I would spend countless hours holed up at Widener, watching as the seasons made their cyclical journey from fall to winter to spring to summer.

Outside the perimeter of Harvard Yard, on Plympton Street, I walked by the oversized crimson red door to the offices of the *Harvard Crimson*, the headquarters of the nation's oldest daily college newspaper, and couldn't help but grin. With my feet firmly planted on the ground, a startling thought struck me. After all those years I had spent wishing I were in Elizabeth's shoes, how much she would have loved to be in mine. Her greatest regret in life was being barred from finishing her education. Women weren't allowed to attend Harvard until 1977, when "sex-blind admissions" were enacted, a decade after Elizabeth's death.

In my own small way, I felt vindicated for both of us, as though our destinies had merged. Elizabeth had shown me the way; now, it was my turn to take the torch. I watched as the sun made its daily descent, rays of possibility on the periphery as the sky transitioned to twilight. I no longer knew what lay beyond the next door, but I would be ready when it opened, for there was beauty in the unknown.

Acknowledgments

Writing is solitary business, but a book is never finished alone. As a first-time author, I began my publishing journey naïve to the mental marathon ahead of me. Behind this beautiful book are many self-doubt spirals, sleepless nights, and severe impostor syndrome. There were many times when I wanted to give up, but the helping hands of so many, and the solace of family and friends motivated me to reach this milestone.

Mom and Dad, thank you for absolutely everything (full stop!), but especially for introducing me to the magical world of words. Every bedtime story, trip to the local library, bookstore visits, (and Winnie The Pooh, Anne of Green Gables, Little House on The Prairie, and Harry Potter themed party/costume), fostered my penchant for books and love of reading from an early age. Thank you for believing in my dream of seeing my own book on shelf someday and cheering me on every step of the way. Couldn't have done it without you. I love you so much.

Grace and Meredith, I won the sibling jackpot when I got you as built-in best friends from birth. I couldn't imagine my life without you and this book wouldn't exist without your endless encouragement and positivity pushing me to keep going. I am so proud to be your sister and forever inspired by the smart, selfless, stunning humans (inside and out) that you are. We did it! I love you.

Geoff, I don't know what I did to deserve someone as incredible as you to do life with. You are so deeply good, in the purest sense of the word, down to your core—I feel like the luckiest girl in the world. Without your steady supply of supportive advice and championship of this pursuit, I never would have made it through the past five years.

Thank you for being there for every tear and triumph. I love you and can't wait to spend forever together.

To my extended family (the Johnsons, Andrews, Youells, De Schulthesses, Mallettes, Hossacks, and Hums), thank you for your steadfast support from the beginning. To my friends who have shared the highs and lows, thank you for reading early (terrible) drafts and understanding when I went MIA, retreating into "hibernation station," at various stages of the publishing process. I have limited room in these acknowledgements, so the old adage, "you know who you are," feels apt here—but please know I will be sending personalized love notes to adequately proclaim my overwhelming gratitude and appreciation. Until then: Thank you. I love you.

To those mentioned in this book: Laura Keohane, thank you for trusting me to tell snippets of our NYC stories (the rest are safe in the vault for us to reminisce about over a bottle of red). To Kristin Tice Studeman, for befriending the Canadian girl who shared a single bed beside you in Carlyle Court one hot summer in the city. Tasha Tacchi, for being my Swiss wife and the kind of friend who'll travel the world with you, even if it's just to see a red door.

To Bryn Turnbull, for your writerly wisdom and shared love of badass broads from bygone eras. To Sarah Miniaci, for your invaluable industry expertise and sparking joy in the journey of bringing this book into the world. Special thanks to Gillian Knap, Jessica Turner, Alexandra Oakes, Marcie Foster, and Lexi McKenna for lending an ear, and your thoughtful touches to these pages.

To Scott Beattie, for unknowingly opening the red door of my dreams and giving me the opportunity of a lifetime. I cannot thank you enough.

Thank you to everyone I have worked with over the years at Elizabeth Arden. To my classmates, professors, and housemates at Western, Ivey, and Harvard—you have a special place in my heart.

To the New York Public Library, Boston Public Library, Toronto Public Library, and Widener Library for the access to research archives and quiet spaces to write. Thank you to librarians, booksellers, publishers, journalists, writers, authors, and readers who share a love of literature and continue to believe in the importance of the written word.

And to Florence Nightingale Graham, for inspiring it all.

About the Author

Louise is a Toronto-based writer. Her work has appeared in *The Globe & Mail*, *The Huffington Post*, *Darling Magazine* and more. A graduate of The Richard Ivey School of Business and Harvard University, she has studied and worked in Hong Kong, Switzerland, New York, and Boston. She's a curious creature with an old soul who sends snail mail, collects typewriters, drinks too much coffee, and delights in slow mornings. Writing has always been her constant in an inconstant world, and eventually, it became a calling that couldn't be ignored. BEHIND THE RED DOOR is her first book.

louiseclairejohnson.com
@louiseclairejohnson

Selected Bibliography

Arden, Elizabeth. The Quest of the Beautiful (Booklet). 1920.

Commire, Anne, and Deborah Klezmer. Women in World History. Gale Research International, Limited, 1999.

"Cosmetics and Skin: Elizabeth Arden." Cosmetics and Skin, https://www.cosmeticsandskin.com/companies/elizabeth-arden.php. Accessed 25 Feb. 2021.

Drachman, Virginia G. Enterprising Women. UNC Press Books, 2002.

"Elizabeth Arden Chooses President and 6-Man Board." The New York Times. 11 Nov. 1966, https://www.nytimes.com/1966/11/11/archives/elizabeth-arden-chooses-president-and-6man-board.html.

Elizabeth Arden: Queen Rules the Sport of Kings. TIME Magazine, 1946.

Fair, Vanity. "Elizabeth Arden Archive | Vanity Fair." Vanity Fair. 14 Apr. 2017, https://www.vanityfair.com/style/photos/2017/04/elizabeth-arden-archive.

"Elizabeth Arden Honored by 1,000; Cosmetics Leader's Funeral Held at St. James Church." The New York Times. 22 Oct. 1966, https://www.nytimes.com/1966/10/22/archives/elizabeth-arden-honored-by-1000-cosmetics-leaders-funeral-held-at.html.

Elizabeth Arden, Inc. The Elizabeth Arden Exercises for Health and Beauty. 1930.

"Elizabeth Arden Is Dead: Made Beauty a Global Business." The New York Times - Breaking News, US News, World News and Videos, 19 Oct. 1966, https://www.nytimes.com/1966/10/19/archives/elizabeth-arden-is-dead-at-81-made-beauty-a-global-business.html.

Encyclopedia.com. Elizabeth Arden (1878–1966). 5 Mar. 2020, https://www.encyclopedia.com/women/encyclopedias-almanacs-transcripts-and-maps/arden-elizabeth-1878-1966.

Forster, Merna. 100 More Canadian Heroines. Dundurn, 2011.

"Liz Arden Sheds Her Prince." Newspapers.Com, The New York Daily News, 1944, https://www.newspapers.com/clip/31784047/1944-elizabeth-arden-2nd-divorce-ny/.

Lewis, Alfred Allan, and Constance Woodworth. Miss Elizabeth Arden. London : W.H. Allen, 1973.

Martin, Edward S. The Wayfarer in New York. 1909.

Peiss, Kathy. Hope in a Jar: The Making of America's Beauty Culture. University of Pennsylvania Press, 2011.

Lowry, Beverly. Her Dream of Dreams. Vintage, 2011.

"Marilyn Monroe's Personal Elizabeth Arden Makeup." The Marilyn Monroe Collection, https://themarilynmonroecollection.com/marilyn-monroe-personal-elizabeth-arden-makeup/. Accessed 25 Feb. 2021.

"Probes Seek Cause of Racing Stable Fire." Newspapers.Com, The New York Daily News, 1936, https://www.newspapers.com/clip/28610874/elizabeth-arden-fire-3may46-ny-daily/.

Roache, Douglas J. "The Elegant World of Elizabeth Arden." Maclean's. 20 Feb. 1965, https://archive.macleans.ca/article/1965/2/20/the-elegant-worlds-of-elizabeth-arden.

Shuker, Nancy. Elizabeth Arden. Silver Burdett Press, 1989.

The Associated Press. "Revlon Is Buying Elizabeth Arden for $419.3 Million." The New York Times - Breaking News, US News, World News and Videos, 16 June 2016, https://www.nytimes.com/2016/06/17/business/revlon-is-buying-elizabeth-arden-for-419-3-million.html.

"The New York Times Archives - NYTimes.Com." The New York Times Archives, 1910-1966. https://archive.nytimes.com/www.nytimes.com/ref/membercenter/nytarchive.html.

Woodhead, Lindy. War Paint: Madame Helena Rubinstein and Miss Elizabeth Arden: Their Lives, Their Times, Their Rivalry. Wiley. London, 2004.

May, Naomi. "From Elizabeth Arden to Essie: Queen Elizabeth II's Beauty Cupboard Contents Revealed." London Evening Standard. 21 Apr. 2020, https://www.standard.co.uk/beauty/queen-elizabeth-beauty-secrets-products-a4419041.html.

Oppedisano, Jeannette M. Historical Encyclopedia of American Women Entrepreneurs. Greenwood, 2000.

"Thomas J. Lewis, 95, Cosmetics Official." The New York Times. 2 Jan. 1971, https://www.nytimes.com/1971/01/02/archives/thomas-j-lewis-95-cosmetics-official.html.

CPSIA information can be obtained
at www.ICGtesting.com
Printed in the USA
LVHW092128270521
688760LV00008B/51/J